Translated Documents of Greece and Rome

E. Badian and Robert K. Sherk, Editors

VOLUME 2

From the end of the Peloponnesian War to the battle of Ipsus

From the end of the Peloponnesian War to the battle of Ipsus

EDITED AND TRANSLATED BY
PHILLIP HARDING

Associate Professor of Classics,
University of British Columbia

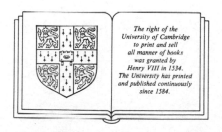

The right of the
University of Cambridge
to print and sell
all manner of books
was granted by
Henry VIII in 1534.
The University has printed
and published continuously
since 1584.

CAMBRIDGE UNIVERSITY PRESS

CAMBRIDGE
LONDON   NEW YORK   NEW ROCHELLE
MELBOURNE   SYDNEY

Published by the Press Syndicate of the University of Cambridge
The Pitt Building, Trumpington Street, Cambridge CB2 1RP
32 East 57th Street, New York, NY 10022, USA
10 Stamford Road, Oakleigh, Melbourne 3166, Australia

First published 1985

Printed in Great Britain at the University Press, Cambridge

Library of Congress catalogue card number: 83–15444

British Library Cataloguing in Publication Data
Harding, Phillip
From the end of the Peloponnesian war to the
battle of Ipsus. – (Translated documents of
Greece and Rome; 2)
1. Greece – History – to 301 B.C. – Sources
I. Title II. Series
938   DF214
ISBN 0 521 23435 2 hard covers
ISBN 0 521 29949 7 paperback

WD

FOR MY FAMILY

Translated Documents of Greece and Rome

SERIES EDITORS' INTRODUCTION

Greek and Roman history has always been in an ambivalent position in
American higher education, having to find a home either in a Department of History or in a Department of Classics, and in both it is usually
regarded as marginal. Moreover, in a History Department the subject
tends to be taught without regard to the fact that the nature of the evidence is, on the whole, very different from that for American, English,
or French history, while in a Classics Department it tends to be viewed
as a 'philological' subject and taught by methods appropriate to Greek
and Latin authors. Even on the undergraduate level the difference may
be important, but on the graduate level, where future teachers and
scholars, who are to engage in original research, are trained, it becomes
quite clear that neither of these solutions is adequate.

One problem is the standard of proficiency that should be required
in Greek and Latin – both difficult languages, necessitating years of
study; and few students start the study, even of Latin, let alone Greek,
before they come to college. The editors recognize that for the student
aiming at a Ph.D. in the subject and at advancing present knowledge of
it there can be no substitute for a thorough training in the two
languages. Nevertheless, they believe that it is possible to extend
serious instruction at a high level to graduate students aiming at reaching the M.A. level and to make them into competent teachers. It is also
possible to bring about a great improvement in the standard of undergraduate courses not requiring the ancient languages – courses that
instructors themselves usually find unsatisfactory, since much of the
source material cannot be used.

In order to use this material, at both graduate and serious undergraduate levels, the instructor must, in fact, be able to range far beyond
the standard authors who have been translated many times. Harpocration, Valerius Maximus, and the *Suda* are often necessary tools, but
they are usually unknown to anyone except the advanced scholar.
Inscriptions, papyri, and scholia can be baffling even to the student
who does have a grounding in the ancient languages.

It is the aim of the series to supply that need for translations of
materials not readily available in English. The principal historical
authors (authors like Livy and Plutarch) are not included; they are easy
enough to find in adequate translations, and the student will have to

read far more of them than could be provided in a general source book. References to important passages in the works of those authors have been given at suitable points, but it is assumed that the instructor will direct the student's reading in them. While doing that reading, the student will now be able to have at his side a comprehensive reference book. Occasionally a passage from an otherwise accessible author (not a main historical source) has been included, so that the student may be spared the temptation of failing to search for it. But most of the material collected in this series would be hard for him to find anywhere in English, and much of it has never been translated at all.

Such translations of documentary sources as exist (and there are some major projects in translation among them, e.g. in the field of legal texts, which are intended to be far more than source books for students) tend to be seriously misleading in that they offer continuous texts where the original is (so often) fragmentary. The student cannot be aware of how much actually survives of the document and how much is modern conjecture – whether quite certain or mere guesswork. This series aims at presenting the translation of fragmentary sources in something like the way in which original documents are presented to the scholar: a variety of type fonts and brackets (which will be fully explained) have been used for this, and even though the page may at first sight appear forbidding to one unaccustomed to this, he will learn to differentiate between text and restoration and (with the instructor's help and the use of the notes provided) between the dubious, the probable, and the certain restoration. Naturally, the English can never correspond perfectly to the Greek or Latin, but the translation aims at as close a correspondence as can be achieved, so that the run of the original and (where necessary) the amount surviving can be clearly shown. Finer points of English idiom have deliberately been sacrificed in order to produce this increased accuracy, though it is hoped that there will be nothing in the translation so unnatural as to baffle the student. In the case of inscriptions (except for those with excessively short lines) line-by-line correspondence has been the aim, so that the student who sees a precise line reference in a modern work will be able to find it in the translation.

Translation is an art as well as a science; there are bound to be differing opinions on the precise interpretation and on the best rendering of any given passage. The general editors have tried to collaborate with volume editors in achieving the aims outlined above. But there is always room for improvement, and a need for it. Suggestions and corrections from users of the series will always be welcome.

The general editors sincerely hope that the present series will make a major contribution to raising the standard of ancient history teaching in the U.S.A. and, indeed, wherever English is the medium of instruction, and that it will help to convey to students not fully proficient in Greek or Latin, or even entirely ignorant of those languages, some of the immediacy and excitement of real (as distinct from textbook) history. Perhaps some will be encouraged to develop their skill in the two languages so as to go on to a fuller understanding of the ancient world, or even to professional study of it.

Harvard University   F.B.
State University of New York at Buffalo   R.K.S.

CONTENTS

Contents

Contents

Contents

VOLUME EDITOR'S INTRODUCTION

The purpose of this volume is to supplement the standard and easily
accessible sources of the history of the Greek world in the fourth century BC.

It is not surprising that a large proportion of the documents translated here are inscriptions from Athens, for the Athenians of the fourth
century, at least while they governed themselves democratically, continued their fifth-century practice of publishing all their public business (peace treaties, laws, casualty-lists, accounts, etc.) on marble
stelai. But by the end of the fifth century this practice had become
widespread in the Greek world, even in states that were not democratic. So the student will find inscriptions from Delphi, Boeotia,
Tegea, Cyrene, Samos, Skepsis, Olynthus and several other places.
Down to the death of Alexander the Great in 323 I was able to use the
selection in M.N. Tod, *Greek Historical Inscriptions*, vol. 2, though it
occasionally needed to be supplemented by recent finds (e.g. nos. 8, 9
and 45). For the period after 323 the selection is entirely my own.

Inscriptions are primary sources of information, but their interpretation often depends upon a narrative account. We have, of course, the
extant histories of Xenophon and Diodorus, but there were many other
historical works, written in the fourth century or later, that pertained to
the fourth century. On the one hand there was the *Universal History* of
Ephorus of Cyme, upon which Diodorus drew. On the other there was
a great variety of monographs, some of which continued Thucydides'
history of Greek affairs (*Hellenica*), while others were on more specific
topics, like the Sacred War or the careers of Philip, Alexander or the
Successors. The writing of local history also increased in popularity,
especially at Athens (the *Atthis*).

Only fragments of these works have survived, and those that have
have done so in a number of ways. Many, for example, were quoted in
extant works or in the scholia that were written in the margins of the
texts of some of these works (especially of the orators Aeschines and
Demosthenes) by ancient scholars from the Hellenistic period
onwards. Others can be found in the compilations of the late Roman or
Byzantine lexicographers (e.g. the *Lexicon* of Harpocration, the *Suda*, or
the *Bibliotheca* of the Patriarch Photius). A few have been preserved on
papyrus, either as fragments of an originally complete text (e.g. the

Hellenica Oxyrhynchia) or as quotations in a commentary (e.g. Didymus' commentary on some passages from Demosthenes). The fragments, however found, are collected in Felix Jacoby's *Die Fragmente der griechischen Historiker*.

In accordance with the aims of this series I have tried to prevent my own opinions from influencing the presentation of these documents, whether epigraphic or literary. Where several dates have been proposed for a document, these have all been indicated in the heading, but the item is always listed under the earliest date. The arguments in support of the various dates and the interpretation of the document, wherever that is controversial, will be found in the fairly full, though by no means exhaustive, bibliography. The student will usually find enough material in English in the bibliography to enable him/her to understand the historical importance of the document and any controversy that surrounds it. I have, however, frequently added works in other languages for the benefit of those who can read them.

In addition to the bibliography, the heading, in the case of inscriptions, provides the following information: place of origin (and discovery, if different), date (or dates) assigned, material and form (including decorative motifs), identification of script and dialect (if necessary) and an indication whether the mason used the chequer pattern (stoichedon) or not. In the next section I list the texts that I have consulted, using an asterisk to mark the one I have translated. Below that follow the principal literary texts that pertain to the material contained in the document. All dates in the heading and elsewhere are BC, unless otherwise noted.

The format of the translation is that prescribed by the general editors of the series. In particular, they are eager that each line of the translation should normally correspond to a line of the inscription. This has been the most difficult part of my assignment. Some problems could be solved in a regular fashion. For example, where (as often) the subject of an active verb came in the following line, I have made the verb passive and the subject the agent. Other difficulties were less tractable and have resulted in a translation that is less elegant than I should have liked. In the case of recurring formulae I have used the same translation, except where this conflicted with the line division. Finally, I have attempted to distinguish between infinitives and imperatives in my translation of inscriptions. Thus, for infinitives (with two exceptions) I have used the translation established in the first volume (e.g. 'commendation shall be given', etc.). However, the perfect infinitives *epsephisthai* and *dedochthai* have been translated as imperatives, in accordance with the standard interpretation of them. Imperatives have been translated in the variety of ways admitted by the English language.

The system of brackets used in the text is outlined below, but some words are in order about restorations. Where letters have been restored in a proper name, these have been enclosed in square brackets. In other cases, the entire word or words that constitute the translation of a Greek word that has been partially restored are italicized, except where the restoration is so slight that there can be no doubt about it. Where the restoration is quite hypothetical, I have either put it in square brackets or relegated it to a footnote. Where there are a variety of suggested restorations, I have usually noted these in the footnotes, with the names of the scholars who have proposed them after each. Otherwise I have tried to restrict the information in the footnotes to explanation of technical terms, identification of important individuals and sundry material of this sort. The footnotes do not constitute a commentary, but I have occasionally given longer notes either as background to a document or summarizing an important theory that has been proposed in a language other than English.

The passages from literary sources are treated in the same way as the inscriptions, but the presentation is less complex.

As far as the rendition of names of people and places is concerned, I have followed the practice established by the editors. Greek names in the text have been transliterated (the letter *chi* is 'ch' not 'kh'), but the names of authors have been given in their latinized form. The difference is usually no more than that between Ctesias and Ktesias, Philochorus and Philochoros, Lycurgus and Lykourgos. Three names have been treated differently, because they are so well known in their Anglo-Latin form – Philip II of Macedon, Alexander the Great and Ptolemy, son of Lagos. Familiar place names and, consequently, their ethnics have been latinized, e.g. Chalcis and Chalcidians rather than Chalkis and Chalkidians. Less well-known names have been transliterated.

ACKNOWLEDGEMENTS

In the production of this volume I have benefited from the assistance and criticism of the Series Editors, E. Badian and R.K. Sherk. In addition the whole work has been greatly improved by the advice of M.F. McGregor. I owe a special debt to my research assistant, Brian Lavelle, and to Barbara Parker, who typed the whole, very difficult text. Much of the cost of their labour was offset by a research grant from the University of British Columbia.

ABBREVIATIONS

AA	*Archäologischer Anzeiger*
ABSA	*Annual of the British School at Athens*
AC	*L'Antiquité Classique*
AClass	*Acta Classica*
AHR	*American Historical Review*
AJA	*American Journal of Archaeology*
AJAH	*American Journal of Ancient History*
AJP	*American Journal of Philology*
AncSoc	*Ancient Society*
Accame, *Lega*	S. Accame, *La lega ateniese* (Rome 1941)
BCH	*Bulletin de Correspondance Hellénique*
Bruce, *Commentary*	I.A.F. Bruce, *An Historical Commentary on the Hellenica Oxyrhynchia* (Cambridge 1967)
Buck	Carl D. Buck, *The Greek Dialects* (Chicago 1955)
Buckler, *Hegemony*	J. Buckler, *The Theban Hegemony* (Harvard 1980)
Bury-Meiggs	J.B. Bury, *A History of Greece*, 4th ed. by R. Meiggs (London 1975)
C&M	*Classica et Mediaevalia*
CAH	*The Cambridge Ancient History* (Cambridge 1923–9)
CP	*Classical Philology*
CQ	*Classical Quarterly*
CR	*Classical Review*
CSCA	*California Studies in Classical Antiquity*
Cargill, *League*	J. Cargill, *The Second Athenian League* (Berkeley, Los Angeles and London 1981)
Cawkwell, *Philip*	G.L. Cawkwell, *Philip of Macedon* (London and Boston 1978)
Cloché, *Dislocation*	P. Cloché, *La dislocation d'un empire* (Paris 1959)
Davies, *Families*	J.K. Davies, *Athenian Propertied Families 600–300 B.C.* (Oxford 1971)
Didymus, *Demosthenes*	*Didymi de Demosthene commenta*, ed. H. Diels and W. Schubart (Leipzig 1904)
Ehrenberg Studies	*Ancient Society and Institutions: Studies Presented to Victor Ehrenberg* (Oxford 1966)
Ellis, *Philip II*	J.R. Ellis, *Philip II and Macedonian Imperialism* (London 1976)
Ferguson, *Athens*	W.S. Ferguson, *Hellenistic Athens* (London 1911)
FGrHist	F. Jacoby, *Die Fragmente der griechischen Historiker* (Berlin and Leiden 1923–)
Fornara	C.W. Fornara, *Archaic Times to the End of the Peloponnesian War*[2] (Cambridge 1982)
GHI	R. Meiggs and D.M. Lewis, *A Selection of Greek Historical Inscriptions to the End of the Fifth Century B.C.* (Oxford 1969)
GRBS	*Greek, Roman and Byzantine Studies*
Hamilton, *Alexander*	J.R. Hamilton, *Alexander the Great* (London 1973)

Abbreviations

Hamilton, *Sparta*	C.D. Hamilton, *Sparta's Bitter Victories* (Cornell 1979)
Hammond-Griffith	N.G.L. Hammond and G.T. Griffith, *A History of Macedonia*, vol. 2 (Oxford 1979)
Heisserer, *Alexander*	A.J. Heisserer, *Alexander the Great and the Greeks* (Norman 1980)
Hell. Oxy.	*Hellenica Oxyrhynchia*, ed. V. Bartoletti (Teubner edn, 1959)
Henry, *Prescripts*	A.S. Henry, *The Prescripts of Athenian Decrees* (Leiden 1977)
IG	*Inscriptiones Graecae* (Berlin 1873–)
IOSPE	*Inscriptiones Antiquae Orae Septentrionalis Ponti Euxini Graecae et Latinae*, ed. B. Latyschev (St Petersburg 1885–1916)
ISE	L. Moretti, *Iscrizioni storiche ellenistiche*, vol. 1 (Florence 1967)
JHS	*Journal of Hellenic Studies*
Larsen, *Government*	J.A.O. Larsen, *Representative Government in Greek and Roman History*[2] (Berkeley and Los Angeles 1966)
Larsen, *States*	J.A.O. Larsen, *Greek Federal States* (Oxford 1968)
MDAI(A)	*Mitteilungen des Deutschen Archäologischen Instituts* (Athenische Abteilung)
MH	*Museum Helveticum*
MacDowell, *Law*	D.M. MacDowell, *The Law in Classical Athens* (London 1978)
Maier, *Mauerbauinschriften*	F.G. Maier, *Griechische Mauerbauinschriften* (Heidelberg 1959)
Marshall, *Confederacy*	F.H. Marshall, *The Second Athenian Confederacy* (Cambridge 1905)
Mitchel, 'Athens'	F.W. Mitchel, 'Lykourgan Athens: 338–322', in *Lectures in Memory of Louise Taft Semple*, 2nd series (Cincinnati 1973)
NC	*Numismatic Chronicle*
OCD	*The Oxford Classical Dictionary*[2] (Oxford 1970)
PCPS	*Proceedings of the Cambridge Philological Society*
PP	*La Parola del Passato*
Parke, *Soldiers*	H.W. Parke, *Greek Mercenary Soldiers* (Oxford 1933)
Parke-Wormell	H.W. Parke and D.E.W. Wormell, *The Delphic Oracle*, 2 vols. (Oxford 1956)
Pečířka, *Enktesis*	J. Pečířka, *The Formula for the Grant of Enktesis in Attic Inscriptions* (Prague 1966)
Pouilloux, *Choix*	J. Pouilloux, *Choix d'inscriptions grecques* (Paris 1960)
P.Oxy.	*Oxyrhynchus Papyri: Memoirs of the Egypt Exploration Fund, Graeco-Roman Branch*, vol. 1– (London 1898–)
Pritchett, *State* 2	W.K. Pritchett, *The Greek State at War*, vol. 2 (Berkeley and Los Angeles 1974)
RA	*Revue Archéologique*
RCHP	C.B. Welles, *Royal Correspondence in the Hellenistic Period* (New Haven 1934)
REA	*Revue des Études Anciennes*
REG	*Revue des Études Grecques*
RFIC	*Rivista di Filologia et di Istruzione Classica*
RhM	*Rheinisches Museum*
RPh	*Revue de Philologie*
Rhodes, *Boule*	P.J. Rhodes, *The Athenian Boule* (Oxford 1972)
Rhodes, *Commentary*	P.J. Rhodes, *A Commentary on the Aristotelian* Athenaion Politeia (Oxford 1981)
Roesch, *Thespies*	P. Roesch, *Thespies et la confédération béotienne* (Paris 1965)

Abbreviations

RSA	*Rivista storica dell'Antichità*
RSI	*Rivista storica italiana*
Ryder, *Eirene*	T.T.B. Ryder, *Koine Eirene* (Oxford 1965)
SEG	*Supplementum Epigraphicum Graecum*
SIG	W. Dittenberger, *Sylloge Inscriptionum Graecarum*[3] (Leipzig 1915–24)
SV 2	H. Bengtson, *Die Staatsverträge des Altertums*, vol. 2 (Munich 1962)
SV 3	H.H. Schmitt, *Die Staatsverträge des Altertums*, vol. 3 (Munich 1969)
Sealey, *History*	R. Sealey, *A History of the Greek City States 700–338 B.C.* (Berkeley, Los Angeles and London 1976)
TAPA	*Transactions of the American Philological Association*
Tarn-Griffith	W.W. Tarn, *Hellenistic Civilization*,[3] rev. G.T. Griffith (Cleveland and New York 1961)
Tod	M.N. Tod, *A Selection of Greek Historical Inscriptions*, vol. 2 (Oxford 1948)
Wehrli, *Antigone*	C. Wehrli, *Antigone et Démétrios* (Geneva 1968)
Westlake, *Thessaly*	H.D. Westlake, *Thessaly in the Fourth Century B.C.* (London 1935)
Will, *Histoire*	E. Will, *Histoire politique du monde hellénistique* (Nancy 1966)
YCS	*Yale Classical Studies*
ZPE	*Zeitschrift für Papyrologie und Epigraphik*

SYMBOLS

( )	indicate an explanatory addition to the text
[ ]	enclose letters or words that no longer stand in the text as it survives, but have been restored by modern scholars
< >	enclose letters or words thought to have been accidentally omitted on the original document
[[ ]]	enclose letters or words that were deliberately erased in ancient times
--	indicate that part of a line of the text is missing
---	indicate that a whole line of the text is missing
|	indicates the end of a line on an inscription
||	indicate the beginning of every fifth line on an inscription
/	indicates the end of a line of verse
//	indicate the beginning of every fifth line of verse
*	indicates the text on which the translation of an inscription here given is based
v	indicates a vacant letterspace on the original document
vv	indicate that there is more than one letterspace vacant on the original document
vacat	indicates that an entire line or a space between entire lines was left vacant
(lacuna)	indicates that a portion of the document is missing
Italics	indicate that only a part of the original word is extant on the document

In the transliteration of numerals, the practice followed has been to use Arabic numerals when Greek numerals were used and to use words when the Greek numerals were written out. Deme names (demotics) customarily appear in the Greek in adjectival form (e.g. Aristophon Azenieus), but I give instead the place name with 'of' (of Azenia). For the identification of the demes and the tribes to which they belong the student should consult J.S. Traill, *The Political Organization of Attica* (Princeton 1975) 109–12.

1   Ancient chronology.

A. The Parian Marble (*FGrHist* 239). Paros, 264/3. Two fragments of a marble stele. **B.** *Chronika* from Oxyrhynchus (*FGrHist* 255). Fragment of papyrus from Oxyrhynchus (*P.Oxy.* 12), late first century BC (?). **C.** Eusebius, *Chronika* (ed. Helm), early fourth century AD.

E. Bickerman, *Chronology of the Ancient World*[2] (London 1980) 87–9; A. Mosshammer, *The Chronicle of Eusebius and Greek Chronographic Tradition* (Lewisburg and London 1979) 29–168.

A. The Parian Marble (extracts)[1]

FRAGMENT A

400/39   l.79   From the time when [the Greeks returned, those who]
| went up-country *with* Kyros,[2] and Sokrates the
philosopher died, after living 70 years, 137 years,[3] when
the archon at Athens was Laches

371/70   l.83   [From the time when the battle at Leuctra] | took place
between the Thebans and the Lacedaemonians, (the
battle) that the Thebans won, 107 years, when the
archon at Athens was Phrasikleides.[4] And A[myntas
dies, and Alexandros, his son, over the Macedonians]
| becomes king[5]

368/7   l.86   From the time when Dionysios the Sicilian died,[6] and
his son Dionysios became tyrant, and [after]
Alexandr[os had died, Ptolemaios of Aloros over the
Macedonians] be|comes king,[7] 104 years, when the
archon at Athens was Nausigenes

366/5   l.87   From the time when the Phocians [seized] the *oracle* at
Delphi [-- 102 years, when the archon at Ath]|ens was
Kephisodoros[8]

FRAGMENT B

336/5   l.2   [-- Philip] *died*, and Ale[xand]er becomes king, 72 years,
when the archon at Athens was Pythodelos[9]

335/4   l.2   From the time when Alexander campaigned against the
Triballi and the Illyrii, | and when the Thebans were in
revolt and were besieging his garrison, he took the city
by storm and razed it to the ground, 71 years, when the
archon at Athens was Euainetos[10]

334/3   1.4   From the time of Alexander's crossing over into Asia
and the battle at the Granicus, and from the time of the
battle that Alexander fought against Dareios at Issus,
70 years, when the archon at Athens was | Ktesikles[11]

332/1   1.5   From the time of Alexander's battle against Dareios
| near Arbela, which Alexander won; and he captured
Babylon, and dismissed the allies, and founded Alexandria, 68 years, when the archon at Athens was Niketes[12]

323/2   1.9   From the time when the war took place for the
Athenians near Lamia against Antipatros, and from the
time of the sea battle | that the Macedonians fought
against the Athenians off Amorgos, in which the
Macedonians were victorious, 59 years, when the
archon at Athens was Kephisodoros[13]

321/20   1.11   From the time when Antigonos crossed over into Asia,
| and Alexander was laid to rest at Memphis, and
Perdikkas invaded Egypt and died,[14] and Krateros and
Aristotle the sophist die|d, 57 years, after living 50
years,[15] when the archon at Athens was Archippos

319/18   1.13   From the death of Antipatros[16] and Kassandros' depar-
ture | from Macedonia,[17] and from the time of the siege
of Cyzicus,[18] which Arrhidaios made, and from the time
when Ptolemy captured Syria and Phoenicia,[19] 55 years,
when the archon at Ath|ens was Apollodoros. In this
same year also the Syracusans chose Agathokles general with absolute authority over the defences in Sicily

317/16   1.15   From the time of the battle at sea between Kleitos | and
Nikanor near the temple of the Calchedonians,[20] and
when Demetrios made his laws at Athens,[21] 53 years,
when the archon at Athens was Demogenes

316/15   1.16   From the time when | Kassandros returned to
Macedonia,[22] and Thebes was built,[23] and Olympias
died,[24] and Kassandreia was founded,[25] and Agathokles
over the Syracus|ans became tyrant,[26] 57 years, when
the archon at Athens was Demokleid[es]

312/11   1.19   From the time when the sun was eclipsed,[27] and
Ptolemy defeated Demetrios at | Gaza, and despatched
Seleukos to Babylon, 48 years, when the archon at
Athens was Po[lem]on.

308/7   1.24   From the time when Demetrios, son of Antigonos, cap-
tured the | [P]eiraeus after a siege,[28] [and Demetrios of
Phaleron was thrown out of Athens, 44 years, when the
archon] at Athens was Kairimos

B. *Chronika* from Oxyrhynchus[29]

344/3–341/40   (Col. 2) [In (the) Olym|piad (that was) the ninth and
one] *hundredth,* | [the victor in the] *stadion* [was]
Arist[o]lykos, | *the Athenian,* and the archons at Athens
5   were [Lykiskos, Py]thodotos, Sosi‖g[ene]s,
Ni[ko]machos. Of that (Olympiad) | in the second year
(343/2), Diony|sios the Second, tyrant | of Sicily, having
10   been deprived of the | rule, sailed to Co‖rinth and
remained there, | keeping a school.[30] And in | the fourth
year (341/40) Bagoas, | the eunuch, having assassin-
15 |ated Ochos, the King of the Persians, ‖ made the
youngest of his | sons, Arses, Ki|ng, while he himself was
in charge of affairs.[31] |

340/39–337/6   In (the) Olympiad (that was) the tenth and one h|un-
20   dredth, the victor in the stadion was An‖tikles, the
Athenian, and the archons at A|thens were
Theo[phrasto]s, [Lysima]chides, Chairo[ndes,
Phry|nichos. | . . . In the third year (338/7) Phi|lip, king
30   of the Macedonians, ‖ won the very famous battle | at
Chaironea | against the Athenians and B[oe]otians;[32]
35 | fighting with h|im was his son Alexander, ‖ [who also
won] great distinction at that time. | [And I]socrates the
orator *d|ied, about nine|ty* [. . . years old].[33] *vv* (vol. 3) *vv*
[Ba]‖g[oas, the] *eunuch,* killed | Ar[ses], the King of the
Persians, | along with his broth|ers, and made Dareios,
5   son of Arsa‖mes, who was of the royal stock, | king in
place of Arses.[34] | . . . And in the fourth year (337/6) the
10   lea‖gue of the Greeks having assem|bled, (the Greeks)
chose Philip | general with absolute authority for the
| war against the Persians.[35]

C. Eusebius, *Chronika*[36]

400/399   The Athenians began to use 24 letters (in their
alphabet), although before they had only 16[37]

380/79   A great earthquake took place and (H)elika and Byra,
cities of the Peloponnese, were swallowed up[38]

1 Ancient chronology

377/6	The Athenians became leaders of Greece
355/4	Alexander, son of Philip and Olympias, is born[39]
347/6	Demosthenes, the orator, is celebrated by universal acclaim
330/29	Alexander captured Babylon, after the death of Dareios,[40] at which point the kingdom of the Persians was destroyed
328/7	Alexander captures the rock of Aornis[41] and crosses the Indus river
327/6	Alexander's war in India against Porus and Taxiles
326/5	(H)arpalos flees to Asia[42]
325/4	Alexander dies in Babylon in the thirty-second year of his life; after him the empire was transferred into many hands
311/10	Lysimacheia was founded in Thrace
308/7	Demetrios of Phaleron went to Ptolemy and gained his request that democracy be restored at Athens[43]
304/3	Seleukos founded the cities of Antiochia, Laodicea, Seleucia, Apamea, Edessa, Beroea and Pella; of these Antiochia was built in the twelfth year of his reign[44]
301/0	Seleukos captured Babylon[45]

1　The Parian Marble (henceforth *MP*) was published in 264/3, in the archonship of Diognetos at Athens. The surviving portion consists of two fragments. The first breaks off in the late 350s and contains a strange assortment of material; the rationale for the inclusion or exclusion of events is often very hard to appreciate. The second fragment begins with the death of Philip of Macedon and continues to the year 299/8; it is concerned almost exclusively with the history of Alexander the Great and his successors. Dates are given by Athenian archons. Four dashes will be used to show that a section of the document has been omitted.

2　Cf. Diod. 14.27 (Ol. 95.1 = 400/399); Eusebius Ol. 94.4 (401/0) and Ol. 95.1 (400/399).

3　The figures are calculated against the year 264/3, the date when the document was published.

4　Cf. Diod. 15.54ff. and Pausanias 8.27–8; 9.1.8.

5　Whilst *MP* and Diodorus disagree radically on the reigns of the fifth-century kings, Perdikkas and Archelaos, from Alexandros II through Alexander III they are less often in disagreement, and, if they are, it is only by one year.

6　Cf. Diod. 15.73.5.

7　Cf. Diod. 15.71.1.

8　The traditional date for the outbreak of the Third Sacred War is the archonship of Agathokles (357/6). Cf. Diod. 16.14.3; Pausanias 10.2.3. It is very likely that *MP* has confused Kephisodoros (336/5) with Kephisodotos (358/7), so that the difference is only one year.

9　All sources date Alexander's accession to 336/5 with the exception of Diodorus, who (17.2.1) puts it in the archonship of Euainetos (335/4). Diodorus' mistake here and some mistakes elsewhere in Book 17 might be the result of his using the

Macedonian year. Since this year began in autumn and was not co-terminous with the official year at either Athens or Rome, Diodorus had a problem in equating them, for the Macedonian year covered parts of two years in each of the other systems. If Diodorus chose to equate the Macedonian year with the official years at Athens and Rome that began in the latter part of the Macedonian year, then the discrepancies in his dates would be explained. See M.J. Fontana, *Kokalos* 2 (1956) 37–49.

10 *Chronika* from Oxyrhynchus (henceforth *Chron. Ox.*) places these events in the first year of the 111th Olympiad, the archonship of Pythodelos (336/5), and is likewise one year behind in its dating of events down to the battle of Issus.

11 *MP* is in error in dating the battle of Issus in the same archon year as Granicus. *Chron. Ox.* and Eusebius also give 334/3 as the date for Issus. Diod. 17.33f. and Arrian, *Anabasis* 2.11.10, give the correct date, autumn 333.

12 Though *MP* has the right year for the foundation of Alexandria, it has placed this after, instead of before, the battle of Gaugamela. It is consequently wrong about the date for the battle of Gaugamela (Arbela), which was about 1 October 331. Diodorus gives the year 331/30 for both the foundation of Alexandria (17.52) and the battle of Gaugamela (17.57–61). Eusebius also dates the foundation to 331, while *Chron. Ox.* gives 330/29 for the battle of Gaugamela. On the site of this battle (Gaugamela not Arbela) see Arrian 6.11.5.

13 Both Diodorus (18.2.1) and *MP* give Kephisodoros as the archon for 323/2 and place the Lamian War and the battle of Amorgos in that year. Only *Chron. Ox.* disagrees, naming the archon for that year Kephisophon and, more seriously, placing the Lamian War in Ol. 115.1, the archonship of Neaichmos (320/19).

14 Although we do not have the details entered by *Chron. Ox.* under this year, we do know that it dates Antipatros' crossing to Asia to attack Perdikkas in Ol. 115.2, the archonship of Apollodoros (319/18). Diodorus (18.26–18.32.4) dates the events here recorded under the archonship of Philokles (322/1) and, in fact, fails to give the names of the archons for 321/20 and 320/19. A lacuna has been suspected, but the fact that *MP* has no entry for 320/19 suggests that there was a basic problem about the chronology of these years that was common to our sources. *Chron. Ox.* gives Neaichmos for 320/19, but, as noted above, erroneously assigns the Lamian War to that year. Eusebius dates Perdikkas' invasion of Egypt to Ol. 114.2 (323/2).

15 There is clearly something wrong here. Aristotle lived 62 or 63 years (384–322) and died in the archonship of Philokles (322/1). Maybe the entry has been misplaced.

16 Cf. Diod. 18.48. It appears that *Chron. Ox.* dates the death of Antipatros to Ol. 116.1 (316/15). At any rate its last entry has been restored as follows: '[In the] first year [of this Olympiad Antipatros] *died* [and] *affairs* passed [into the hands of Polyper]chon . . .'

17 Cf. Diod. 18.54. He went to Antigonos in Asia.

18 Cf. Diod. 18.51–53. Arrhidaios was the satrap of Hellespontine Phrygia.

19 Cf. Diod. 18.43, where Ptolemy's invasion is dated 320/19.

20 Cf. Diod. 18.72.4 (318/17).

21 Cf. Diod. 18.74.3 (318/17).

22 Cf. Diod. 19.35.36 (317/16); 19.35.49f. (316/15). For Eusebius, Kassandros' rule in Macedon begins in Ol. 115.4 (317/16) (Hieronymus) or Ol. 116.1 (316/15) (Armenian).

23 Cf. Diod. 19.54.1–3.

24 Cf. Diod. 19.51.

25 Cf. Diod. 19.52.2.

26   Dated by Diodorus (19.2.1) to the archonship of Demogenes (317/16). Eusebius under Ol. 114.2 (323/2) has the entry 'Agathokles assumes the tyranny at Syracuse'.

27   There is no necessary inference that the eclipse was associated with the battle and Diodorus does not mention one in his account (19.80ff.). Consequently, we do not know the exact location from which the eclipse was visible. However, the only total eclipse that was visible in the Greek world around this time took place on August 15, 310. Its line of totality passed through central Asia Minor, southern Greece and Sicily, thereby passing over Paros.

28   Diodorus (20.45) describes Demetrios' capture of the Peiraeus but dates it in the archonship of Anaxikrates (307/6).

29   The *Chronika* from Oxyrhynchus in Egypt covers the period 355/4–316/15. It was written sometime in the Roman period, possibly near the end of the first century BC. The lack of any clear principle in its choice of material suggests that it was excerpted from a larger work. It dates by Olympiads and Athenian archons.

30   Cf. Diod. 16.70.1–3.

31   Cf. Diod. 17.5.3. Diodorus' date for Arses' accession is imprecise, but that of *Chron. Ox.* (341/40) must be wrong. The Akkadian lists of Persian Kings give 338/7–336/5 for Arses' reign. For the possibility that Arses took the royal title Artaxerxes IV see E. Badian, *Greece and the Eastern Mediterranean*, ed. K.H. Kinzl (Berlin and New York 1977) 40–50.

32   Cf. Diod. 16.84–6.

33   Cf. [Plut.] *Lives of the Ten Orators* (= *Moralia* 837ef); Dion. Halic. *de Isoc.* 1 (98 years); Lucian, *Macrob.* 23 (99 years).

34   Cf. Diod. 17.5.4–5, whose text names the father of Dareios Arsanes. His date (336/5) is consistent with the tradition against *Chron. Ox.*

35   Cf. Diod. 16.89.3.

36   From the time of Hellanicus of Lesbos (5th century BC), the Greeks had been assembling chronological systems such as the lists of the priestesses of Hera, archons at Athens, and (later by Aristotle) victors at the Olympic Games. In the Hellenistic period such scholars as Eratosthenes and Sosicrates extended their research to include all the civilizations of the known world (e.g. Egypt, Lydia, Macedonia) and the obvious need arose to relate these lists to one another. Thus the art of comparative chronography was developed, the last and greatest practitioner of which was Eusebius. Beginning, like a good Christian, with the year of Adam, Eusebius established the comparative chronology of the civilized world by inscribing each list on a rod (canon) so that, as each civilization arose, its chronology could be aligned with those that preceded. On the margins or in the centre were rods carrying snippets of historical information. The fact that those snippets could easily be misplaced by a year or two (or sometimes more) is amply demonstrated by the frequent disagreement between our two basic texts of Eusebius, the version of Hieronymus (St Jerome) and an Armenian version. No attempt can possibly be made to represent Eusebius' style in the present selection, but it is well illustrated by Mosshammer. A table showing the differences between the major chronographic sources for the period 336/5–302/1 can be found in F. Jacoby, *FGrHist* 2BD (Commentary on nos. 106–261), pp. 698–701.

37   See no. 6 below. (Of course, the Athenian alphabet never used only 16 letters.)

38   Cf. Diod. 15.48.1–4; Strabo 1.3.18.

39   Cf. Plut. *Alexander* 3.5–9; J.R. Hamilton, *Plutarch Alexander: A Commentary* (Oxford 1969) 7.

40   Cf. the Parian Marble at the year 332/1 and n. 12.

41 Cf. Plut. *Alexander* 58.5; Arrian 4.28.8–30.4; Diod. 17.85; Curtius 8.11.1–25.
42 Harpalos fled twice; the first time in 333 to Megara (Arrian 3.6.4–7); the second and more famous occasion (probably the one intended here) was to Athens in 324 (cf. no. 120 below).
43 Cf. the Parian Marble at the year 308/7. Eusebius is strangely confused about this event.
44 On Seleukos' foundations see A.H.M. Jones, *The Greek City* (Oxford 1940) 7–10.
45 Cf. the Parian Marble at the year 312/11.

2   Alliance between Athens and Eretria. Athens, 404/3 *or* 394/3.

Two fragments of a marble stele, Ionic letters (but o=ou in lines 3, 5, 6, 9, 12, 13; e=ei in lines 6, 9, 14, 17), stoichedon (except in lines 1 and 2, which have larger letters).

IG II² 16+; Tod 103, pp. 16–18; *SV* 2.229, pp. 176–7; *P. Krentz, *AJP* 100 (1979) 399. Cf. Xen. *Hell.* 4.2.17; Diod. 14.82.3.

S. Perlman, *CP* 63 (1968) 260 n.28; Rhodes, *Boule* 82–5; Bury-Meiggs 339; Krentz, *AJP* 100 (1979) 398–400; D. Knoepfler, *AJP* 101 (1980) 462–9.

Fragment A (after Bengtson, *SV* 2)

[Alliance] of the Eretrians | and the Atheni[ans]. | Resolved by the Boule.[1] [Akamantis[2] held the prytan|y], Chelonion,[3] [son of]
5   Theog[--], *was sec||retary*, Euboulide[s[4] was archon (394/3), --] | *presided.* Gnathio[s made the motion: They shall be allies, the E|retrians and the A|then|ians --] | (lacuna)[5]

Fragment A (after Krentz)

[Alliance] of the Eretrians | and the Atheni[ans]. | Resolved by the Boule. [Akamantis or Pandionis held the prytan|y], Chelonion, [son of]
5   Theog[--, (demotic)] *was sec||retary*, Euboulide[s (patronymic) (demotic)] | *presided.*[6] Gnathio[s made the motion: They shall be allies, the E|retrians and the A]then[ians --] | (lacuna)

Fragment B

[-- to the best] of their ability. [And whatever se|ems to be better] to the two cities in joint [de|liberation], *this* shall be valid. The oath shall be
5   sworn | [for the Athenians] by the generals [and th||e Boule and the] Knights, and for the Eretrians *by the* | [generals and] the council and *the Knigh|ts* [and the other] magistrates. *And* there shall exist [-- | --].[7] And there shall be sworn (that which is) *customar|y* (as an) [oath] amongst

7

10 themselves *by each of the t‖wo* (parties). [And] as ambassadors [shall be chosen] right away by the [B|oule ten] *men*, five from the *Boul|e*, [and five from the] *citizens not in office*, to *acce|pt* [the oaths] *from* the Eret[r]ian[s --]

1   The enactment formula is peculiar for the absence of the People. There are, how-ever, other Athenian decrees of the early fourth century that have the same formula, though they are mainly honorific (cf. no. 20). Most scholars assume that the decree 'must have received the ratification of the Assembly' (Tod, p. 17). For a discussion of the problem see Rhodes, *loc. cit.*
2   Both Akamantis and Pandionis fit the space, but the secretary for Pandionis in the archonship of Euboulides was Platon of Phlya, son of Nikochares (cf. no. 20).
3   The name (derived from the word that means 'tortoise') is not common at Athens, but is found three times in inscriptions from Thasos.
4   If this document does belong to the year of Euboulides, then the alliance it records should be very early in his year, for in that summer 3000 hoplites 'from all Euboea' and 100 cavalry from Chalcis fought at Corinth (Xen. *Hell.* 4.2.17; Diod. 14.82.3) and there were also Euboeans at the battle of Coronea (Xen. *Hell.* 4.3.15). That is, if it is a reasonable assumption that alliance should precede military involvement (cf. Knoepfler 462 n. 2).
5   About 7 lines long.
6   By thus removing Euboulides as archon and making him instead the chairman Krentz removes the grounds for dating the document to 394/3. On the basis of the enactment formula (see n. 1 above) Krentz suggests that this was a decree of the Thirty Tyrants, and so dates it to 404/3.
7   '[the alliance for eternity]' (Krentz); '[the alliance for a hundred years]' (Knoepfler). Earlier editors believed this was an alliance for all time but thought that clause was lost in the lacuna.

3   Rewards for the liberators of Athens from the Thirty. Athens, 404/3 *or* 403/2 *or* 401/0. Four fragments of a marble stele, inscribed in front and back, Ionic letters (except e=ei and o=ou in the text of the decree), stoichedon.

IG II^2 10; Tod 100, pp. 8–13, + *SEG* 12.84; D. Hereward, *BSA* 47 (1952) 102–17; *P. Krentz, *Phoenix* 34 (1980) 298–306.[1] Cf. Xen. *Hell.* 2.4.25; Aristotle, *Ath. Pol.* 40.2; [Plut.] *Lives of the Ten Orators* (= *Moralia* 835f–836b).

W.S. Ferguson, *CAH* 5.372–5; D. Whitehead, *Liverpool Class. Monthly* 9 (1984) 8ff.

[Lysiades (patronymic)] *was secretary* [(demotic),| Eukleides (demotic)]os was archon.[2] | [Resolved by the Boule and the People --][3] *held the prytany*, Lysiades was secretary, Demophilos *presided* | [-6-[4] made the motion: Because they are good men with regard to the] *People*,[5] all those who joined in the return from Phyle or to those who *returned*
5   ‖ [from Phyle gave assistance by donating money or supplies,][6] *let it be*

voted by the Athenians. There shall be for them and their descendants | [equality of taxation and the right of possession of land and house in Athens,][7] and the magistrates shall *use* in their case the same laws | [as also in the case of the Athenians. All those who did not join in the return,] but joined in fighting the battle at Munychia, *and* | [captured the Peiraeus[8] or remained loyal to the democratic forces in Peiraeus][9] *when* the reconciliation was brought about and carried out the duties | [assigned to them, there shall be for them and their descendants equality of taxation at Athens and] *the right of giving security*[10] *just as* for the [A]thenians. And the [. . . .][11]

10	Chairedemos	farm(er)	Bendiphanes	tray-(maker)
	Leptines	coo(k)	Emporion	farm(er)
	Demetrios	carpen(ter)	Paid[i]kos	bread-s(eller)
	Euphorion	mulet(eer)	Sosias	full(er)
	Kephis[o]doros	builder	Psammis	farm(er)
15	Hegesias	garden(er)	Egersis	
	Epameinon	mule-tend(er)	Ona[.]mes	[--]
	[. . .]opos	oil-(seller)	Eukolion	labour(er)
	G[l]au[k]ias	farm(er)	Kallias	statu(e-maker)
	[. . . .]on	nut-(seller)	*vacat*	
20	[Diony]sios	farm(er)	Of Aigeis:	
			Athenogi[t]on	[--]

1   This is the only published text of the decree that makes use of the information provided by the new fragments added by Hereward, which have rendered all previous texts obsolete.
2   So Krentz. All previous editions have centred the prescript on the stone and read: '[Lysiades] *was secretary*, [-]os was archon'. On this approach there were only two possible candidates for archon – Pythodoros (404/3) and Xenainetos (401/0).
3   '[Hippothontis]' (Tod).
4   '[Archinos]' (Tod).
5   '[In order that the met]ics [may receive fitting rewards]' (Tod).
6   'or to those who *returned* [gave assist|ance for the return to Peiraeus]' (Tod).
7   '[citizen|ship and they shall be assigned forthwith to the ten tribes]' (Tod).
8   'a[nd joined | in saving] the [Peiraeus for the Athenians]' (Tod).
9   '[and were present in the city]' (Tod). The restoration 'remained loyal to the democratic forces in Peiraeus' (Krentz) must fit somewhere into the body of the decree, for it is found intact on one of the new fragments as a heading. This raises to four the number of categories of those honoured.
10   '[there shall be for them equality of taxation while they live at Athens and the right of intermarriage and the] *right of giving security*' (Tod).
11   The text of the decree breaks off at this point. It is followed by lists of names, to each of which is attached a designation of occupation only. There are three columns of names on the front of the stele, six or seven on the back. The total of names must have been in excess of 1000. The names were probably grouped by categories. The people listed are most likely all non-citizens. For some discussion of the occupations represented see P. Cloché, *REG* 30 (1917) 392–403, M.N. Tod,

Epigraphica 12 (1950) 3–26, and Hereward 113–14. For the sake of example I have given a few names from the back of the inscription, following the text in Tod.

4   Dedicatory epigram for Lysandros. Delphi, end of fifth *or* second half of fourth c. Two fragments of a limestone statue base that formed part of a large group, Ionic letters, non-stoichedon, elegiac couplets (lines 1–4), one line for each verse. The last line is an additional elegiac pentameter.

Fouilles de Delphes 3 (1) (Paris 1932) 50; Pouilloux, *Choix* 46, pp. 157–8; **GHI* 95C, pp. 287–90. Cf. Pausanias 10.9.7–10; Plut. *Lysander* 18.

He dedicated his statue [upon] this monument, when, victorious /| with his swift ships, he had destroyed the power of the sons of Ke[k]rops, /| Lysandros (is his name), having crowned unsacked Lacedaemon, /| his fatherland with its beautiful dancing-grounds, as
5   the acropolis of Greece. //‖ He from sea-girt Samos composed the poem. Ion (is his name).

5   Athens honours loyal Samians.[1] Athens, 403/2. Marble stele, Ionic writing, stoichedon (sometimes observing syllabic division of words).

IG II[2] 1; Tod 97, pp. 1–4; **Pouilloux, *Choix* 24, pp. 92–6. Cf. Xenophon, *Hell.* 2.2.6, 2.3.6.

P. Foucart, *REA* 1 (1899) 181–207; Bury-Meiggs 317.

[Resolved by the Boule and the People, Pand]ionis held the prytany, Agyrrhios[2] of K[ollyt]os | [was secretary, Eukleides was archon, Ka]llias of Oa presided, Kephisophon [made the motion: | Commendation shall be given to the Samians because they are] good men toward the Athenians, and *everything* | [shall be confirmed that the] Athenian
5   [People previously] voted to the Sa[mian] People; ‖ [the Samians shall send, as] they *themselves* request, to Lacedaemon, whomever [they | themselves wish; and since they] *ask* the Athenians to help in the negotiation, (the Athenians) shall also choose | [ambassadors, and these men] *are to negotiate* along with the Samians whatever good they can [and | are to deliberate in common with] them (the Samians). And the Athenians commend the Ephesians and the Not[ians | because they welcomed warmly] (those of the) Samians who were in exile. Intro-
10   duction shall be made of the embassy ‖ [of the Samians to the] *People* to transact any business they require. Invitation shall be issued for

| [dinner] at the Prytaneion tomorrow [to the] *embassy* of the Samians. Kephisophon | [made the motion: Let all the rest] (be) as (resolved) by the Boule; and let the Athenian People vote validity | [to what was] previously *voted* regarding the Samians, exactly as the Boule, after deliberation, | introduced as a recommendation [to the People]. And
15   invitation shall be issued to the embassy of the Samians for dinner ‖ [at the Prytanei]on tomorrow.[3] *vv.*|

1   This decree and another honouring a certain Samian, Poses, and his sons were inscribed at the same time (after the restoration of the democracy) and on the same stele as Fornara no. 166, the recommendations of which are confirmed in line 5.
2   On the career of Agyrrhios see R. Sealey, *Historia* 5 (1956) 178ff.
3   One explanation of this curious rider is that the normal courtesy of invitation to hospitality or dinner in the Prytaneion had been omitted from the original pro-bouleuma. (On 'probouleuma' see Glossary.) Another is that in the probouleuma Kephisophon had invited the Samians to 'hospitality', although, as citizens, they qualified for the honour of 'dinner' in the Prytaneion. In either case, as usual in Athenian inscriptions, if an amendment added anything to, or altered anything in, the motion, the changes were embodied by the secretary in the decree when it was inscribed, but the amendment was also inscribed just as it had been moved in the assembly.

6   The Athenians adopt the Ionian alphabet. 403/2.

Photius, *Lexicon*, and the *Suda s.v. Samion ho demos* (Theopompus, *FGrHist* 115F155).

A.G. Woodhead, *The Study of Greek Inscriptions*[2] (Cambridge and New York 1981) 12–23.

In the archonship of Eukleides Archinos[1] persuaded the Athenians to use Ionian letters . . .[2]

1   The text at this point is very corrupt in both the sources. The name is an emendation. For Archinos see no. 7.
2   From this time onwards the Ionic alphabet gradually superseded the local alphabets throughout the Greek world, especially when Attic (later Koine) became the standard dialect of the Hellenistic world. Local alphabets existed in the fourth century, however (e.g. Arcadian at Tegea (see no. 122).

7   Athens honours the heroes of Phyle. Athens, 403/2.

Five fragments of a marble stele, Ionic letters (but o=ou, except in the epigram), stoichedon with four different letter sizes: in descending order of size these are (1) prescript, lines 1–2; (2) epigram in elegiac couplets, lines 73–6; (3) list of names, lines 3–72; (4) decree, lines 77ff.

7   Athens honours the heroes of Phyle

*A.E. Raubitschek, *Hesperia* 10 (1941) 284–95 (with a line drawing of the arrangement of the fragments p. 289). Cf. Xen. *Hell.* 2.4.2f.; Aesch. 3.187, 190; Dem. 24.135; Nepos, *Thrasybulus* 2–4.

P. Cloché, *La restauration démocratique à Athènes en 403 avant J.-C.* (Paris 1915) 15–18.

[The following occupied Phyl]e | [and restored the democracy].[1]

(There follows a list of names arranged by tribes in two columns, probably of 35 lines each. The list thus runs from lines 3 to 72. There are about 58 names.[2] The first column probably contained the entries for the tribes Erechtheis, Aigeis, Pandionis, Leontis and Akamantis, though only the last three letters of Akamantis are preserved. Of the 30 names listed only two can be restored. '[Thrasyboulos, son of Lykos, of Steir]ia' is suggested as the first entry under the tribe Pandionis,[3] and '[Theokles, son of Leu]kios, of Souni[on]' is the third entry for the tribe Leontis. More remains of the second column. Under Oineis (restored), no names are preserved, but there are several patronymics and the demotic Phylasios ('of Phyle') occurs five times. Under Kekropis (restored) there are the beginnings of three names and the middle of a fourth. The name Hippothontis is largely preserved. Under it can be restored the names 'Archino[s, son of Myronides, from Koile]'[4] and 'Oinei[des]'. 'Aiant[is]' has three entries and Antiochis (restored) has six. After a *vacat* there is a separate heading, probably '[From] E[leutherai]'.[5] This is followed by three unpreserved names.)

| These [men for their courage have been honoured with crowns by the indigenous] /| people [of Athens. For once, when men with unjust]
75   //|| *ordinances* [were ruling the city, they were the first for their deposition] /| *to take the initiative*, [even though it meant risking their lives]. /|

Resolved by *the* [Boule and the People, Pandionis held the prytany, Agyrrhios of Kollytos was secretary, Eukleides | was archon], Keph[isophon of Paiania presided, Archinos made the motion --] | [6]

1   Essential to this restoration are: (1) the identification of the epigram as the one quoted by Aeschines 3.190; (2) the presence of five men from the small deme of Phyle in the list of names, which suggests that the events recorded took place in the vicinity of Phyle; (3) the frequency of the expression 'to occupy Phyle', which became proverbial (cf. Arist. *Ploutos* 1146); (4) the equally common formula for 'restored the democracy'.
2   Though the exact number of names inscribed is uncertain, since the preserved fragments do not join each other, it is unlikely (in Raubitschek's opinion) to have been much larger, certainly not as many as the more than 100 that are implied by Aeschines 3.187. Xenophon (*Hell.* 2.4.3) says Thrasyboulos had 70 followers, while Pausanias (1.29.3), who Raubitschek believes may have seen this monument, says he left Thebes with only 60.

3 The restoration is based upon the regular ordering of the tribes (in which Pandionis
   is third), the preserved ending of the demotic and the number of letter spaces.
4 Archinos' presence at Phyle is thus confirmed beyond question. See the discussion
   in Cloché 16.
5 'Eleutherai was not an Attic deme, but its inhabitants must have been considered as
   Athenians' (Raubitschek 294).
6 The essential points of the honours that must have been proposed in this decree are
   recorded by Aeschines 3.187. He names Archinos as the proposer. If Kephisophon
   of Paiania is correctly restored as the president, he can have held that post only
   when his tribe (Pandionis) was in prytany. He was a member of the Boule in the
   archonship of Eukleides (403/2), for he appears as secretary in the second decree
   inscribed on *IG* II^2 1, the decree honouring Poses and his sons. Kephisophon's name
   might be restored in the list of honorands on line 25, immediately after that of
   Thrasyboulos, where the demotic 'of Paiania' is a certain restoration.

8   Theozotides and the Athenian orphans. 403/2.

A. Decree of Theozotides. Athens, 403/2. Marble stele, inscribed on front and left side,
Ionic letters (except o−ou), stoichedon. *R.S. Stroud, *Hesperia* 40 (1971) 280–301.
B. Lysias, *Against Theozotides*. Papyrus, Hibeh, third century AD. Grenfell and Hunt, *The
Hibeh Papyri* 1 (London 1906) 49–55, no. 14; *Lysias*, ed. L. Gernet and M. Bizos (Budé)
2.234–6, 257–9.

A. The decree of Theozotides

FRONT
Resolved by the *Boule* [and the] *People*, Antioch‖[i]s held the prytany,
[8]s was secretar|y, Kallisthene[s] presided, [Theo]zotides^1 | made the
5   motion. All those Athenia[ns] who *died by viol‖ent* death in the oligarchy
    help|ing the democracy,^{2} to the *children* of these men | *for the sake of* the
    benefaction of their fathers towards | the Ath[en]ia[n] *people* [and] (for the
10 sake of their) *bravery*, | *to distribute* to the *children of* [all] *these* an ‖ *obol* [a]
    day as *maintenance*. And [just as] t|o *orphans* there is *rendered* [by the law
    from] the | Prytanei|on] . . .^{3}

LEFT SIDE^4
5   Kleoboulos, | son of Androkles, | Androkles, | son of Androkles, ‖ both
    of Aphidna. | Lysanias, | son of Olympi[chos,] | Hippon, | son of
10 [O]lympichos, ‖ both of Kydathen[ai]on. | Athenaios, | son of
15 Philonau|tos, of Alope|ke. ‖ Charikle[s], | son of Chairede|mos, |
20 Chairede|mos, ‖ son of Chairede|mos, | Kol[-c.4-]|s.^{5}

B. Lysias, *Against Theozotides*^{6}

FRAGMENT A
5   [--] *by this law* [--] these, and especially ‖ [on account of] *this* [judge-

ment],[7] *hat|ing* both the illegitimate and the | *adopted* neither lawfully
no|r in a holy manner. For it seems to me that of the *or|phans* [it is even]
10   more the illegitimate ‖ [who deserve to be maintained][8] by the city than
the | [legitimate]. For, [as for the] legitimate, | [their father when he
dies][9] *leave|s* (them) [heirs to his fortune], *but* [as for the] illegit-
imate | . . .[10]

FRAGMENT B

25   Of their *patrimony* -- | [-] of *his* service as a *mercenary* [--‖-] *that man* left
behind for them [--. | But this] is the most terrible of all things if | [the]
finest of the proclamations contained | in the *laws* is misrepresented | by
30   Theozo[tid]es and a falsehood ‖ *established.* For at the Dionysia | *whenever*
the herald publicly proclaims the | *orphans* with their patronymics[11] and
35   adds | [that] the fathers of these | youths died in the w‖ar, fighting for
their | country as brave men, | [and] (that) the state maintained these
(youths) *un|til* (they reached) manhood, will he then separately, | con-
40   cerning the adopted and the *il‖legitimate*, make an announcement saying
that these | were not maintained (by the state) owing to Theozotides,
| or by *making a* similar *proclamation* about all | [the orphans, will] he
45   [speak falsely | of the] adopted and the *ill‖egitimate*, by passing over their
upbringing in *silence?* | What an outrage and what a *great disgrace* [this
will be for the city]! But *after* Kle|[omenes--], *gentlemen* of the jury, | [--]
occupied *the Acropolis* | [-][12]

1   On Theozotides' family and career see Davies, *Families* 6915.
2   This surely refers to the overthrow of the Thirty. See Stroud 285–7. The word
     demokratia appears here for the first time on stone in Athens.
3   There are eleven lines of text following, but they are so poorly preserved as to
     make translation meaningless. It is clear, however, that Theozotides is referring to
     the established procedures regarding war-orphans as a model for his proposal. For
     a review of what is known about the public support of war-orphans see Stroud
     288–90.
4   Three separate masons with very different styles inscribed the names on the left
     side. This, together with the difference between the lettering on the side and that
     on the front, leads Stroud to suggest (283) that the names were added after the
     decree had been inscribed.
5   The deme of his demotic is either Kollytos or Kolonos.
6   The fragments of Lysias' speech against Theozotides that have been preserved
     suggest that the law that Lysias was opposed to had, at least, the following pro-
     visions: (1) orphans of citizens should be raised by the state, but bastards and
     adopted children should not; (2) pay for the cavalry on campaign should be
     reduced from one drachma to 4 obols a day. The only element common to both
     these provisions is economic retrenchment.
7   Supplied by Jander (*app. crit.* Budé).

8   Supplied by Fuhr (*app. crit.* Budé).
9   Supplied by Fuhr (*app. crit.* Budé).
10 End of fr. A, col. 1. Nothing translatable remains of col. 2.
11 Cf. Aeschines 2.154.
12 End of fr. B, col. 1. Nothing translatable remains of col. 2.

9   The revised Athenian law-code (the calendar of sacrifices). Athens, 403/2–400/399.

One (C) of eleven fragments of several large marble stelai that were designed to be joined together by clamps to form at least two free-standing walls, one 120 mm thick, the other *c.* 92 mm thick, inscribed on front and back (except fr. E, which was inscribed on only one surface and is 144 mm thick). Attic letters (on the front), Ionic letters (on the back surface, a large part of which had been erased and re-inscribed), stoichedon (except that line 1 forms a heading in larger letters and the names of months are inscribed in letters intermediate in size between those of the heading and those of the text).

J.H. Oliver, *Hesperia* 4 (1935) 21;*F. Sokolowski, *Lois sacrées des cités grecques* (Paris 1962) no. 10, pp. 27–31. Cf. Lysias 30, *passim*; Andocides 3.81–5.

Oliver, *Hesperia* 4 (1935) 5–32; S. Dow, *Hesperia* 10 (1941) 31–7; C. Hignett, *A History of the Athenian Constitution* (Oxford 1952) 299–305; A.R.W. Harrison, *JHS* 75 (1955) 26–35; E. Ruschenbusch, *Historia* 5 (1956) 123–8; S. Dow, *Proc. Mass. Hist. Soc.* 71 (1953–59) 3–36; *idem*, *Historia* 9 (1960) 270–93; *idem*, *Hesperia* 30 (1961) 58–73; D. MacDowell, *Andokides on the Mysteries* (Oxford 1962) 194–9; R. Stroud, *Drakon's Law on Homicide* (Berkeley and Los Angeles 1968) 20 8, esp. 26 n.32; J.D. Mikalson, *The Sacred and Civil Calendar of the Athenian Year* (Princeton 1975) 29–31, 46; R.S. Stroud, *The Axones and Kyrbeis of Drakon and Solon* (Berkeley and Los Angeles 1979) *passim*; K. Clinton, *AJP* 100 (1979) 1–12.

Fragment C (back), cols. 2 and 3[1]

30	The following sacrifices are made every other year a[--].[2]
	In Hekatombaion[3]
	On the fifteenth
	From the Tribe-
	kings' (laws)[4]
35	For the tribe of the G(e)leontes,[5]
	for the Leukotainians'
	trittys, a sheep
4dr.	without a mark
4dr.2ob.	The priestly perquisite
40	for the Tribe-kings

	1dr.	For the back
		To the herald for the shoulder,
	4ob.	feet, head
		On the sixteenth[6]
45		From the Tribe-
		kings' (laws)
		For the tribe of the G(e)leontes,
		for Zeus of the brotherhood and
		Athena of the bro-
50		therhood, two oxen
	50dr.	without a mark
	16dr.	The priestly perquisite
		for the Tribe-kings,
		the leg.
55		To the herald for the chest,
	2dr.3ob.	feet, head.
		For the rearer (of the animals), of barley
		bushels
		[---]
60	12dr.	To Themis[7] a sheep
	15dr.	To Zeus of the forecourt a *sheep*
	12dr.	To Demeter a sheep
		To Pherrephatta[8]
	17dr.	a ram
65	15dr.	To Eumolpos a sheep
	15dr.	To Delichos[9] the *hero* [a sheep]
	15dr.	To Archegetes[10] [a sheep]
	15dr.	To Polyxen[os a sheep]
		To Threptos[11] [a ram]
70	17dr.	of select quality
	15dr.	To Dioklo[s a sheep]
	15dr.	To Keleos [a sheep]
		The Eumolp[idai]
		[make] these [sacrifices]
75		to the priestess [of Demeter]
	100dr.	
		From the *stelai*[12]
	3dr.	A young pig [-]
	12dr.	To Hesti[a a sheep]
80	12dr.	To Athen[a a sheep]
	10dr.	To the Gr[aces --]
		[A sheep] to Her[mes]
	15dr.	*who presides over games*

	10dr.	[---]
85	15dr.	To He[ra[13] a sheep]
	15dr.	To Z[eus a sheep]
		[---]

1   The revision of the Athenian law-code was begun in 410 after the restoration of the democracy. It was carried out by a commission of 10 anagrapheis, of whom only Nikomachos is known. Some of the laws they republished without revision on separate stelai, e.g. Drakon's law on homicide (Fornara no. 15). The bulk of their work was inscribed in Attic letters on the front side of the two free-standing walls in a somewhat crude, inelegant fashion. This was largely Sacred Law, though we do have part of a trierarchic law on the front side of the fragment translated here. This publication antedates the period of the Thirty Tyrants and so is not relevant to this volume. The commission resumed its work in the archonship of Eukleides and continued down to 400/399. Their attention seems to have been devoted to a detailed publication of the Sacred Calendar, which was inscribed in Ionic letters (cf. no. 6), in elegant stoichedon pattern on the back side of the walls and continued on to another wall (fr. E) that was inscribed on one side only. The largest and best preserved fragment (C) is the one translated here. The walls were set up inside the Royal Stoa in the Agora. Some confusion exists as the result of the demonstration that a large part, if not the whole, of the back surface had already been inscribed and required wholesale erasure before the Sacred Calendar could be cut on it. For an explanation see A. Fingarette, *Hesperia* 40 (1971) 330–335.

2   This heading runs over the second and third columns only and does not pertain to col. 1, which was most likely concerned with yearly sacrifices. The end of the line is restored by Oliver as '[at] A[thens]' but by Dow as '*from* (the Greek word '*a[po'*) [the archonship of Laches (400/399), earlier series of festivals]'.

3   The first month of the Athenian year, around midsummer.

4   The formula, and others like it, has been shown by Dow to indicate not the funds from which the monies listed in the margin were dispensed, but the legal source from which Nikomachos and his colleagues derived their information.

5   One of the four ('Ionian') tribes of pre-Kleisthenic Athens. The others were Argadeis, Hopletes and Aigikoreis. Cf. Sealey, *History* 23.

6   The date of the festival of Synoikia (unification of Attica).

7   All the following gods and heroes are associated with the festival of the Eleusinia.

8   I.e. Kore (Persephone), daughter of Demeter.

9   Read now Melichos. See Clinton 6 n.17.

10 Iacchos.

11 Triptolemos.

12 Cf. Lysias 30.17.

13 Or 'Her[akles]'. See Clinton 6.

10   Extract from an inventory[1] of the treasures of Athena and of the Other Gods.[2] Athens, 398/7. Marble stele (inscribed front and back), Ionic letters, stoichedon (except line 1, which forms a heading).

IG II[2] 1388.

W.S. Ferguson, *The Treasurers of Athena* (Cambridge, Mass. 1932) 110–40.

Gods. | [The following, the treasurers of the] *sacred* treasures of Athena
and of the O|*ther* [Gods, who held office in] the archonship of
[Euthykl]es (398/7), (namely) Epichares of Euonym|[on, Protokles of
5 Ikari]a, Kephisophon of Paiania, Charias of P||[elekes, Demokles] from
[Kephale], D[i]ogeiton of Acharnai, *vv* | [Diomedes of Phlya, Aris]tokles
of Hamaxanteia, Philokrates | [of Aphidna, Anthemion] of Anaphlys-
tos, for whom Mnesiergos of Athmo|[non was secretary,] handed over
10 to the treasurers who held office in Souniades' | [archonship (397/6),
(namely) -8-]atos of Euonymon, Charias of Araphen, Di||[-18-], Eubios
of Aithalidai, Euathlos from Ker|[ameis, -13-], Philotades of Dekeleia,
vv | *vacat* [Xenon of Anaphly]stos, for (all of) whom Morychos of
Boutadai was secretary, | *having taken* (them) *over* from the previous
treasurers who held office in [Arist|okrates'] archonship (399/8),
15 (namely) Sokrat[e]s of Lam[pt]rai and his *fellow magistrate*||*s*, [for whom
Chairi]on of Eleusis was secretary, in the temple of the
He|[katomped]on, in number and weight: Of the golden Nike:[3] First
s|*helf*: head, diadem, a pair of earrings, chaplet, necklace, two studs of
go|ld, left *hand*, bracelet, little gold pieces; weight *of these*, 2044 dr. 3 ob.
20 Second shelf: breastplate, breastband; wei||ght of these, 2010 dr. Third
shelf: folded portion of the chiton, two buckles, fee|t [two]; weight of
these, 1939 dr. 3 ob. Fourth shelf: | right [hand], bracelet, crown, pair
of ribbands; weight of the|se, [1]968 dr. Fifth shelf: golden wing for the
25 *b*|*ack*, two legs; weight of these, 4002 dr. 3 ob. Censer || *of silver*, which
Kleostrate, daughter of Nikeratos, dedicated, bronze *sup*|*ports* included;
weight of these, 1300 dr. Unworked gold: weight | [of this, 3] ½ ob.
Bracelets of thin gold, [2], Polyhippe, daughter of Meleteon | of
[Acharn]ai dedicated (them); weight of these two, 1 dr. 4 ob. Collar of
twisted metal, *plat*|*ed with gold*, silver underneath; weight of this, 58 dr.
30 4 ob. Crown of go||ld, prize for valour for the Goddess; weight of this,
272 dr. 3½ ob. Wine-pourer|s *of silver*, 3; weight of these, 1382 dr. 2 ob.
Crown of go|ld, which Lysandros, son of Aristokritos, the Lacedaemo-
nian dedicated;[4] | weight of this, 66 dr. 5 ob. Crown in the form of an
olive branch, made of gold, which Gelon, son of T|[les]onidas, of
35 Pellene dedicated; weight of this, 17 dr. 3 ob. Cro||wn in the form of an
olive branch, made of gold, which Hierokles of Phaselis dedicated;
wei|ght of this, 64 dr. Crown in the form of an olive branch, made of
gold, which the city dedica|ted, the victory-prize for the competition in
the cithara; weight of this, 85 dr. Cro|wn in the form of an olive branch,
made of gold, which Aristomache, daughter of Aristokles, dedicated;
40 | *weight* of this, 26 dr. 3 ob. Circular ring of gold, which Platth||[is] of
[Ae]gina dedicated, weight of this 1½ ob. Crown of gol|d, [which the]
Nike has on her head, the Nike on the hand of the stat|ue of gold,
unweighed.[5] Phocaean staters, 2. Phocaean sixths,[6] | [12]. Persian

shekels[7] of silver, 11. Golden stand, unweig|hed. *Mixing bowl,* silver under-
45   neath, overlaid with gold, unweighed. Phocaean sixth, || [one. Two]
seal-stones, one on a ring of gold, the | [other] *silver.* Bronze bowls, 100.
Bronze weights, 12. *Dagg|er* with [ivory] *sheath;* this was dedicated by the
Boule (that held office in) | [the archonship of Antigenes (407/6)].
Drinking cup of Zeus Polieus, made of silver; [w|eight of this, 199 dr.].
Belonging to Artemis of Brauron, *gold vessels* | [---][8]

1   The treasurers of the sacred treasures issued only inventories in the fourth century,
     not accounts as they had in the fifth. See Ferguson 128.
2   The treasurers of Athena and the treasurers of the Other Gods were amalgamated
     into one board in 406. They remained so until 385/4, when they were again sepa-
     rated. In 342/1 they were once more combined and stayed that way for the rest of
     the fourth century. In the period from which this extract is taken, although the great
     majority of the sacred treasures had been moved into the Hekatompedon (the cella
     of the Parthenon), the treasurers produced three lists yearly of treasures whose
     provenance was the Parthenon, the Opisthodomos and the Hekatompedon respect-
     ively. See Ferguson 104–27.
3   This is the sole survivor of the 8 golden Nikai that had been created between 434
     and 406. The others had been melted down in the last years of the Peloponnesian
     War. The creation of a new Nike was begun in 377, from the melting down of golden
     crowns (see next note), and this was dedicated in 374. Later in the 330s Lykourgos
     saw to the creation of others, all of which were finally melted down by Lachares at
     the end of the century. See Ferguson 122 n.2. Cf. Fornara nos. 119, 164 and n.4.
4   Dedicated in 403. This and most of the other crowns listed here disappear after
     378/7 and the likelihood is that they were melted down for the creation of the new
     golden Nike of 374.
5   The statue is that of Athena Parthenos. This crown is regularly listed as unweighed.
6   That is, the sixth part of a stater.
7   One Persian shekel = 7½ Attic obols (Xen. *Anab.* 1.5.6).
8   The last part of the front face is lost. It most likely contained the list of the silver
     hydriai, nineteen of which (at least) were in existence. By 391/90 their number had
     been increased to twenty seven. Cf. *IG* II² 1400, 23–32, and Ferguson 113–15. The
     inscription continues on the back with a separate list of the 'uncatalogued and
     unweighed [annual dedications]'.

11   Internal politics in Athens, Corinth, Thebes and Argos as the real cause of the Corinthian War. 397/6 (early 396) *or* 396/5.

A. The Oxyrhynchus Historian (London fragment 1–3). Fragments of papyrus from
Oxyrhynchus (*P.Oxy.* 842), late second or early third century AD. **Hell. Oxy.* 6.1–7.5.
B. Polyaenus, *Strategemata* 1.48.3. **C.** Harpocration, *Lexicon s.v.* Hagnias (Androtion,
FGrHist 324F18; Philochorus, *FGrHist* 328F147). Cf. Xen. *Hell.* 3.5.1; Pausanias 3.9.8;
Isaeus 11.8.

R. Sealey, *Historia* 5 (1956) 178–203; I.A.F. Bruce, *Emerita* 28 (1960) 75–86; D. Kagan,
PP 80 (1961) 321–41; S. Perlman, *CQ* 13 (1963) 64–81; Bruce, *Commentary* 50–63; R.
Seager, *JHS* 87 (1967) 95–115; G.A. Lehmann, *ZPE* 28 (1978) 109–26; *ZPE* 30 (1978)
73–93; Hamilton, *Sparta* 178–208.

11 Internal politics as the real cause of the Corinthian War

A. The Oxyrhynchus Historian

(6.1) About *the* [same] *time*[1] a trireme sailed out | from Athens [without the] approval of [the] *People*. It *was* | Demain[et]os[2] (who was) in *charge* of it. (He had) communicated [in] | secret with the Boule about the
5 *affair*, as it is said, || since (some) of the citizens had joined with him. With [these] | he went down to Peiraeus, *launched* a ship from the | ship-sheds and putting to [sea tried to sail] *to* Kon[on]. (2) An up|roar *occurred* after this. Those of the Athe|nians who were angered [were the]
10 *notables* and the re||spected, and they were *saying* [that] they (Demainetos and his associates) would *destroy*[3] the city by starting a *war* [against the Lac]edaemon[i]ans. The *members of the Boule* were thrown into a panic *by the* uproar and summoned a meeting of the Assembly, maintaining the pretence (that they) had had no part in the affair. When the people
15 || were assembled, those of the Athenians who were of the group led by Thrasyboulos, Aisimos and Anytos arose (and) instructed the People that they would (in)cur great danger for themselves, unless they absolved the city of responsibility. (3) Of the Athenians, those who
20 were reasonable and owned property were || happy with things as they were,[4] whilst the popular majority was at that time cowed and was persuaded by those who were giving advice.[5] So they sent to Milon,[6] the harmost of Aegina, and *told* (him) to make every *effort* to punish Demai[ne]tos, because (it was) *without* the city's approval (that) he had
25 done || this. Beforehand, [however,] almost all the time they were *stirring up trouble* and in many ways *were acting in opposition* to *the* Lacedaemo[nian]s. (7.1) For they kept on sending weapons [and] *crews* for the ships that were with K[onon], and ambassadors had been *sent*
30 || to the Great King p[7] [-- those led by --]krates[8] and Hagnias and Tele[sag]oros. These were caught by Pharax the previous navarch,[9] who sent them off to the L[a]cedaemonians, and they put them to death. (2) And they persisted in this opposition on the instigation of
35 the group led by || Epikrates[10] and Kephalos.[11] For those were the men who were especially desirous (of involving) the city (in war) and they had maintained this (policy), not from the time when they had con- versed with Timokrates and (Col. 2) [had taken] the money, [but already long] before. And yet some *say* that the money that he (Timokrates) brought [was the cause] of *the alliance* [between these men and] those in Boeotia and those *in the* [other] previously named [cities],
5 || not knowing that *all* [these men] *happened* for a long time to be hostile [to the Lacedaemo]ni[a]ns and to be on the look-out for a way to *involve their cities in a war*. For hostility was felt by the Argives and the *leaders* [of the] Boeot[ians] towards the Lacedaemonians, because their political
10 *opponents* || were treated by them (the Lacedaemonians) as friends, and

(hostility was felt) by those in Athens who were eager to rid the Athen[i]ans of their inactive and peaceful state and to lead them [on] to war-making and *ambitious activity*, in order that it might be possible for them to enrich themselves from the public treasury . . . Well now, these men, in the cities aforementioned, for the reasons given rather than because of Pharnabazos and his money were aroused to hostility
35 ‖ towards the Lacedaemonians.

B. Polyaenus, *Strategemata* 1.48.3

Since Konon was in alliance with Pharnabazos when Agesilaos was laying Asia waste, he persuaded the Persian to send money to the political leaders of the cities of Hellas, in order that, after receiving it, they might persuade their fatherlands to begin the war against the Spartans. And they (the political leaders) did persuade (their fatherlands to begin the war), after they had been bribed, and the Corinthian War broke out. The Lacedaemonians, for their part, recalled Agesilaos from Asia.

C. Harpocration, *Lexicon s.v.* Hagnias

Androtion in the fifth book of his *Atthis*, and Philochorus, say that this man (Hagnias) and his fellow-ambassadors were captured and put to death by the Lacedaemonians.

In the translation of this papyrus I have marked off only the first ten lines, then every fifth line, since this is the practice of Bartoletti in the Teubner text.

1 The date of this event is one of the most crucial chronological problems in the Oxyrhynchus History. Essential to its solution are the first sentences of the poorly preserved section immediately following the passage translated. Enough of these is extant to indicate that the author passed on to narrate the events of the spring (most likely) or summer of the eighth year. Since the author began his history where Thucydides left off, the eighth year cannot refer back to that point. Clearly he has chosen some other epochal year; the question is, which one? See Bruce, *Commentary* 66–72, for a well-reasoned discussion of the contending views. More recently the topic has been treated (in German) by G.A. Lehmann in the articles cited.
2 Cf. Aeschines 2.78, where a Demainetos, who is probably to be identified with this one, is identified as a member of the clan Bouzygai. See Bruce, *Commentary* 50–1, for the further career of Demainetos, and for the possible family relationship see Davies, *Families* 3276.
3 Bartoletti. 'Would bring disrepute upon' (Grenfell and Hunt).
4 Or 'acquiesced in the present state of affairs'. For the divergent views over what 'the present state of affairs' refers to see Bruce, *Commentary* 53–4.
5 For an interpretation of the internal politics involved see Sealey 179–85.
6 The name is Cheilon in Aeschines 2.78, if the reference is to the same incident.

7   This is the initial letter of a Greek word, which has been restored as 'previously'
    (Meyer), 'first' (Bury), 'five' (Richards), 'again' (Kalinka).
8   The possible restorations are Hippokrates, Autokrates or (less likely) Aristokrates.
9   Cf. Xen. *Hell.* 3.2.12–14. The date of the embassy is most likely spring or summer
    397.
10 See Davies, *Families* 4859, and Bruce, *Commentary* 56.
11 See Bruce, *Commentary* 56–7.

12   The activities of Konon. 397/6–394/3.

A. Photius, *Bibliotheca* 44b20–38 (Ctesias, *Persica, FGrHist* 688F30). **B.** Didymus, *Demosthenes*, col. 7.28ff. on Dem. 10.34 (Philochorus, *FGrHist* 328F144–6). F. Jacoby, **FGrHist* 3b (text) and 3b Suppl. 1 and 2 (Commentary and Notes), 328F144–6. **C.** The Oxyrhynchus Historian (London fragment 4.2–3, 10, 14). **Hell. Oxy.* 9.2–3, 15, 19. **D.** *SIG* 126; Tod 106, pp. 21–2; **Die Inschriften von Erythrai und Klazomenai*, ed. H. Engelmann and R. Merkelbach (Bonn 1972) 51–2 (with a photograph of a squeeze). Erythrae, 394/3. Fragment of a stele (now lost), Ionic letters, stoichedon. Cf. Xen. *Hell.* 4.3.10–12; 4.8.6; Diod. 14.79.4–8, 81.4–6, 83.4–7, 84.3–5, 85.2–4; Pausanias 6.7.6; Plutarch, *Artaxerxes* 21; Isocrates 4.142; Nepos, *Conon* 4.

G.L. Cawkwell, *NC* 16 (1956) 69–75; I.A.F. Bruce, *CQ* 11 (1961) 166–70 and *PCPS* 8 (1962) 13–16; G.L. Cawkwell, *JHS* 83 (1963) 152–4; R. Seager, *JHS* 87 (1967) 99–104; Bruce, *Commentary* 72–6, 97–102, 122–7; E. Costa, *Historia* 23 (1974) 48–56; Hamilton, *Sparta* 187–92, 227–32.

A. Photius, *Bibliotheca* 44b20–38 (epitome of Ctesias' *Persica*)

The reasons why King Artoxerxes (*sic*) was at odds with Evagoras, king of Salamis: both the messengers of Evagoras to Ktesias for the purpose of receiving the letters from Aboulites, and the letter of Ktesias to him about reconciling him to Anaxagoras, king of the Cyprians. The arrival of the messengers of Evagoras at Cyprus, and the return to Evagoras of the letters from Ktesias. And the speech of Konon to Evagoras[1] concerning the journey up-country to the King, and Evagoras' letter about what was demanded by him. And the letter of Konon to Ktesias, and the tribute from Evagoras to the King, and the return of the letters to Ktesias. The discussion of Ktesias with the King about Konon, and the letter to him. The return of gifts from Evagoras to Satibarzanes, and the arrival of the messengers to Cyprus, and Konon's letter to the King and Ktesias. How the messengers from the Lacedaemonians, who had been sent to the King, were imprisoned. The King's letter to Konon and to the Lacedaemonians, which Ktesias himself conveyed. How Konon became commander of the navy through the influence of Pharnabazos.

B. Didymus, *Demosthenes* col. 7.28ff. on Dem. 10.34

DEMOSTHENES 10.34

For, as for me, whenever I see someone who is fearful of the man in
Sousa and Ekbatana and who says that he (the man in Sousa) is ill-
disposed to the city, even though in the past he helped in putting the
city's affairs in order and just recently was making offers (if you did not
accept them, but voted rejection, it was not his fault),[2] and (when I see
this same man) saying something different about the plunderer of the
Greeks, who near at hand, at our doors, in the very centre of Greece, is
so increasing in power, I am amazed and I fear him, whoever he may be,
because he does not fear Philip.

DIDYMUS, *DEMOSTHENES* COL. 7.28ff.

... Therefore that it is not reasonable | that they are being reminded by
30   [D]emosthenes of this ‖ peace[3] has been seen, but rather of some other
be|nefaction and [probably the one] concerning Ko[non] the [son of]
Timothe|[os because] this [man with] *the* armaments from
Phar[naba]zos, | which he used, in the sea-battle near Cn[i]dus | *over-*
35   *whelmed* the [La]cedaemonians. ‖ Phi[lochorus] *will confirm these* facts
also. For [under the heading], '*The archonsh|ip of* [S]ou[niade]s of
Acharnai (397/6)' he writes [as follows --[4]]: K[o]non --] with *many*
[*ships*[5] -- Cy]prus | [-- Pharnabazos the] *satrap* [of Phr]ygia | [--] the
40   *same* [-- ‖ --][6] he sailed [-- | --] of triremes [-- | --] of the gulf [-- | -- he]
45   brought up [from S]yria [-- | ---] ‖ and *bringing together* the *ships* [from the]
King [near L]orym[a | on the] Cher[so]nese[7] and *thence with all* (these)
attack|ing unexpectedly the *navarch* of the [Lac]edae[monian]s | [--] and
50   when a sea-battle took place *he was victorious* [and] fifty triremes ‖ *were*
captured and Peisandros was kil|led. After this sea-battle Konon |
restored the [Long] Walls too for the Athenian[s], | *against the will* of the
Lacedaemonians, a|s the same historian records also.

C. The Oxyrhynchus Historian 9.2–3

THE NAVAL WAR 396/5

20   (9.2) [--- ‖ -- to the ships of the Lac]edaemonians and their | [allies came
Pollis],[8] who had arrived as navarch from Lace|[daemon to take over
the navarchy of] Archelaidas, *since he had been app|pointed* [his successor.[9]
And at the] same time Phoenician | [and Cilician] ships [had come] to
25   Caunus, *ninety* (in number), of which ‖ [ten sailed from Cili]cia, while
the rest | [--] of them the Sidonian | [ruler[10] --] *for the King* to the men of
that | [land --] *regarding* the navarchy. Phar|[nabazos --] (the next two
lines are too fragmentary to be translated) [-- the] *camp.* (9.3) But

K[o]non in (his) direction | [--] *perceiving*, after taking up | [-- and]
35   manning the triremes | [-- as] *quickly as possible* the river, the Cau‖[nian
(river)[11] as it was called], sailed [to] the C[a]unian *lake* | [--] of
Pharnabazos and Ko‖[non --phe]rne[s],[12] a Persian [--] | (The rest of
col. 3 and the whole of col. 4 are too fragmentary to be intelligible.)

The Oxyrhynchus Historian 15.1–3

REVOLUTION AT RHODES, SUMMER 395[13]
(15.1) [--] *ea|ch day he held a review* [of his soldiers] under *a|rms* in the
harbour. [His expressed purpose for this was] that they might not,
through *in|activity*, [become] less effective [in] war, but (really) he
5   *wa‖nted* to make the Rhodians [eagerly] prepared, [if at any time] they
saw [them] *present*, under *arms*, at that time to undertake *their* assignment.
[After] *he had made* everyone [accustomed] to seeing the *review*, he [him-
self], taking twenty [of the] triremes, sailed off [to Caunus], because he
10   *wished* ‖ [not] to be present at the death [of the magistrates], but to
Hieronymos and Nikophemos[14] *he gave orders to take care of* affairs, since
they were his *associates*. (2) [And they,] after waiting that day, *when the*
troops were present [for] *the review* on the following day, as usu‖al, led some
15   of them along [under] arms into the harbour, while others (they
stationed) just [outside] the agora. Those of the Rhodians who were
party to the *conspiracy*, when they judged the time was ripe for attempting their *task*, gathered together into the agora, (armed) *with* daggers.
20   And Dorimachos,[15] ‖ one of them, mounted the stone from which
usually the herald made proclamations, and shouted out at the top of
his voice: 'Fellow citizens,' he said, 'let us attack the tyrants as quickly
as possible.' And the rest, after he had shouted out for assistance, with
25   their daggers (in hand) leaped upon the tri‖bunal of the magistrates
and killed the Diago[re]ans and eleven other citizens. After accomplishing that, they called the Rhodian citizens to an assembly. (3) They
had only just assembled, when Konon returned from Caunus with his
30   triremes. Then those ‖ who had perpetrated the massacre dissolved the
existing constitution and established a democracy. Some few of the
citizens were exiled. And so the Rhodian revolution ended in that way.

The Oxyrhynchus Historian 19.1–3 (col. 15.32–col. 16.29)

THE NAVAL WAR, SUMMER, AND AUTUMN 395
(19.1) And Konon, since Cheirikrates[16] had already taken over (the
command) of the ships of the Lacedaemonians and their allies, for he
35   had arrived as navarch in succ‖ession to Pollis, manned twenty of his
triremes and, putting out from Rhodes, sailed to Caunus. Because he

wished to communicate with Pharnabazos and Tithraustes and to get
money,[17] he went inland from Caunus to (see) them. (2) It happened

40   that his sold‖iers were at that time owed many months' pay.[18] For they
were being paid by the generals insufficiently, as is always the case with

5   those fighting on the King's behalf. For (even) in the ‖ Decelean War,
when they (*sc.* the Persians) were the allies of the Lacedaemonians, it
was in an altogether unsatisfactory and niggardly fashion that they
were in the habit of providing money, and on many occasions this
would have led to the dissolution of the fleet of the allies, had it not
been for Kyros' eager support. And the King is to blame for this, for he,

10   ‖ whenever he enters a war, sends down some money at the beginning
to the leaders but takes little thought for the time that follows, and
those who are in charge of affairs, since they are unable to make payment from their own pockets, sometimes *watch helplessly* the dissolution

15   of their own ‖ *forces*.[19] (3) Anyway, that is the way it turns out usually.
But Tithraustes, on the arrival of Konon at his court, who told him that
there would be a danger of ruining their plans through lack of money,

20   in which respect those fighting for the King ought not re‖asonably to
fail, sent some of his entourage to give pay to the soldiers. They took
with them two hundred and twenty[20] silver talents, money that had
been taken from the property of Tissaphernes. Then Tithraustes, after

25   spend‖ing a little more time in Sardis, went up-country to the King,
appointing as generals in charge of affairs Ariaios and Pasiphernes,
and handing over to them for the war the remaining silver and gold,
which they say amounted to seven hundred talents.[21]

D. *SIG* 126. Erythrae honours Konon[22]

[Resolved] by the Council and the ‖ [People. K]onon shall be registered
‖ [as a] *benefactor* of the Erythraeans ‖ [and as a] proxenos, and (the

5   privilege of) a front ‖ seat (at public events) shall be his at Ery‖[thr]ae
and immunity from taxation ‖ for all goods, both ‖ for (their) importation

10   and export, ‖ both in time of war and in time of peace. ‖ And he shall be
an Erythraean, ‖ [if] he wants. And there shall exist ‖ *these* (privileges)
both for himself and for (his) *de‖scendants*. And there shall be made ‖ [of

15   him] a statue[23] of bronze ‖ [overlaid with gold] and it shall be set up
‖ [wherever] Konon [decides] *vv* ‖ [--] and [--] ‖

---

1   Konon had escaped to Evagoras' court after the battle of Aegospotamoi. Cf. Diod.
13.106. The events recorded here are treated by Diodorus under the year 399. Cf.
Diod. 14.39.
2   The parenthesis is Demosthenes'. This is a reference to Artaxerxes' appeal (probably in 345) for help against Egypt, which Athens and Sparta refused.

3   Didymus' entry at this point is concerned with an explanation of the clause 'even
     though in the past he helped in putting the city's affairs in order'. He rejects the
     view, held by some, that this refers to the first peace-initiative of Antalkidas in
     392/1.
4   Diels and Schubart restore 'in his fifth book'.
5   Suggested by Diels and Schubart, who restore this whole line to read 'having
     sailed with many ships to Cyprus'.
6   Diels and Schubart here restore the name of the archon Euboulides (394/3), in
     whose archonship the battle of Cnidus took place (August 394). But see Jacoby's
     commentary at this point. Philochorus' account of these important years is not
     likely to have been so brief. Didymus has compressed his source.
7   The south-west tip of Asia Minor. Cf. Diod. 14.83.4–7 for a similar account of the
     battle of Cnidus.
8   For the chronology of the Spartan navarchy at this time see Bruce, *Commentary*
     66–73.
9   Restored by W.L. Newman (*ap.* Bruce).
10   Cf. Diod. 14.79.8.
11   The river Calbis.
12   Perhaps Pasiphernes; cf. 19.3 (translated below). Possible also is Artaphernes; cf.
     Diod. 14.79.5.
13   Sometime between 398 and 395 the Rhodians expelled the Spartans and admitted
     Konon and his fleet (cf. Diod. 14.79.6; Pausanias 6.7.6). The government was then
     taken over by the family of Diagoras, on whom see Bruce, *Commentary* 98–9.
14   Cf. Diod. 14.81.4.
15   Otherwise unknown.
16   Cheirikrates' navarchy should have begun sometime in 395. He was replaced by
     Agesilaos' brother, Peisandros, for he was navarch at the battle of Cnidus (August
     394). This chronology would be quite acceptable, were it not that Xenophon (*Hell.*
     3.4.29) dates Peisandros' appointment as navarch in the late summer of 395. See
     Bruce, *Commentary* 123.
17   Cf. Diod. 14.81.4–6, who adds that Konon went on to Babylon and conversed with
     Artaxerxes. This is denied by Nepos, *Conon* 3, and Justin 6.2.12–13, who says: 'And
     so Conon, after importuning the King for a long time by letter without success, at
     last went to him in person, but was prevented from seeing him and conversing with
     him, because he was not willing to do obeisance to him in the Persian manner.'
     See Bruce, *Commentary* 123–5.
18   Fifteen months, if we can believe Isocrates 4.142.
19   Cf. Isoc. 4.142.
20   Hardly sufficient for fifteen months of arrears. If we accept the rate of pay offered
     by Kyros at the close of the Peloponnesian War as a guideline (4 obols a day; cf.
     Xen. *Hell.* 1.5.7), then the pay for the crews of 90 triremes, at 200 men to a trireme
     for 15 months, would amount to slightly more than 800 talents.
21   The next chapter, not translated here, recounts the mutiny of Konon's Cypriot
     mercenaries and Konon's successful suppression of it. These chapters indicate
     graphically a problem that was to become increasingly frequent for generals in the
     fourth century, and not only for those in the service of the Great King, namely that
     they were insufficiently and irregularly funded.
22   Erythrae revolted from Athens in 412 and remained loyal to Sparta until
     immediately after the battle of Cnidus.
23   Statues of Konon were set up at Ephesus and Samos (cf. Pausanias 6.3.16) and
     later in Athens along with one of his son Timotheos (cf. *IG* II^2 3774$^+$ (Tod 128)).

13   The battle of Sardis. 396/5.

The Oxyrhynchus Historian (London fragment 6.4–6). *Hell. Oxy.* 11.4–6. Cf. Xen. *Hell.*
3.4.22–4; Xen. *Ages.* 1.30–2; Diod. 14.80.2–4.

C. Dugas, *BCH* 34 (1910) 65–73; Bruce, *Commentary* 82–4 and Appendix 1; D. Nellen,
AncSoc 3 (1972) 45–54; J.K. Anderson, *CSCA* 7 (1974) 27–53; V.J. Gray, *CSCA* 12 (1979)
183–200.

(11.4) [--][1] hoplites, and five hundred light-armed troops,[2] and [as
commander over] *these* [he set] Xenokles,[3] the [S]partiate, [having
given instructions that whenever they[4] were] marching past them [--] *to*
5   *be drawn up* for battle [--] ‖ getting *the army* on the move *at dawn*, he
(Agesilaos) led it *forward* [once more.] And [the] barbarians *followed
along*, as was their custom, *some* of them harassing the Greeks, *some riding
their horses around* them, others *pursuing* (them) *over* the plain in no good
10   *order*. (5) X[e]nokles, ‖ when *he judged the moment right* for closing with the
enemy, *aroused* the Peloponnesians from the ambush (and) *began to press
forward*[5] *at the double*. As for the barbarians, as each group perceived the
Greeks running towards (them), they took to flight over the whole
15   plain. When Ag[esil]aos saw them in panic, ‖ he sent from his army the
light-armed soldiers and the cavalry to pursue them. And these,
together with those who had risen up from the ambush, attacked the
barbarians. (6) After pursuing the enemy for no very long time, for *they
20   were* not *able* to cat‖ch them[6] since many (of them) were *on horseback* and
lightly armed, they did manage to kill about six hundred,[7] then, giving
up the *pursuit, they made their way* to the very camp of the *barbarians*. They
25   caught the watch *off its guard* and quick‖ly took (the camp). From them
(the barbarians) they captured *a large amount* of food, many men, a great
deal of equipment and much money <some> (of which) belonged to *the*
men, *but* some (of which) *belonged to* Tissaphe[rnes] himself.[8]

1   The preceding part of chapter eleven is very fragmentary, but clearly narrates
    Agesilaos' march from Ephesus to the Hermus valley. For the route described by
    this author and the discrepant account of Xenophon (*Hell.* 3.4.20–1) see Dugas
    59–65 (with a good map facing p. 58).
2   Diodorus (14.80.2) says that Xenokles had 1400 soldiers in all for his ambush. Most
    likely, then, he had 900 hoplites.
3   Cf. Xen. *Hell.* 3.4.20.
4   'They' are either the enemy or, more likely, Agesilaos and his army, since the
    ambush was sent ahead.
5   This is the reading of the papyrus, but the first editors (Grenfell and Hunt), followed
    by Bartoletti, alter it to read, 'he began to run'.
6   The papyrus here has 'themselves'.
7   Diod. 14.80.4 gives 6000.
8   This account of the battle of Sardis, when compared with those by Xenophon and
    Diodorus, presents a good exercise in source-criticism.

27

14   Alliance between Boeotia and Athens. 395.

A. *IG* II² 14; Tod 101, pp. 14–15; *SV* 2.223, pp. 168–70. Athens, 395. Two fragments of a marble stele, Ionic letters (but e=ei, o=ou), stoichedon (except lines 1–3 which form a heading). **B.** Scholion to Aristophanes, *Ecclesiazusae* 193 (Philochorus, *FGrHist* 328F148). Cf. Xen. *Hell.* 3.5.7–16; Andocides 3.25; Lysias 16.13; Paus. 3.5.4.

Bruce, *Commentary* 52, 121; R. Seager, *JHS* 87 (1967) 96–9; S. Perlman, *CP* 63 (1968) 260–1; Bury-Meiggs 338–9; Hamilton, *Sparta* 205.

A. *IG* II² 14

Gods. vv | Alliance *of the* Boeo[tians and the A]thenia[ns for | all] time.[1] *vv* | [If] anyone comes against [the Athenians] for the purpose of making
5   war [either ‖ by] land or by *sea*, the Boe[otians] shall give assistance | with all their strength, *in* whatever *way* is reques|ted by the Atheni[ans, to the best of their] ability. And *i|f* [anyone] comes against [the Boeotians] for the purpose of making war either [b|y land or] by [sea],
10   assistance shall be given by the Athen[i|]ans with all their strength, in whatever] way is request|ed [by the Boeotians, to the best of their] *ability*. And if there be *any* [r|esolution either to add to or] *delete from* (this treaty) by the Athen[ian|s and by the Boeotians in joint deliberatio|n --]

B. Aristophanes, *Ecclesiazusae* 193–6

Another point:[2] This League! When we were considering it, / people kept on saying that the city would be ruined, if it should not come about. / But when indeed it was made, they grew vexed with it,[3] and the politician / who persuaded them to it, took to his heels right away.[4]

SCHOLION
Concerning the league Philochorus records that an alliance of the Athenians[5] and Boeotians was made two years before.[6]

---

1   Alliances 'for all time' instead of for a specific number of years became increasingly popular in the fourth century. Cf. Tod, p. 15.
2   Praxagora is speaking.
3   After the initial success at Haliartus, the allies were defeated at Nemea and at Coronea, both in 394. This could account for the change in opinion and provides an additional argument for dating the production of the play to the spring of 393, before Konon had arrived in Athens.
4   The politician is unknown. He could be Thrasyboulos. He cannot be Konon.
5   This is an emendation for the manuscript reading 'Lacedaemonians'.
6   I.e. before the production of the play. The date of that is not absolutely certain, but is usually placed in the spring of 393. Cf. n. 3 and Jacoby, *FGrHist* 3b.Suppl. 2.519.

15   The Boeotian constitution. 395.

The Oxyrhynchus Historian (London fragment 11.2–4). *Hell. Oxy.* 16.2–4. Cf. Xen. *Hell.* 5.1.33; Thuc. 5.31.6, 5.36–8 (esp. 38.2–3).

P. Cloché, *REG* 31 (1918) 315–43; *idem, Thèbes de Béotie* (Namur 1952) 71–4; Larsen, *Government* 31ff.; *TAPA* 86 (1955) 40–50; Roesch, *Thespies* 36–43; Bruce, *Commentary* 102–9 and Appendix 2; Sealey, *History* 404–5; P. Salmon, *Étude sur la Confédération béotienne* (Brussels 1978) *passim*.

(16.2) At that time (395) (political) affairs were organized *throughout* Boeotia as follows:[1] Councils had been established *at that* (col. 12) *time*, four [in] each of the cities.[2] To these (councils) *not* [all] the *citizens could belong, but* (only) those who *possessed a certain* amount *of property*.[3] Each
5   of these councils [by] turn *presided* and *deliberated in advance* ‖ on (the state's) *business* and introduced (proposals) to the (other) *three*, and [whatever] they all agreed upon became their final decision. (3) [Their] local affairs they continued to manage in this way, but as for the government *of* [Boe]otia (as a whole), it was organized in the following manner: All the inhabitants of the area had been divided [into] *eleven* dis-
10   tricts, ‖ and each of these (districts) provided one Boeotarch[4] [as follows]: the Thebans contributed four, two on behalf of [the] city and two on behalf of the Plataeans and (the people) of Skolos, Er[y]thrae and Skaphai and the other regions that earlier shared in the citizenship of
15   Plataea,[5] but were at that time depend‖ent upon the state of Thebes;[6] two Boeotarchs were provided by the people of Orchomenus and Hysiae, two by the Thespians along with Eutresis and Thisbae, one by the people of Tanagra, and yet another by the people of Haliartus and Lebadea and Coronea, who was sent by each of the cities in turn; in the
20   same way (one Boeotarch) c‖ame from Akraiphnion, Kopai and Chaeronea.[7] (4) This was the way in which the districts contributed the magistrates. They provided councillors also, sixty for each Boeotarch,[8] and they themselves (i.e. the citizens of the districts)[9] paid these men (the councillors) their daily expenses. There had also been imposed
25   on each district a military levy of about one thousand ‖ infantry and one hundred cavalry.[10] Put quite simply, (it was) in proportion to (the number of) magistrates (they provided) that they drew upon the federal treasury and paid their taxes and sent judges,[11] and they had their share of all (aspects of the federation) in like manner, both the obligations and the privileges. Well then, that is the way the whole
30   nation governed its affairs, and the common assemblies ‖ of the Boeotians, (when they met) together, held their sessions on the Cadmea.

1   This form of federal government had most likely been established in 447, after the

battle of Coronea, which led to the complete withdrawal of the Athenians. See Thuc. 1.113.2–4. It was dissolved under the terms of the King's Peace (387/6), see Xen. *Hell.* 5.1.33.

2   These councils looked after local affairs only. On the question which cities managed their own affairs and which did not see Bruce, *Commentary* 104.

3   Usually considered to be the equivalent of the hoplite census.

4   These officials held the supreme command in military affairs, cf. Diod. 15.52; Pausanias 9.1.6. Whether one of them held the overall command, as is implied by Thuc. 4.91, or whether decisions were made on the basis of a majority vote (Pausanias 9.13.6), is debated.

5   Cf. Strabo 9.2.24 and Pausanias 9.2.1, 9.4.4.

6   Presumably since the capture of Plataea in 427, but perhaps as early as 431. Cf. Bruce, *Commentary* 106.

7   For these cities and their relationship to one another see Bruce, *Commentary* 106–8.

8   Thus there were 660 councillors in the federal council.

9   The reference of 'they themselves' is disputed. Some (e.g. Cloché, *Thèbes de Béotie* 73) want this to refer to the councillors themselves. But this is grammatically difficult. The other two possibilities are that it refers either to the local authorities or to the federal government.

10 For a study of the military organization see P. Salmon, *AC* 22 (1953) 347–60, and Bruce, *Commentary* 162–3.

11 Apparently both the financial and the legal systems were organized on a federal basis. Cf. Bruce, *Commentary* 163.

16   Alliance between Athens and Locris.[1] **Athens, ?395.** Fragment of a marble stele, Ionic letters (but e=ei in lines 5 and 8, o=ou, except in line 10), stoichedon.

IG II² 15+; Tod 102, pp. 15–16; *SV* 2.224, pp. 170–1.

Bruce, *Commentary* 118–19; R. Seager, *JHS* 87 (1967) 99 n. 34.

[---|---] *just as* for the C[orinthian|s --.[2] Alliance of the Athe]nians and
L[ocrians for | all time. If anyone comes against the Ath]enians for the
5   purpose of making war [either b‖y land or by sea], the Locrians[3] *shall
give assistance* with all their strength, [i]n whatever way is requested by
the Atheni]ans, to the best of their ability. [And i|f anyone comes
against the Locrians for the purpose of making] *war* either by land or
by [s|ea, the Athenians shall give assistance with all their] strength, in
whatever way [is reques|ted by the Locrians, to the best of their ability].
10   And whatever else is resolved by the A[the‖nians and the Locrians]
deliberating together, this [shall be] va|lid.[4] *vv*

1   No literary source refers to this alliance, but its existence should cause no surprise. The immediate cause of the Corinthian War was a border dispute between Locris and Phocis. Locris was allied with the Boeotians, who were in turn allied with

Athens, while Phocis became an ally of Sparta. Cf. Xen. *Hell.* 3.5.3f.; Pausanias 3.9.9f.; *Hell. Oxy.* 18.1–5.

2   Before the text of the alliance itself most likely came the concluding words of the decree ratifying it.

3   In his account of the border dispute between Locris and Phocis, Xenophon (*Hell.* 3.5.3) identifies the Locrians as the Eastern (Opuntian or Epicnemidian) Locrians, while the Oxyrhynchus Historian (18.2) and Pausanias (3.3.9) call them the Western (Ozolian) Locrians. Consequently it is not clear which of the two we are dealing with in this document.

4   The close similarity between the script and the formulae of this document and no. 14 argue strongly that they belong to the same period, late summer 395.

17   Fortification of Peiraeus. Athens, 395/4 *and* 394/3. Masonry block, Ionic letters (but o=ou), non-stoichedon.

IG II² 1656 and 1657;[1] Tod 107, pp. 22–4; *Maier, *Mauerbauinschriften* 1 and 2, pp. 21–3. Cf. Xen. *Hell.* 4.8.10; Diod. 14.85.3.

R.L. Scranton, *AJA* 43 (1939) 301ff.; P. Funke, *ZPE* 53 (1983) 186ff.

IG II² 1656

In Diophantos' archon|shi(p) (395/4). In the course of Skirophorion[2]
5 | month. For the dai|ly (paid) work. For yoke-||teams bringing the stones, | (cost of) hire: 160 (drachmas). | For iron tools, (cost of) hi|re: 52 (drachmas).

IG II² 1657

In the archonship of Euboulides (394/3), | (for laying of stones) begin-ning from the mark[3] | (and extending) up to the central pill|ar of the
5   gates by || the Sanctuary of Aphrodite, on the right-|hand (side) as one goes out: 790 (drachmas). Co|ntrac(tor): Demosthenes of B|oeotia, (as) also for the trans|portation of the stones.

1   These are the first two of a series of such records, *IG* II² 1656–64.

2   The last month of the Attic official year, roughly midsummer. It shows that the Athenians had begun the refortifications before the battle of Cnidus, and certainly before Konon's return (393).

3   Where or what this was is unknown.

18   Spartan victory at Corinth.[1] 395/4[2] *or* 394/3.[3]

Scholion to Demosthenes 20.52 (Androtion, *FGrHist* 324F47, and Ephorus, *FGrHist*

70F209). Cf. Xen. *Hell.* 4.2.16–23; Diod. 14.83.1–2.

W.K. Pritchett, *Studies in Ancient Greek Topography* 2 (Berkeley and Los Angeles 1969) 73–84; Bury-Meiggs 339–40; Sealey, *History* 390–2.

Demosthenes 20.52

But when the great battle against the Lacedaemonians took place at Corinth . . .

SCHOLION
Hypereides has spoken about this battle in his speech against Diondas (Hyper. F95–6). Both in Ephorus (*FGrHist* 70F209) and in Androtion (*FGrHist* 324F47) it is recorded that the Spartans won a crushing victory over the Athenians.[4]

1   Many modern texts refer to this as the battle of Nemea.
2   Jacoby, following K.J. Beloch, *Gr. Gesch.*[2] 3.2.217.
3   Cf. no. 19.
4   Diodorus (14.83.2, 84.2) says Athens and her allies lost 2800 men in this battle.

19   Monuments for the Athenian casualties at Corinth and Coronea. Athens, 394.

A. *IG* II[2] 5221. Upper part of a marble stele, Ionic letters (three letter sizes: (1) the heading; (2) the tribal names; (3) the lists of the dead), stoichedon in the lists. **B.** *IG* II[2] 5222; *Tod 104, pp. 18–20. Upper part of a marble stele (inscribed on the epistyle beneath a crowning member), Ionic letters (larger in the heading), non-stoichedon. **C.** *IG* II[2] 6217; *Tod 105, pp. 20–1. Gabled stele of marble (inscribed beneath a relief showing a horseman striking a fallen enemy), Ionic letters (but o=ou). Cf. Lysias 16.15; Xen. *Hell.* 4.2.17; Diod. 14.83.2, 84.2; Pausanias 1.29.11.

W.K. Pritchett, *Studies in Ancient Greek Topography* 2 (Berkeley and Los Angeles 1969) 83; Bury-Meiggs 339–40; Sealey, *History* 391–2.

A. *IG* II[2] 5221[1]

[OF THE ATHENIANS THE FOLLOWING] *DIED* AT CORINTH AND IN BOEOTI[A] [--][2] of Akamantis of Oineis of Kekropis of Hippothontis of Aiantis of Antiochi[s]
[--]isikrates The general Kallip[--]eias The general [--]
[--]ipp[--] Mnesikl[-- Tho]ukle[ides --]

B. *IG* II² 5222³

These cavalrymen died at Corinth: The phylarch Antiphanes, Melesias, Onetorides, Lysitheos, Pandios, Nikomachos, Theangelos, Phanes, Demokles, Dexileos, Endelos. At Coronea: Neokleides.⁴

C. *IG* II² 6217⁵

Dexileos, son of Lysanios, from Thorikos,⁶ | was born in the archonship of Teisandros (414/13), | died in the archonship of Euboulides (394/3) | at Corinth, one of the five cavalrymen.⁷ |

1 This is clearly just a small part of a very large document, listing all the Athenians who died in these two battles. Beneath the heading (here rendered in capitals) the tribal names head ten separate lists of casualties. For a line drawing of the extant portion see A. Brueckner, *MDAI*(A) 35 (1910) 221.
2 Here can be restored the names of the tribes Erechtheis, Aigeis, Pandionis and Leontis.
3 I have made no attempt to indicate the line divisions of this inscription, rather translating the text as Tod prints it. In fact, the document is only two lines long, each of the lines breaking into three parts. For a line drawing showing the disposition of the letters and the crowning member see A. Brueckner, *MDAI*(A) 14 (1889) 407.
4 This is hardly likely to be a full list of the Athenian cavalry who died in these two battles, eleven and one respectively. Most likely it commemorates the casualties of one tribe only – Akamantis, to which Dexileos belonged (see item C).
5 For photographs of this very famous monument from the Ceramicus see Bury-Meiggs 340 and Sealey 391.
6 A deme of the tribe Akamantis.
7 The reference of the last phrase is unclear.

20   Athens honours Dionysios I of Syracuse. Athens, 393. Marble stele (with a relief of Athena holding out her right hand to a female figure, representing Sicily), Ionic letters (but o=ou), stoichedon (lines 1–4 larger letters, lines 5ff. smaller letters).

IG II² 18; *Tod 108, pp. 24–6. Cf. Lysias 19.19–20.

R. Sealey, *Historia* 5 (1956) 183; R. Seager, *JHS* 87 (1967) 103; E. Costa, *Historia* 23 (1974) 51 and n. 72; Bury-Meiggs 385–405 (the career of Dionysios).

In the archonship of Euboulides (394/3), when P[andio]|nis held the sixth prytany,¹ *vv* | in which Platon, son of Nikochares, of Phly[a] *was*
5 *sec*|*retary. vv* || Resolved by the Boule.² Kinesias³ made the motion: With *regard* [to what An]|drosthenes⁴ says, commendation shall be given to

Di[o]n[ysios th|e] *ruler* of [Sic]ily[5] and Leptines, [the] *bro|ther* of
Dion[y]s[ios,] *and* Thearides, the [brothe|r] of Dionys[ios, and
Poly]xenos, the [brother-in-la‖w of Dionysios --][6]

1   This is the first extant example of a new type of prescript, in which an ordinal
    number is added to the name of the tribe in prytany. See Henry, *Prescripts* 24–5.
2   ' . . . apparently not submitted to the Ecclesia for ratification as a decree . . . ' (Tod
    p. 25). A decree needed the approval of the People. Cf. no. 2 n. 1.
3   This is perhaps ('no doubt', Tod p. 25) the dithyrambic poet ridiculed by Lysias
    (21.20 and fr. 73) and by Aristophanes (*Birds* 1373–1404, *Lysistrata* 860, *Frogs* 1437
    and *Ecclesiazusae* 330). See A.W. Pickard-Cambridge, *Dithyramb, Tragedy and Comedy*[2]
    (Oxford 1962) 43–5.
4   Nothing more is known of this man.
5   This is the title by which Dionysios is regularly addressed in Athenian decrees.
6   Why Dionysios and his family were being honoured we do not know, but it is
    tempting to infer that it had something to do with drama – from the name of the
    proposer; the time of year in which the motion was made (close to the Lenaean
    festival); the place where the inscription was set up (in the Theatre of Dionysos); and
    Dionysios' known interest in poetry. On the other hand, at this point in the Corin-
    thian War, it would make good diplomatic sense for Athens to court the favour of
    an ally of Sparta.

21   Two treaties between Amyntas III and the Chalcidians. Olynthus, *c.* 393 (first treaty); later, but before 382 (second treaty and the heading of the first).

Upper part of a marble stele (inscribed
on both faces), Ionic script of the Euboean type with occasional
Atticisms, stoichedon.

SIG 135; *Tod 111, pp. 30–4; *SV* 2.231, pp. 178–80; Pouilloux, *Choix* 25, pp. 96–8. Cf.
Xen. *Hell.* 5.2.11–18; Diod. 14.92.3; 15.19.2–3.

A.B. West, *The History of the Chalcidic League* (Madison 1918) 97–102; M. Gude, *A History
of Olynthus* (Baltimore 1933) 24–8; M. Zahrnt, *Olynth und die Chalkidier* (Munich 1971)
122–4; Hammond-Griffith 172–80 (Hammond).

(OBVERSE FACE – FIRST TREATY)[1]
Treaty with Amyntas, the son of Errhidaios.[2] | Treaty between
Amyntas, the son of Errhidaios, | and the Chalcidians. They shall be
5   allies | with each other as regards all men ‖ for fifty years.[3] If anyone
attacks Amyn|tas, coming into *his* [territory for the purpose] of making
war, | [or] attacks the Cha[lcidians, assistance shall be given] by the
Chalcidi|[ans] to Am[yntas and by Amyntas to the Chalcidians ---]

(REVERSE FACE – SECOND TREATY)
And exportation is to be permitted both of pitch and of timber | for all
kinds of construction and for shipbuild|ing, with the exception (of the

wood) of the fir, (provided that what is exported be) whatever the
5 | League does not need. Even (in the case) of fir, the League ‖ shall be
permitted to export (it), provided that it advise Amyntas before
ex|porting, and pay the prescribed dues. | Exportation of other (com-
modities) shall be permitted, as well as tr|ansit, provided (those con-
cerned) pay the dues, the Chalcidi|ans (when they export) from
10 Macedonia and the Macedonians (when they export) from ‖ Chalcidice.
With the Amphipolitans, the Bott[i]|aeans, the Acanthians (and) the
Mendaeans, they shall not *ma|ke* friendship, neither Amyntas nor the
Chalcid[ians], | *separately*, but with *common* [con|sent, if] it is decided by
15 both parties, jointly ‖ [they shall take] *them* [into alliance]. The oath of
allian|ce: [I shall observe the] *agreements* (made) *by* the Chalcid[ia|ns,
and if anyone attacks A]myntas, [(coming) into | his territory for the
purpose of making war, I shall assist Am]yn[tas ---]

1 In the case of this document I have followed (without prejudice) the view of Zahrnt,
who argues that the text on the reverse is not a continuation of that on the front, but
that in fact there are two treaties. The first is a mutually beneficial alliance made
between equals, while the second is clearly more advantageous to the Chalcidians,
both in the commercial clauses and in the provision concerning Amphipolis,
Bottiaca, Acanthus and Mende. Zahrnt concludes that at some time after the first
treaty the Chalcidians were strong enough to extract from Amyntas the concessions
contained in the second. This was most likely in the 380s, when the Chalcidic
League was economically and politically strong. Cf. D.M. Robinson and P.A.
Clement, *The Chalcidic Mint and the Excavation Coins found in 1928–1934* (Baltimore
1938) 156, and see the speech of the Acanthians at Sparta in 382 (Xen. *Hell.* 5.2.16f.)
2 The Macedonian spelling of Arrhidaios. This heading was added later, in the same
writing as the text on the obverse.
3 It was more characteristic of fifth-century treaties to stipulate a time period. Early
in the fourth century treaties began to be concluded in perpetuity (cf. no. 14).

22 Athenian mercenary forces at Corinth. 393–391.

A. Harpocration, *Lexicon s.v.* Mercenary force in Corinth (Androtion, *FGrHist* 324F48;
Philochorus, *FGrHist* 328F150). **B.** Scholion to Aristophanes, *Plutus* 173. **C.** Justin,
Epitoma 6.5.2. **D.** Polyaenus, *Strategemata* 3.9.57. Cf. Demosthenes 4.24; Diod 14.91.2–
3; Xen. *Hell.* 4.4.9; 4.4.16; 4.5.11–19; 4.8.7.

Parke, *Soldiers* 48–57; F. Jacoby, *FGrHist* 3b. Suppl. 1.521; G.T. Griffith, *Historia* 1 (1950)
236–56; C.D. Hamilton, *Historia* 21 (1972) 29–30; Bury-Meiggs 342–3.

A. Harpocration, *Lexicon s.v.* Mercenary force in Corinth

Konon first assembled this (force), Iphikrates and Chabrias[1] later took
it over. And by using this (force) they (the Athenians) cut to pieces the

mora of the Lacedaemonians, under the generalship of Iphikrates and Kallias,[2] as both Androtion and Philochorus report.

B. Aristophanes, *Plutus* 173

Isn't it he who keeps the mercenary force in Corinth?[3]

SCHOLION
They say that the Corinthians employed the mercenary force[4] because of the superiority of the Athenians in the alliance. But the man who established the mercenaries at Corinth was Konon the Athenian general,[5] after he had destroyed the Lacedaemonians, to guard against their (the Lacedaemonians') attack.

C. Justin, *Epitoma* 6.5.2

When they learned this (i.e. the return of Agesilaos and his victory at Coronea), the Athenians were afraid that, now that the Lacedaemonians were once again victors, they might be reduced to their former state of servitude. And so they assembled an army and ordered that it be led by Iphikrates, who, although only twenty years old, was a young man of great natural ability.

D. Polyaenus, *Strategemata* 3.9.57

After two thousand of the mercenaries had defected to the Lacedaemonians,[6] Iphikrates sent a secret letter to the leaders encouraging (them) to be mindful of the prearranged moment, at which time he expected the allied forces from Athens. (He did this), knowing that the letter would fall into the hands of those who were guarding the roads. When the guards took the letter to the Lacedaemonians, they set out to arrest the defectors. And they barely escaped, because they had become untrustworthy to the Athenians and seemed (to be so) to the Lacedaemonians.

1 Not at the same time: Iphikrates in 393 and Chabrias in 389 (as his successor).
2 Kallias was commander of the hoplites and took no part in the battle. Whether Iphikrates was general or not is discussed by Parke 51–2. Both the quotation from Justin (C) and Xen. *Hell.* 4.5.13 suggest that he was not.
3 At this time (spring 388) Chabrias was the leader of the mercenary forces.
4 The scholiast is obviously confused.
5 He was not, of course, an Athenian general in 394/3.
6 This is taken by Parke, pp. 52–3, as an indication that the mercenary force may have been larger than the 1500 suggested by our other evidence.

23 Athens rejects the Great King's peace. 392/1.

A. Didymus, *Demosthenes* col. 7.11–28 on Demosthenes 10.34 (Philochorus, *FGrHist* 328F149a). **B.** Anon. Argument to Andocides 3 (Philochorus, *FGrHist* 328F149b). Cf. Xen. *Hell.* 4.8.12ff.; Andocides, *On the Peace, passim*; Demosthenes 19.277f.

F. Jacoby, *FGrHist* 3b.Suppl. 1, pp. 515–21; 3b.Suppl. 2, pp. 413–19; R. Sealey, *Historia* 5 (1956) 184–5; Ryder, *Eirene* 1–38; G.L. Cawkwell, *CQ* 26 (1976) 70–7.

A. Didymus, *Demosthenes* col. 7.11–28[1]

[By the] *previous* res|toration *some* say *he means* the *p|eace* that came down in the time of Antialk[idas,[2] the L]ac[onian,] | *incorrectly*, [at least as] *it*
15   *seems* to me. For, (as for) that (peace), ‖ *not only* [did] the Ath[e]n[ians not accept] it, but, entirely | *the opposite*, they rejected it [as an impious] *transgression* | against themselves, [as Philo]chorus *recounts* in these very wo|rds, *under the heading*, 'In the archonship of Philok[le]s of Anaphly|stos' (392/1): 'And the peace, the one in the time of Antial-
20   kidas, was sent ‖ down by the King. (But) the Athenians did *not* accept it, | because there had been written in it that *the* Greeks *who in* [A]sia *were liv|ing* should all in the King's *household* | be accounted members. Furthermore *the ambassadors* who | *agreed* (to these terms) in Lacedaemon
25   were sent into exil‖e, on the motion of Kallistratos.[3] They did *not even* wait | for the judgement. (They were) Epikrates of Kephisia, An|dokides of Kydathenaion, Kratinos of Sphettos, Eu|boulides of Eleusis.'

B. Anon. Argument to Andocides 3

Since the war in Greece was going on for a long time ... the Athenians despatched ambassadors to the Lacedaemonians with full powers (to negotiate), amongst whom was also Andocides.[4] And, after some proposals had been put forward by the Lacedaemonians and they had despatched their own ambassadors, a resolution was passed to the effect that the *demos* would make a decision about the peace within forty days. And on these terms Andocides advised the Athenians to accept the peace ... Well now, Philochorus says that the ambassadors both came from Lacedaemon and returned without accomplishing anything, since Andocides did not succeed in persuading (the Athenians).[5]

1   This is part of Didymus' commentary on the same passage of Demosthenes (10.34) that is translated in no. 12.
2   The spelling in our other sources is uniformly Antalkidas. Jacoby prefers the spelling Antialkidas on the basis of this passage and the usage in two Spartan documents.
3   Most likely Kallistratos of Aphidna. See R. Sealey, *loc. cit.*

4   Cf. [Plut.] *Lives of the Ten Orators* (= *Moralia* 835a).
5   If this is a true quotation, it can be fitted into the fragment quoted by Didymus only
after the sentence ending 'in the King's household'.

**24   Arbitration between Miletus and Myus. Miletus, between 391
and 388.** Two non-contiguous fragments of a marble stele, Ionic letters,
stoichedon (with irregularities).

SIG 134; *Tod 113, pp. 36–9.

F. Adcock and D.J. Mosley, *Diplomacy in Ancient Greece* (London 1975) 210–14; L.
Piccirilli, *Gli Arbitrati Interstatali Greci* 1 (Pisa 1973) 155–9.

5   [--] Dionys|[---|--] satr|[ap --] *they were quar‖relling* [over the land] in the
       Maeandr|[ian plain --] to become | [--] dispute[1] | [--] of the city | [--] the
10   King and [-‖-- St]rouses[2] *in* | *order that* [the jurymen of the Ionians],[3] *after*
31   *coming togeth|er* [--] | (lacuna)[4] [--] and after the institution of the tria|l by
       the Milesians and the Myesians and after the | witnesses had testified
       for both | sides and an inspection had been made of the boundaries of
35   th‖e land, when the jurymen were on the point of giv|ing their judge-
       ment, the Mye[s]ians withdrew their suit. | The advocates (for the two
       sides) put this in writ|ing and gave (it) to the cities that | were sitting
40   in judgement on the case, to serve as evid‖ence. Since the Myesians had
       withdrawn from the cas|e, Strouses, on learning (this) from the Ionian
       j|urymen, in his capacity as satrap of Ionia, g|ave his *final decision* that
       the land belonged to the Miles[i]|ans. The advocates of the Milesians
45   were Nymph[-3-‖---]

1   Some part of the word 'dispute' is extant, most likely a noun.
2   If, as is likely, this is the satrap whom the literary sources call Strouthas, the arbi-
     tration can be dated approximately, since he superseded Tiribazos as Satrap of
     Lydia/Caria in 392 and was recalled in 388. See Xen. *Hell.* 4.8.17–19; Diod.
     14.99.1–3.
3   It appears from lines 40ff. that Strouses (Strouthas) had referred the dispute to the
     member-states of the Ionian League, each of which sent five jurymen (therefore fifty
     in all) to decide the suit.
4   Lines 15–31 contain the names (largely preserved) of the jurymen of six of the twelve
     cities of the Ionian League. The names of five of these cities are extant – Erythrae,
     Chios, Clazomenae, Lebedus and Ephesus. Presumably the jurymen from Phocaea,
     Teos, Colophon, Samos and Priene were listed in the *lacuna* and in lines 13–15.
     Miletus and Myus naturally did not send jurymen. Translation continues in the
     middle of line 31.

25   Athens resumes alliance with Thasos. Athens, 391/90 *or* 390/89 *or* 389/8 *or* 387/6.[1] Four fragments of a marble stele, Ionic letters (but o=ou), stoichedon.

IG II[2] 24. Cf. Dem. 20.59; Xen. *Hell.* 4.8.25–31; Diod. 14.94; Lysias 28 and 29.

R. Seager, *JHS* 87 (1967) 110; Bury-Meiggs 343; G.L. Cawkwell, *CQ* 26 (1976) 270–7.

FRAGMENT D
For the Thasians [Archippos and Hipparchos,[2] the sons of Archip]pos.

FRAGMENT A
[--] and [--|--] sufficient [--|Th]asians a five per cent tax[3] [--|--] a five per
5   cent tax *pay*[-- on] *mer*‖*chandise* a five per cent tax [--|--] when
10   [Thras]yboulos *was commander* [--|---|---|---]. ‖ *About* the other (matters?)
[-- the] *Bo*|*ule* shall *choose five* [men --] | *the embassy* of the Tha[sians --|-]
15   they shall appoint[4] [--] to | grant and *submit to legal proceedings* [--‖---]

FRAGMENTS B, C
[-- towards the] *Boule* [and the People, i|f] *they want* [anything] from the
People of [Ath]en[s --|- and] if anyone kills Arch[ippos or Hippar|chos],
5   the *brother* of Archippos, *he shall be exiled* [from the city] ‖ of the Athenians
and from the *other cities*, [as many as] | are allies of the [Ath]enians.
Inscription shall be made [of this] | decree on a marble stele by the [sec-
retary of] t|he Boule and it shall be set up [in the] *city*. There shall be
given [--] f|or the inscription of the stele to the *secretary* [by the]
10   t‖reasurer of the Boule twenty drachmas. [And it shall be possible] | for
Archippo[s] *and* Hippar[chos] to approach [the] | Boule, if they want
anything, the first (to do so) [after the sacrifices]. | And (the People)
shall confirm by vote *an archon for* [Thasos, right] | away, and as seer
15   Stho[rys],[5] since [--‖--] of these. Invitations shall be issued to
[Ar]chipp[os and the] *othe*|*r* ambassadors of the Thasi[ans] (to come)
[to] the Pr[ytaneion on the] *mor*|*row* for hospitality. *vv* | *vacat*

1   This decree honours the leaders of an embassy from Thasos. The embassy must be
dated after Thrasyboulos' expedition to Thrace and the Hellespont (for there is a
reference back to that in line 6) and before the Great King's Peace. On the evidence
of line 6, however, it is clear that formal ties were resumed between Athens and
Thasos at the time of Thrasyboulos' expedition (cf. Dem. 20.59). This expedition is
dated by Merkelbach (*ZPE* 5 (1970) 32) to 389/8, by Seager to 390/89 and by
Cawkwell to 391/90.
2   *IG* II[2] is part of a decree granting Athenian citizenship to '[Archippos?] the
Thasia[n] *an*|*d* Hipparchos'.
3   On the restoration of the 5% tax see Thuc. 7.28.4. Cf. R. Meiggs, *The Athenian Empire*
(Oxford 1972) 369. For its continuation after the death of Thrasyboulos cf. no. 26.

4   Or 'produce', or 'prove', or 'publish'.
5   *IG* II² 17 honours Sthorys of Thasos and grants him Athenian citizenship for his
    help to Athens before the battle of Cnidus.

26   Athens honours Clazomenae. Athens, 387/6. Three contiguous
fragments of a marble stele (surmounted by a relief representing two
bulls facing each other), Ionic writing of the early fourth century (o=ou
nine times; e=ei twice), stoichedon (except line 1, which forms a
heading).

IG II² 28; Tod 114, pp. 39–41; *R. Merkelbach, *ZPE* 5 (1970) 32–6. Cf. Xen. *Hell.* 5.1.31.

R. Seager, *JHS* 87 (1967) 110; Bury-Meiggs 343–4; S. Ruzicka, *Phoenix* 37 (1983) 104–8.

Theodotos was archon (387/6), Paramythos, son of Philagros, of Erchia
was secretary. | Resolved by the People.[1] Theodotos was archon,
Kekropis held the prytan|y, Paramythos was secretary, Daiphron pre-
sided. Poli|agros made the motion: Commendation shall be given to
5   the people of Clazomen‖ae, because they show good will towards the
city of Athens | now as (they have) in the past. Concerning the matters
that they report,[2] let it be re|solved by the People that, if the Clazo-
menians *pay* the | five per cent tax (established) in the time of
Thrasyboulos, (then) *with regard to* the making of treaties or not w|ith
those in Chytum[3] and (with regard to) the [hostages], who are held by
10 the C[lazom]‖enians, (the hostages) from Chytum, complete authority
[shall belong to the People of Claz]|omenae, and it shall not be per-
mitted to the [People of Athens either] | to restore the exiles *without*
(the consent of) [the People of Clazome]|nae, or [to expel] *any* of those
who remain. [Concerning a gov]|ernor and garrison [the People] *shall*
15 *make a decision righ‖t* away, whether it is necessary to instal (them) *in*
[Clazomenae or whether | the People of Clazomenae] shall have absol-
ute authority in these matters, | (to decide) whether they want to
receive (them) [or not. As for the ci|ties] from which the
Clazome[nians] acquire their grain, [Phocaea, Chi|os and S]myrna, it
shall be permitted *for them* (the Clazomenians) under the terms of the
20 treaty [into their harbour‖s to sail. --[4]] and his fellow generals [shall
| see to it] *that* [the] same treaty [with Pharnabazos[5]] exist | [for the
Clazomenians] as for the Atheni[ans. It was voted[6] | by the People that
they (the Clazomenians),] without *paying* [any other] *taxes* [or | admit-
25 ting a garrison] or [being subject to] a governor, [shall be ‖ free, just like
the Athen]ians [--]

1   The decree was moved in the assembly without a probouleuma from the Boule.

2 This decree must date early in the archonship of Theodotos, i.e. before the Great King's Peace. News must have reached the Clazomenians, however, that Antalkidas had reached an agreement with Artaxerxes and was returning west with Tiridates.
3 Oligarchs from Clazomenae.
4 Either Dionysios or Leontichos fits the space. Both are known to have been generals in this year (Xen. *Hell.* 5.1.26) and both were operating in the Hellespont (Xen. *Hell.* 5.1.28).
5 Restored by Merkelbach, *ZPE* 5 (1970) 34–5.
6 If this is correctly restored it records the result of the vote taken in accordance with line 13. Cf. Fornara no. 128, pp. 141–2 lines 29–32 and n. 4.

27 Leukon, king of the Bosporos. 387–347.

A. *IOSPE* II 4; *Tod 115 (A), pp. 42–5. Fragment of a gabled stele of grey marble, Ionic letters, stoichedon, Panticapaeum (Kertch) **B.** *IOSPE* II 343; *Tod 115 (C), pp. 42–5 Shaft of a double herm of white marble, Ionic letters, stoichedon, Taman peninsula.
C. *IOSPE* II 6; *Tod 115 (B),[1] pp. 42–5. Marble base, Ionic letters, stoichedon, Panticapaeum (?). Cf. Dem. 20.29–40; Aeschines 3.171–2.

E.H. Minns, *Scythians and Greeks* (Cambridge 1913) 563ff.; M.I. Rostovtzeff, *Iranians and Greeks in South Russia* (Oxford 1922) 67ff. and *Social and Economic History of the Hellenistic World* (Oxford 1941) 1.594–602; S.M. Burstein, *Historia* 23 (1974) 401–16. See also R. Werner, *Historia* 4 (1955) 412–44; V.F. Gajdukevič, *Das bosporanische Reich*, trans. G. Janke (Berlin 1971) 65ff.

A. Tod 115 (A)

Resolved by the Arcadians[2] that Leukon, | [son of Sat]yros, the Pantikapaitan | [---]

B. Tod 115 (C)

Demarchos, son of Skythes, | dedicated (this) to Aphrodit[e] | of the
5 Sky,[3] guardian | of Apatouron,[4] || when Leukon | was ruler of the Bospor[os] | and of Theodosia.[5] |

C. Tod 115 (B)

Stratokles on behalf of his father | Deinostratos, who was priest to Apollo the Healer, | dedicated (this), when Leukon was ruler of the
5 Bosporos | and of Theodosia and was king of the Sindoi, || Toretai, Dandarioi and Psessoi.[6]

1 The order of these inscriptions in Tod has been reversed to conform to their probable chronological relationship.

2 Most likely the Arcadian League, organized by Epameinondas in 370. See Burstein
413 n. 51.
3 For this title cf. Herodotus 4.59.
4 Cf. Strabo 11.2.10.
5 The city of Theodosia was overcome by Leukon sometime between 370 and 354. Cf.
Burstein 416.
6 These inscriptions document the growth of Leukon's power.

28   Political change at Erythrae. Sometime between 387/6 and 355.

A. An Athenian decree for Erythrae. Athens, *c.* 387/6 (found at Erythrae). Fragment of
a marble stele, Ionic letters, stoichedon. S. Şahin, *Belleten* 40 (1976) 565–71; *SEG*
26.1282; S. Hornblower, *Mausolus* (Oxford 1982) no. M14. **B.** Erythrae honours
Idrieus,[1] son of Hekatomnos. Erythrae, between 365 and 355. Marble stele, Ionic
letters, stoichedon. *E. Varinlioğlu, *ZPE* 44 (1981) 45–7. Cf. Tod 155, pp. 163–5
(Erythrae honours Maussollos of Caria);[2] H. Engelmann and R. Merkelbach, *Die
Inschriften von Erythrai und Klazomenai* 1 (Bonn 1972) 8, pp. 53–6.

Bury-Meiggs 418–20; Hornblower, *Mausolus* 107–10.

A. An Athenian decree for Erythrae

[---|-] in [Er]ythra[e], *let it be resolv|ed* by the People. It shall not be per-
5   mitted | for a reconciliation to be made by any of the generals ‖ at all
with those in the ci|ty[3] without (the consent) of the People of Athe|ns.
Nor (any) of the exiles, w|ho have been driven out by the Erythra-
10 |eans, shall anyone be permitted to re‖store to Erythrae without (the
consent) of the | People of Erythrae.[4] Concern|ing (the matter of) not
surrendering (the) Er|ythraeans to the barbari|ans,[5] answer shall be
15   made to the Ery‖thraeans that it has been resolved *by th|e* People of
Athens [--|---]

B. Erythrae honours Idrieus, son of Hekatomnos

[--] *vv* | generals.[6] *vv* | *vacat* Resolved by the Council. Of the generals
(and) the Prytaneis | (and) the Epimenioi[7] (a) motion: | Idrieus, son of
5   Hekatomnos, of Mylasa, s‖ince he is a good man regarding the | city of the
Erythr[a]eans, shall be | a benefactor and proxenos | of the city of the
Erythraeans. There has | been given to him also exemption from tax-
10   ation ‖ for all that he imports or export|s, and (the privilege of) the front
seat at public festivals, | and (the right of) sailing in and sailing out
during both | war and peace without violation | and without formal
15   treaty, and (his) lawsuits (shall have) priority of ju‖dgement. And he
shall be also a citiz|en, if he wants, and he shall join a *cl|an*, whichever

he *wishes*. [There shall exist] *the|se* (privileges) for himself and (his) *descendants* [--]

1 Brother of Maussollos of Caria; he succeeded his sister Artemisia in 351/50 and ruled until 344/3.
2 This decree (now lost) votes honours to Maussollos that are similar to those accorded Idrieus in (B), though they are not as precisely set out. In addition, however, Maussollos and his sister-wife (Artemisia) are to have statues erected to them. Probably this honour was voted to Idrieus in the missing portion of (B). The similar form of the two inscriptions suggests that they were contemporary. A date sometime during Athens' Social War (357/5) is usually accepted, but see Hornblower, suggesting *c.* 365 as a possible alternative.
3 Of Erythrae. Probably the acropolis is meant. Presumably there was civil war at Erythrae.
4 This suggests that the democratic faction was in control at this time.
5 The most probable time for this to be a possibility is the time of the King's Peace (387/6) or slightly before.
6 The last word of another document.
7 'A board of high officials or a committee of the Council or of the Assembly who held office for a month' (Varinlioğlu 47).

29 Athens honours Hebryzelmis. Athens, 386/5. Marble stele (crowned by a relief showing a female figure between two horsemen), Ionic letters (except o=o and ou throughout, e=ei in lines 8, 17 and 22), stoichedon (except line 1, which forms a heading).

IG II² 31; *Tod 117, pp. 47–50.

A. Höck, *Hermes* 26 (1891) 453–62; S. Casson, *Macedonia, Thrace and Illyria* (Oxford 1926) 196, 199, 206; M. Cary, *CAH* 6.72, 106; J. Wiesner, *Die Thraker* (Stuttgart 1963) 130–1; R.K. Sinclair, *Chiron* 8 (1978) 47–9.

In the archonship of Mystichides (386/5). | [Resolved] by the *Boule* and the People: [Erechth|eis] *held the prytany*. [Ch]eilon of Kephisi[a]
5 *pre|sided*, Neon of [Ha]l[a]i was secretary, [E||ua]n[dr]os made the motion: Commendation shall be given to Heb[ryze||lm[i]s, the king of the Odrysians,[1] because *he | is a good* man toward the People *of* [Athe]|ns, *and* he shall have (the privileges) that his *ances|tors* (had), *all* (of them).
10 And commendation shall be given also to [-6-||-2-] and [-7-]non, the general [and | --][2] of Hebryzelmis, *the ki|ng*. And a stele *shall be set up, inscribed*| by the secretary of the Boule with what *has been vot|ed*, [on the]
15 *acropolis*. For the inscription [of the] || stele the *apodektai* [shall *disburse*] *thir|ty drachmas* to the secretary of the *Boul|e*. Three *men* [shall be chosen] from the Ath[e]n[ians] | *at large*, to report *to* [Heb]|ry[zel]mis [what]
20 has been voted by the *People*, and to *re||port also* about the ships[3] that

43

(are) *nea*|r Pl[-5- and] about the other matters *that are request*|*ed* by the *ambassadors from king* He[bryz]el[m]is, who *have come* to the People of A[the]|ns. *Commendation shall be given* also to T[e]isand[r]o[s and]

25 || Lysa[n]dros,[4] because they are both *good* men [towar|d] the People of Athens and [--]

1   In the second half of the fifth century the Odrysians (situated in the Hebrus valley) became the dominant kingdom amongst the Thracians. The Athenians made an alliance with Sitalkes in 431 and gave citizenship to his son Sadokos (Thuc. 2.29, 67.2). In 391 or 390 Thrasyboulos made an alliance for Athens with Amadokos I (Medokos) and brought about a reconciliation between him and Seuthes II (Xen. *Hell.* 4.8.26; Diod. 14.94.2; *IG* II² 21). Hebryzelmis was, most likely, the successor to Medokos, probably coming to the throne at the time of this document. He reigned until Kotys, son of Seuthes II, became king in 383.
2   The word missing here is a further qualification of the man who was general.
3 ● 'Presumably an Athenian squadron, lying somewhere off the Thracian coast' (Tod). But Sinclair (p. 48) prefers Höck's restoration 'about the ships *that* (are) *sailing around* (the coast)'.
4   These men and the service they performed are equally unknown. It is possible, however, that they were Greeks in the service of Hebryzelmis.

30   Dissolution of Mantinea. 385 *or* 384.[1]

Harpocration, *Lexicon s.v.* The dissolution of the Mantineans (Ephorus, *FGrHist* 70F79). Cf. Xen. *Hell.* 5.2.1–7; Diod. 15.5.12; Strabo 8.3.2; Isoc. 4.126, 8.100; Polybius 4.27.6; Pausanias 8.8.6–9.

M. Cary, *CAH* 6.60–1; D.G. Rice, *Historia* 23 (1974) 166–71; R. Seager, *Athenaeum* 52 (1974) 40; Bury-Meiggs 346; G.L. Cawkwell, *CQ* 26 (1976) 72–3; Sealey, *History* 405–6.

Isocrates in the (speech) *On the Peace* (8.100), speaking about the Lacedaemonians, says 'they dispersed the Mantineans'. And Ephorus in his twentieth (book) says that the Lacedaemonians dissolved the city of the Mantineans into five villages.[2]

1   Diodorus (15.5) treats the attack on Mantinea under the year 386/5 (15.2.1), and the dissolution of the city in the following year, the archonship of Dexitheos (385/4). Xenophon does not give a precise date. So it is an open question whether the city fell in the winter of 385 or the spring of 384.
2   Xenophon (*Hell.* 5.2.7) gives the number of villages as four.

31   Alliance between Athens and Chios. Athens, 384/3. Five fragments of a marble stele (with a relief), Ionic letters (e or ei=ei; o or ou=ou inconsistently), stoichedon (with anomalies in lines 19, 24, 34–43).

IG II² 34;[1] Tod 118, pp. 50–2; *SV* 2.248, pp. 196–8; Pouilloux, *Choix* 26, pp. 98–100. Cf. Diod. 14.94.4; Isocrates 14.28, 4.163.

Marshall, *Confederacy* 10–11; Accame, *Lega* 9–14, 34–5; A.P. Burnett, *Historia* 11 (1962) 3; I.A.F. Bruce, *Phoenix* 19 (1965) 281–4; G.L. Cawkwell, *CQ* 23 (1973) 56; J. Cargill, *League* 52.

Alliance of the Athe[nians and Chians. When Diei]|t[r]ephes *was archon*[2] (384/3), [when Hippothont|is] *held the first prytany,* [in which -9-], son of

5 [S|teph]ano[s from] Oio[n[3] was secretary] | (lacuna) || [---] | these things [--][4] *are mindful of the co|mmon* agreements [that] *have been written* by the Hell|enes, (namely) *that they will maintain,* like | the Athenians, the *peace*[5]

10 [and the] *friendship* || and the oaths and [the] *treaties* [that are in exist-ence], | which were sworn by the King *and* [the Athenians and] | the Lacedaemonians and the other [Hellenes], | and have come[6] professing

15 (their) good (intentions) *to th|e* People of Athens and all He||llas and the King, let it be voted by the Peop|le. Commendation shall be given *to the* [People] of Chi|os and to the ambassadors [who] *have come*; there shall continue | in existence the peace and *the* oaths and the | *alliances* that are

20 now *in existence*; the Chians shall be tre||ated as allies on terms of free-dom and auton|omy, provided that they do not transgress (any of) the (terms) on the s|telai, (terms) that have been inscribed concerning the peace, | in any way, and provided that, if anyone else transgresses (them), t|o the best of (their) ability they refuse to obey; there shall be

25 set up a s||tele on the acropolis *in front of* the stat|ue,[7] and on this shall be written: if anyone c|omes against the Athenians, the Chians shall give assistance with all (their) *stre|ngth* to the best of (their) ability, [and], if anyone comes [again|st the Chi]ans, the Athenian[s] shall give

30 assistance with all (their) *strength* || [to the best of] (their) ability. The oath shall be sworn to those [who have com|e from Chios] by the Boule *and* the [general|s and the] taxiarchs, in Chi[o]s [by the Council | and the] *other* magistrates. *There shall be chosen* [five | men] *to sail* [to Chios to

35 ad||minister the oath to the] city [of the Chians. The existence of t|he alliance shall be for all] time. [Invit|ation shall be issued to the embassy] of the Chi[ans] (to come) [for | hospitality to the Prytane]ion on the *morrow. vv* | [The following were chosen] as ambassadors:

40 Kephalo[s[8] of Kol||lytos, -c.5-] from [A]lopeke, Aisimo[s[9] .. | -c.10-]s, of Phrearrhoi, Demokle[ide|s -c.4-]. *The following* were the Chian ambas-sadors: Bryon, Ape|[-c.8-]ritos, Archelas. *vv.*

1 This alliance was possibly published at Athens in two copies, though it is hard to
   see why. At least, it is clear that fragment A of *IG* II² 35 reproduces (with minor
   orthographic differences and a longer stoichedon line) the material contained in
   lines 7–25 of the translation. The text used for these lines is, therefore, a conflation
   of the two documents. While most scholars treat the two inscriptions as simultane-

ous publications, Accame (*Lega* 34–5) has suggested that *IG* II² 35 was a later re-affirmation of the treaty of 384/3, possibly set up in 378/7 at the time of the foundation of the Second Athenian Confederacy. Cf. nos. 34 and 37 and see Cargill, *League* 52.

2   This translation has been substituted for the usual formula, 'In the archonship of', in order to preserve the line-division of the original.
3   Oion Dekeleikon, not Oion Kerameikon. See J. Traill, *The Political Organization of Attica* (*Hesperia* Supplement 14, Princeton 1975) 124.
4   In this space must stand some such phrase as 'since the Chians'.
5   The King's Peace.
6   To be understood here is the same phrase as in line 6. See n. 4.
7   The statue of Athena Promachos.
8   Kephalos is the politician mentioned by the Oxyrhynchus Historian, cf. no. 11. He was also the proposer of *IG* II² 29, 'Athens rewards Phanokritos of Parion'.
9   Aisimos was a colleague of Thrasyboulos. Cf. no. 11.

32   The occupation of the Cadmea. 382/1.

Scholion to Aelius Aristeides 13.172 (Androtion, *FGrHist* 324F50). Cf. Xen. *Hell.* 5.2.31; Diod. 15.20.2; Plut. *Pelopidas* 5.3.

M. Cary, *CAH* 6.63–4; D.G. Rice, *Historia* 23 (1974) 179–82; G.L. Cawkwell, *CQ* 26 (1976) 64–5.

Aelius Aristeides 13.172

. . . and they (the Athenians) displayed not (just) one form of benefaction, but omitted none, receiving them in their flight and collaborating with them in their return . . .

SCHOLION
The fugitives[1] were four hundred, as Androtion says.

1   That is, the Thebans who fled to Athens after Phoibidas had seized the Cadmea.

33   Alliance between Athens and Thebes. Athens, 378/7. Fragment of a marble stele, Ionic letters (but o=ou, except once in line 19), stoichedon.

IG II² 40; *SV* 2.255, pp. 203–5; A.P. Burnett, **Historia* 11 (1962) 4–8. Cf. Xen. *Hell.* 5.4.34–6.3; Diod. 15.28; Plut. *Pelopidas* 14–15.1.

Accame, *Lega* 38–44; Burnett, *Historia* 11 (1962) 1–17; J. Buckler, *Historia* 20 (1971) 506–8; A. MacDonald, *Historia* 21 (1972) 38–44; D.G. Rice, *YCS* 14 (1975) 95–130; Bury-Meiggs 349–51; Cargill, *League* 52–6, 105.

[-- the oath] *is to be sworn* by seventeen [m|en from Thebes].[1] *Invitation shall be issued* to the two Theb[an | ambassadors --] (to come) for hospitality to the [P|rytaneion on the morrow. Ste]phanos[2] made the motion.

5 Concerning the matters || [that are raised by those who] have come on embassy [to the] *allies,* | [let all the rest (be) as (proposed) by the] Boule. In addition commendation shall be given to | [-21-] and Theopompos[3] an|d [-8- and the] *trierarch* Aristom[a]cho|[s[4] and invitation shall be

10 issued] (to come) [for] *dinner* to the Prytanei[on || on the morrow. Commendation shall be given] also to Antimachos the Ch|[ian[5] and -6- the My]tilenean and invitation shall be issue|d (to come) [for dinner[6] to the Pr]ytaneion on the morrow. An|d their [names] *shall be recorded* by the secretar|y [of the Boule on the] stele,[7] in accordance with the decree of

15 th||e [Boule. And concerning the] treaty on this stel|e, (the treaty) [with the Thebans,[8] if] it is apparent that there is a difference | [between] (the text) [of this stele and the] stele [on the] *Acropolis, after passing a res|olution* [about] these (differences), [the Boule] shall introduce a motion to t|he

20 [People. --] of the Mytilenean,[9] th||e [Boule shall pass a resolution] and introduce a motion to the Peo|ple. [For the] *inscription* of the stelai *there shall be prov|ided* [by the apodektai] *thirty* drachmas for ea|ch, [and let the] secretary of the Boule [have] (them) [inscribed].

---

1 Burnett. A. Wilhelm (cited by Burnett 5) suggested two restorations on the basis of Thuc. 5.18.9. The first, 'seventeen from each of the cities', the second, 'seventeen men from each of the two (cities)'. For the seventeen oath-takers see Buckler 507–8.

2 Several earlier editors read the name Kephalos here, but see Burnett 5 n. 5.

3 Identified by Burnett with the Theopompos who took part in the liberation of the Cadmea (Plut. *Pelop.* 8.2) and fought at Leuctra (cf. no. 16). But see Cargill, *League* 54.

4 Clearly an Athenian.

5 The restoration 'Chian' is certain. See Burnett 4. What part Antimachos and the men from Mytilene played in the negotiations is not known, though it is possible they represented the allies.

6 The restoration 'dinner' rather than 'hospitality' is required by the space. This formula normally applied to Athenian citizens. Cf. no. 5 n. 3.

7 Burnett. 'Their [stelai] *shall be inscribed* by the secretar|y [of the Boule on the] *Acropolis*' (A. Wilhelm); 'Their [stelai] *shall be set up* by the secretar|y [of the Boule on the] Acropolis' (Accame). See the discussion of this difficult passage by Cargill (*League* 54–5).

8 Burnett. 'In accordance with the decree of th|e [Boule concerning the] treaty on the stel|e [of the allies]' (Kirchner, Bengtson).

9 Because of the two appearances of the word 'Mytilenean' on the stone, it was at first thought that this document recorded a treaty between Athens and Mytilene. Later, when Kirchner edited the inscription for *IG* II[2], he entitled it 'Treaty with the Thebans and the Mytileneans'.

34 Alliance between Athens and Byzantium. Athens, 378/7. Two fragments of a marble stele, Ionic letters (but o=ou and e=ei, except in line 14), stoichedon.

IG II² 41; Tod 121, pp. 56–7; *SV* 2.256, pp. 205–6. Cf. Diod. 15.28.3. For the friendship between Athens and Byzantium from 390/89 onwards cf. Xen. *Hell.* 4.8.27; Demosthenes 20.60; Isocrates 14.28.

Accame, *Lega* 16–17, 32ff.; A.P. Burnett, *Historia* 11 (1962) 3; G.L. Cawkwell, *CQ* 23 (1973) 50–1; D.G. Rice, *YCS* 24 (1975) 99; Bury-Meiggs 351; Cargill, *League* 32, 52, 169ff.

[-- of the Athen|i]ans[1] both now [and in the] *pre|ceding* period *contin|ue* [to
5   be], *let it be voted* [by the People]: || The Byza[ntines] shall be [Athenian]
     | allies *and* (allies) [of the other] a|llies. The [alliance] *s|hall be for them*
     [on the same terms as for the Chians]. | The oath shall be sworn [to
10 them by the Boul|e] and [the generals and th|e] *commanders of the cavalry*
15 [-- | ---] | (lacuna) | [-- invitation shall be issued to the amb||assadors of
     the Byz]ant[ines] (to come) [for hospit|ality] to the Prytaneion on *the
     mor|row*. The inscription of the *stel|e* (shall be the responsibility of) the
20 secretary of the Boule. | *vacat* || The following were chosen as ambas-
     sadors: | Orthoboulos[2] from Keramei[s], Exekestides[3] from Pallene,
25 | Xenodokos from Acharnai, | Pyrrhandros[4] from Anaphlystos, ||
     Alkimachos from Angele. | The following were the ambassadors from
     Byzant[i]|um: Kydon,[5] Menestratos, | Hegemon, Hestiaios, *vv* |
     Philinos.[6]

1   Presumably in the preceding space stood some form of the usual explanatory
    clause, maybe similar to the one found in no. 37. Then the sense of the clause would
    be, 'Since the Byzantines continue to be well disposed to the city of the Athenians
    now, as they have been in the past'.
2   See Lysias 16.13.
3   Cf. no. 59 n. 1.
4   Cf. nos. 35 and 38 and see Aeschines 3.139.
5   See Xen. *Hell.* 1.3.18, 2.2.1.
6   Probably the Byzantine Philinos, who was honoured as proxenos and benefactor by
    the Athenians about this time (*IG* II² 76).

35 'Charter of the Second Athenian Confederacy'. Athens, 378/7 (spring 377). Twenty fragments of a marble stele (inscribed on front and left side), Ionic letters (but o=ou except in lines 30, 50 and 118, e=ei, or eta in lines 121, 128), stoichedon (lines 7–77, but line 24 has one extra letter and in line 69 the letters are more widely spaced; lines 1–6 form a heading).

IG II^2 43; Tod 123, pp. 59–70; *SV* 2.257, pp. 207–11; Pouilloux, *Choix* 27, pp. 100–5; A.G. Woodhead, *AJA* 61 (1957) 367–73; *Cargill, *League* 14–47. Cf. Diod. 15.28.2, 29.7, 30.2, 36.4–5; Isoc. 14.44.

Marshall, *Confederacy* 14ff.; Accame, *Lega* 48ff.; R. Sealey, *Phoenix* 11 (1957) 104–9; Ryder, *Eirene* 54–7; G.L. Cawkwell, *CQ* 23 (1973) 47–60; Cargill, *League* 51–7, 97–160; C. Hamilton, *Traditio* 36 (1980) 83ff.; G.L. Cawkwell, *JHS* 101 (1981) 41–7.

FRONT

In the archonship of Nausinikos (378/7), | Kallibios,[1] son of
Kephisophon, | of Paiania was secretary. | *vacat* When Hippothonti[s]
5 (held the) *seventh* pryta‖ny.[2] Resolved by the Boule and the Peop|le,
Charinos of Athmon[on][3] presided. | Aristoteles[4] *made the motion*: To
the good *fortune* of the A|thenians and *of the allies* of the Athenia|ns, in
10 order that (the) Laced[aemo]nians may allow the Helle‖nes, free *and*
autonomous, to live | in peace, holding in security the [land] (that is)
15 the|ir [own]: [[-- | --- | --- ‖ --]].[5] *Let it be voted* by the People: If anyone
wis|hes, [of the Hel]lenes, or of the barbarians who | are living on [the
mainland],[6] or of the islanders, *as* | *many as* are [not] *subject to the King*,
[to be] an ally | of the Athenians and of their allies, it shall be permitted
20 *to hi*‖*m* (to do so), remaining *free* and autonomous, liv|ing under what-
ever constitution he wants, neith|er receiving a *garrison* nor having a
governor | *imposed* upon him nor paying tribute,[7] but (he shall become
an ally) on | the same terms (as those) on which (the) Chians[8] and (the)
25 Theba‖ns[9] and the other allies (did). For those who have | made alliance
with (the) Athenians and | their allies, the People shall give up the
pro|perties, however many there are found to be, either privately or
30 p|ublicly, held by Athenians in the *land* [of those who] ma‖*ke* the
alliance, *and* [concerning these] (properties) | shall give a pledge [--][10]
it happens (that) | of the cities [that are making] this allian|ce with
(the) Athen[ians] there are stelai at Athen|s unfavourable (to them),
35 the Boule that is at the time in ‖ office *shall have* the authority to destroy
(them). After N|ausinikos' archonship it shall not be permitted, either
pr|ivately or publicly, for any Athenian to p|ossess in the lands of the
40 allies | either a house or a plot of land, either by purcha‖se, or as the
result of a mortgage, or by any other mean|s at all. If anyone does buy
or acquire or take (such property) | on mortgage by any means what-
ever, it shall be permitted for any | of the allies who wants to lay an
indictment before the del|egates (to the Council) of the allies. The
45 delegates, after sel‖ling (the property), are to give[11] [one] *half* (of the
proceeds) to the (man) who laid the indictment, while the r|*est is to be*
(the) *common* (property) of the allies. If anyon|e *comes* for the purpose
of making war against those who have made | the alliance, either by
50 land or by se|a, the Athenians and their allies will give assistance ‖ to

them, both by land and by sea, | with all (their) strength to the best of
(their) ability. If any|one proposes or puts (a proposal) to the vote, (be
he) a magistrate or a private individ|ual, contrary to this decree, that it
is necessary to abrogate any of t|he enactments mentioned in this

55 decree, *l*|*et* it be (the penalty) for him to be deprived of (his) civic rights,
and | let *his property* become public property and the *Goddess* | (is to have)
the *tithe*, and let him be tried among (the) Athen[ia|n]s and *the* allies[12]
on the charge of dissolving the | alliance, and let them punish him with

60 deat‖h or exile from whatever land the Athenians and the allie|s con-
trol. [If] he is condemned to death, let him not be bu|ried in [Att]ica,
nor in the (land) of the al|lies. (As for) this *decree*, let the secretary | of

65 the Boule have (it) *inscribed* on a stele of mar‖ble and have (the stele)
placed beside (the statue of) Zeus Eleu|therios.[13] The money shall be
given for the in|scription of the *stele*, (namely the sum of) sixty
drachmas, | out of the Ten Talents,[14] by the treasurers of the Godd|ess.

70 On this stele he shall inscr‖ibe the names both of the cities that are
(already) | allied and of whatever (city) becomes | an ally. These things
(then) shall be inscribed, and there shall be chosen | by the People
three ambassadors right awa|y (to go) to Thebes, to persuade the

75 Thebans to (do) what‖ever good they are able. The following were
chosen: | Aristoteles of Marathon, *v* Pyrrhandro|s of Anaphlys[t]os,[15]
Thrasyboulos of Kollytos.[16] |

The following states (are) allies of (the) Athenians.[17] | Chians,
80 Tenedians, Thebans, ‖ Mytileneans, Chalcidians, | [M]ethy[m]neans,
Eretrians, | Rhodians, Poiessians, Arethousians, | Byzantines,
85 Carystians, | Perinthians, Ikians, ‖ Peparethians, Pal[-7-], | Sciathians,
90 [-9-], | Maroneans, [-9-], | Dians, [-9-], | Par[i]ans, O[-9-], [-9-], ‖
Athenitai, P[-8-], [-9-]. | Aristoteles made the motion:[18] [--] *sin*|*ce first*
[--] | of their own free will *they join* [-- the things] *that have* | *been voted* by the
95 People and the [--] ‖ of islands into the *alliance* [--] | to the [--] of the
things that *have been voted* [-- | ---]

LEFT SIDE
100 Of (the) [-2 or 3-]raians | the People,[19] | Abderites, ‖ [Thasi]ans,
105 | [Chalci]dians | from [Thrace], | Ainians, | Samothracians, ‖
Dikaiopolitans, | Acarnanians, | of (the) Cephallenians | Pronnoi;
110 | Alketas, ‖ Neoptolemos, | [[-*c*.6-]],[20] | Andrians, | Tenians, |
115 [Hes]tiaeans, ‖ Mykonians, | Antissaians, | Eresians, | Astraiousans, | of
120 (the) Ceans ‖ (the) Iulietae | (the) Karthaians | (the) Koressians,
125 | Elaiousians, | Amorgians, ‖ Selymbrians, | Siphnians, | Sikinetans, |
130 Dians | from Thrace, ‖ Neopolitans. | *vacat* | Of (the) Zacyn[th]ians | the
People | in the Nellos.[21] |

35 'Charter of the Second Athenian Confederacy'

1 Kallibios was a trierarch about this time; cf. *IG* II^2 1604.87 and Davies, *Families* 3773.
2 Spring 377.
3 Since Athmonon is a deme of the tribe Kekropis, Charinos does not belong to the tribe in prytany. Thus he marks the first datable example of the standard fourth-century practice, whereby nine Proedroi were chosen during each prytany (one from each of the nine tribes not in prytany) to prepare the agenda and supervise meetings of the assembly. Cf. Aristotle, *Ath. Pol.* 44.2–3. For the date of the change from 'chairman of the prytany' to 'chairman of the Proedroi' see G. Glotz, *REG* 34 (1921) 1–19, D.M. Lewis, *ABSA* 49 (1954) 31–4, and Henry, *Prescripts* 27 n. 32.
4 See Diogenes Laertius 5.1.35.
5 These lines were deliberately erased in antiquity. The most commonly accepted restoration is that of Accame, *Lega* 51. It runs: 'in its entirety and so that there may continue in validity for all time the Common Peace that was sworn by the Greeks and the King in accordance with the agreements'. For criticism of this restoration and different suggestions for the erasure of these lines see Cawkwell, *CQ* 23 (1973) 60 n. 1, and Cargill, *League* 28–32.
6 Or '[Europe]' (Wade-Gery *ap.* Tod, *addenda*).
7 See no. 36.
8 See no. 31.
9 See no. 33.
10 Tod and most editors, following Schaefer, read 'to them' in this space. But see Cargill, *League* 18 n. 3, who prefers to end the sentence at the word 'pledge' and to read, 'If for anyone' (i.e. of the allies) in the space.
11 The last five letters of the word 'selling' and the first five of the word 'give' (both forms of the same Greek verb) were originally omitted by the mason and later inscribed above the line.
12 Whether this involves a joint court or two separate trials is in contention. See Cargill, *League* 121–2.
13 In the Agora, near the Stoa of the King.
14 Presumably a special fund reserved for certain public expenses. It is mentioned again in no. 40 line 18. See Rhodes, *Boule* 103 n. 7.
15 Cf. nos. 34 and 38.
16 He helped restore the democracy in 403 (Dem. 24.134). For his family-tree see Davies, *Families* 7305.
17 The following list was inscribed in several hands. The Chians, Thebans, Mytileneans, Methymneans, Rhodians and Byzantines are in the same hand as inscribed the decree itself. The Chalcidians, Erctrians, Arethousians, Carystians and Ikians were added soon after in smaller letters, arranged stoichedon. The Perinthians, Peparethians, Sciathians, Maroneans and Dians form another group, inscribed 'in a crude and thick script' (Tod, p. 66). Other hands added the other names. For a detailed study see now Cargill, *League* 32–9. A problem exists regarding the number of allies in the League. The names listed here total no more than 60, yet Diodorus (15.30.2) gives the number 70 and Aeschines (2.70) gives 75. Cargill argues in favour of 60 (*League* 45–7).
18 The purpose of Aristoteles' additional motion is not clear. Proposed restorations are too hypothetical. See Cargill, *League* 39 and 99.
19 The former restoration 'the People of the Corcyraeans' was shown to be impossible by Bradeen and Coleman (*Hesperia* 36 (1967) 102–4), who suggested 'the People of the Theraeans'. Their suggestion is accepted by Cargill, *League* 40–1.
20 Fabricius' restoration of the name Jason (of Pherae) in this space was challenged

by A.G. Woodhead (*AJA* 61 (1957) 367–73) and is not accepted by Cargill, *League* 43–4, but is supported by Cawkwell (1981) 44f.

21   The names on this side were all added at the same time and inscribed by the same hand, with the exception of lines 97–9 and 131–4. See Cargill, *League* 39–44 and 51–67 (for a history of the growth of the confederacy). On the identification of the 'People in (on?) the Nellos' see now F.W. Mitchel, *Chiron* 11 (1981) 73–7.

36   A new name for tribute. ?378/7.

Harpocration, *Lexicon s.v.* Syntaxis (Theopompus, *FGrHist* 115F98). Cf. Plut. *Solon* 15.2.

C.H. Wilson, *Athenaeum* 48 (1970) 302–26; Cargill, *League* 124–7; F.W. Mitchel, *Class Views* 28 (1984) 23–37.

They used to call also the payments of phoroi (= tribute) 'syntaxeis' (= contributions), since the Greeks were distressed by the name of 'phoroi'. It was Kallistratos[1] who gave them this name, as Theopompus says in the tenth (book) of the *Philippika*.

1   Presumably Kallistratos of Aphidna.

37   Methymna joins the Athenian Confederacy.[1] Athens, 378/7.
Marble slab, Ionic letters (but o=ou throughout, e=ei once in line 3), stoichedon (from line 5; line 22 has one extra letter).

IG II^2 42; Tod 122, pp. 57–9; *SV* 2.258, pp. 212–13.

Marshall, *Confederacy* 56 n. 3; Accame, *Lega* 44ff.; D.M. Lewis, *ABSA* 49 (1954) 33–4; G.L. Cawkwell, *CQ* 23 (1973) 50–1; Cargill, *League* 52, 107.

[Resolved by the Boule and the People -- | --] *held the prytany*, Kal[1-7-] from [Alo]|peke was secretary, Simo[n --]|ios presided, Astyphilos[2] made the motion: Concerning | the matter raised by the Methymneans,
5   sinc||e they are allies[3] and well disposed to the cit|y of the Athenians, (the) Methymneans, in order that | also with the other allies of the Ath|enians they may be in alliance, they shall be inscr|ibed by the
10   secretary of the Boul||e, as the other allies also have | been inscribed. The oath shall be sworn by the em|bassy of the Methymneans, the
15   same | oath as the other allies also | swore, to the delegates of the al||lies and to the generals and the | hipparchs. The oath shall be sworn to the Methymn|eans by the delegates of the allies | and by the generals and
20   the hipparch|s in the same terms. It shall be the concern of Ai[si]||mos[4] and the delegates on the *sh|ips*[5] that the oath be sworn by the magis-

trates of the M[eth]|ymneans, just as (it was sworn) by the other allies.
| Commendation shall be given to the city of the Methymn|eans and
25   invitation shall be issued to the ambassadors of the || Methymneans (to
come) for hospitality. *vv* | *vacat*

1   The Methymneans were inscribed on the 'Charter of the Confederacy' in the same
hand as the body of the document. Cf. no. 35 line 81 and n. 17. Thus they were
already members by the time no. 35 was inscribed. Yet the references in this document to 'the other allies who have been inscribed' and to the 'delegates of the allies'
at Athens and 'on the *ships*' suggests that the confederacy has already been
organized. The usual explanation of this problem is that Methymna applied for
membership and was accepted after the passage of no. 35, but before its inscription.
For a contrary view see Cawkwell in the article cited. See now Cargill, *League* 107 n.
24.
2   This man has been identified with the son of Euthykrates of Araphen, but he is not
the only Astyphilos known in this period, so the identification is not certain. Cf.
Davies, *Families* 7252(C).
3   The Methymneans were, therefore, already in alliance with the Athenians, like the
Chians, Byzantines and others. Exactly when they became allies of Athens is not
known, but it was not until after 390/89, when they were still loyal to Sparta (Xen.
Hell. 4.8.29).
4   Cf. nos. 11 and 31.
5   'Ships' is the restoration of both Sauppe and Wilhelm (*ap.* Tod) and is commonly
accepted. Other suggestions (also *ap.* Tod) are 'places' (Mylonas), 'oaths' (Judeich),
both of which are one letter too long for the space.

38   Alliance between Athens and Chalcis.[1] Athens, 378/7. Marble slab, Ionic letters (but o=ou throughout, e=ei in lines 8 and 21), stoichedon (in lines 1–3 the letters are larger and more widely spaced to form a heading and line 17 has an extra letter).

IG II^2 44; Tod 124, pp. 70–2; **SV* 2.259, pp. 213–14. Cf. Diod. 15.30.1.

Marshall, *Confederacy* 57; Accame, *Lega* 70ff., 74ff.; Cargill, *League* 33–4, 38, 102, 154–5.

[Ar]istoteles, son of Euphiletos, | of [Ach]arnai was secretary.[2] | [In]
the archonship of Nausinikos (378/7). | *Resolved* by the Boule and the
5   People, Leonti[s] || *held the prytany*, Aristoteles was secretar|y, [of the]
Proedroi the one (who) put (the motion) to the vote (was) Pantareto|[s]
of [--]ia, Pyrrhandros[3] made the motion: Concerning the matters *r*|*aised*
by the Chalcidians, they[4] shall be introduced *t*|*o* [the] People at the first
10   assembly, and the *o*||*pinion* of the Boule shall be added, (namely) *that it
is the* | *opinion of the* Boule to accept the alliance (offered) *b*|*y* [the]
Chalcid[ia]ns with good fortune, on the terms on which *it is of*|*fered* by
the Chalcidians. The oath shall be sworn by *the* | *city* to (the)

15   [Cha]lci[di]a[n]s and by the Chalcidian[s] to the [A]‖the[nian]s *and*
there shall be inscribed on a stele of marb|le *and set up*, in [Athe]ns on
(the) Acropolis | [and] *in* [Chal]cis [in] the sanctuary of Athena, (the
text of) t|*he oath* and [the] alliance. There shall be *alli|ance* between (the)
20   [Ath]enian[s] *and* (the) Chalcidians *as follows*: ‖ *Alliance* between (the)
Chal[cid]ians in Eu[b]oea [and] | (the) [Atheni]ans. (The)
Chalcidi[ans] shall possess their own (territory) *in fr|eedom* [and]
autonomy and [-- | --],[5] neither having a garrison imposed upon them
25   [by] | (the) [Athenians], nor paying tribute, nor ad‖mitting [a governor]
contrary to the decrees [of th|e allies. If] anyone *comes for the purpose* (of
making) war [again|st the land --][6]

1   *IG* II² 155 has been identified by E. Schweigert (*Hesperia* 7 (1938) 626) as a copy of
this decree. Both were probably set up on the Acropolis. Cf. no. 31 n. 1 and *IG* II²
216/7, a decree regulating the handing over of sacred treasures from one board of
treasurers to its successor. But see Cargill, *League* 61 n. 30.
2   Not the same man as the proposer of no. 35, whose deme was Marathon.
3   Cf. no. 34 n. 4.
4   I.e. the Chalcidians.
5   Variously supplemented (*ap.* Tod): 'not subject to tribute' (Dittenberger); 'at their
own discretion' (Hiller); 'having their own lawcourts' (Foucart); 'making the treaty
of their own volition' (Wilhelm); 'being their own masters' (Accame).
6   The inscription becomes untranslatable after this point, but enough remains to
indicate that what followed was some variant of the standard formula for a defensive
alliance. Cf., for example, no. 14.

39   Reorganization of Athenian finances. 378/7.

A. Valuation of the rateable property in Attica for the purpose of the capital levy
(eisphora). (1) Polybius 2.62.7; (2) Harpocration, *Lexicon s.v.* That six thousand talents
was the assessment (of the rateable property) of Attica (Philochorus, *FGrHist* 328F46).
Cf. Demosthenes 14.19. **B.** Number of citizens liable to the capital levy. Harpocration,
Lexicon s.v. One thousand two hundred (Philochorus, *FGrHist* 328F45). Cf. Isoc. 15.145;
Demosthenes 14.16, 20.28, 21.154. **C.** Organization of those liable to the capital levy
into groups (symmories). (1) Harpocration, *Lexicon s.v.* Symmoria (Philochorus, *FGrHist*
328F41); (2) Photius, *Lexicon s.v.* Naukraria (Cleidemus, *FGrHist* 323F8). Cf. Demosthenes 14.17.

G.E.M. de Ste Croix, *C&M* 14 (1953) 30–70; F.W. Walbank, *A Historical Commentary on
Polybius* 1 (Oxford 1957) 268–9; A.H.M. Jones, *Athenian Democracy* (Oxford 1957) 83–6;
R. Thomsen, *Eisphora* (Copenhagen 1964) 24–37, 45–104, 194–249; E. Ruschenbusch,
ZPE 31 (1978) 275–84.

A. Valuation of the rateable property in Attica

(1) POLYBIUS 2.62.7
For who has not learned concerning the Athenians that at the time

when, together with the Thebans, they embarked upon the war against the Lacedaemonians[1] . . . at that time, deciding to base the levies for the war upon worth, they made a valuation of the whole land of Attica and the houses and likewise the remaining property. Nevertheless, the total valuation of the worth (for taxation purposes) fell short of six thousand talents by two hundred and fifty.[2]

(2) HARPOCRATION, *LEXICON* s.v. That six thousand talents was the assessment (of the rateable property) of Attica
For that six thousand talents was the rateable value of Attica . . . also Philochorus (says) in the tenth (book)[3] of (his) *Atthis*.

B. Number of citizens liable to the capital levy

HARPOCRATION, *LEXICON* s.v. One thousand two hundred
Isaeus in the speech *Against Ischomachos* . . . The wealthiest of the Athenians were one thousand two hundred (in number), and these also performed the liturgies.[4] Mention is made of these both by the other orators and by Philochorus in the sixth (book).

C. Organization of those liable to the capital levy into groups

(1) DEMOSTHENES 27.7
For in the tax-paying groups they agreed on my behalf to pay a tax-assessment of five hundred drachmas on each twenty-five minas.

HARPOCRATION, *LEXICON* s.v. SYMMORIA
Demosthenes, *Against Aphobos* 1 (27.7). It was not the whole citizen-body, as amongst us, that was divided into tax-paying groups at Athens, but only the wealthy and those capable of paying taxes to the city . . . The Athenians were for the first time divided up by symmories in the archonship of Nausinikos[5] (378/7), as Philochorus says in the fifth (book) of (his) *Atthis*.

(2) PHOTIUS, *LEXICON* s.v. NAUKRARIA
Cleidemus[6] says in his third book that after Kleisthenes established ten tribes in place of four, they happened to be divided into fifty parts which they called naukrariai, in the same way as they now call (the units in) the division into a hundred parts 'symmories'.[7]

1   Usually taken to refer to the hostilities that began in 378/7 rather than to the
    Corinthian War. Support for this can perhaps be found in C (1).
2   Polybius' precise figure of 5750T is surely based upon documentary evidence (cf.
    n. 5 below). It is rounded out to 6000 by Demosthenes (14.19). At least that is the
    usual view, though it is surprising to find the accurate historian Philochorus (see
    A (2)) using the less precise figure (if such it was). See the discussion in Thomsen
    89–96 and de Ste Croix 36–41. At any rate the difference is small and around 6000T
    was the sum upon which the state based its levy of ½, 1 or 2 per cent (cf. Dem. 14.27).
3   The reading of the manuscript (tenth) would date Philochorus' reference to the
    time of Demetrios Poliorketes. Jacoby emends to 'sixth' and brings the date of the
    reference up to the 350s.
4   There is a radical difference of opinion among scholars whether the 1200 richest
    men, who were liable for the trierarchic liturgy, were also the only ones who paid the
    capital levy or whether a larger group (say 6000), which included the 1200, paid the
    eisphora. See, for example, the discussions in Jones and Ruschenbusch.
5   It is clear from this and from Dem. 22.44 that a major reform of the tax-system took
    place in this year.
6   The translation is by C.W. Fornara. Cf. Fornara no. 22A, pp. 25–6.
7   The symmory-system was used both for the paying of eisphora and for the perform-
    ance of the trierarchic liturgy. It was possibly extended to the latter by the law of
    Periandros in 358/7. There were only 20 trierarchic symmories, with 60 men in each
    (Dem. 14.16). Exactly when the 100 symmories for the eisphora were introduced
    and whether, in fact, they were relevant to this period at all is debated. See Thomsen
    84–96; Jones 83–6; Ruschenbusch 275–84. Our understanding of this whole matter
    is complicated by the fact that at some time before 362 a procedure was introduced
    whereby the three richest men in each symmory were required to advance the tax
    for their symmory to the state and then collect the money from the other members.
    This system was called proeisphora. See especially Isaeus 6.60 and [Dem.] 50.8–9
    and the discussions in Thomsen 220ff. and de Ste Croix 58ff. Despite this system, it
    was still possible for arrears of eisphora to exist; cf. Dem. 22.44, 24.162.

40   Athens honours Straton, king of Sidon. Athens, 378/7 *or* 368/7 *or* 364 *or* 360. Marble stele, Ionic letters, stoichedon.

IG II² 141; *Tod 139, pp. 116–19.

A.C. Johnson, *CP* 9 (1914) 417–23; R.P. Austin, *JHS* 64 (1944) 98–100; G.L. Cawkwell, *CQ* 13 (1963) 138; M.J. Osborne, *ABSA* 66 (1971) 319; R.A. Moysey, *AJAH* 2 (1976) 182–9.

[---] of the Atheni[ans] and he saw to it that as | splendidly as possible
were conveyed the ambass|adors to the Persian King, (the ambas-
sadors) whom the People had sen|t.[1] And reply shall be made to the
5   man who has come f‖rom the king of the Sidonians that, if also | for the
future he is a good man | toward the People of Athens, no|thing will he
fail to get from the Athenian|s, of the things that he may want. And he
10   shall be proxen‖os of the People of Athens, Strato|n,[2] the king of Sidon
(that is), both himself | and his descendants. This decree is to be

in|scribed by the secretary of the Boule | on a marble stele within ten
15   days,[3] and || is to be placed on the Acropolis. For the i|nscription of the
stele there shall be given by the | treasurers to the secretary of the Boule
3|0 drachmas from the Ten Talents.[4] There are to be com|missioned in
20   addition by the Boule tokens[5] f||or the king of the Sidonians, in order
| that the People of Athens may know if any communication | is sent by
the king of the Sidonians, when he wa|nts (something) from the city,
25   and the king of the S|idonians may know whenever someone is sent t||o
him by the People of Athens. Invitation shall be issue|d for hospitality
to the man who has come from | the king of the Sidonians at the
Pryta|neion for tomorrow. *vacat* | Menexenos[6] made the motion: (Let)
30   all the rest (be) a||s proposed by Kephisodotos.[7] (Regarding) all those
Sido|nians with permanent residences in Sidon and holding citi|zen-
ship (there), who reside for the purposes of tra|de at Athens, it shall not
be permitted in their case for the resident | aliens' tax to be exacted, nor
35   for the choregia || to be assigned to anyone, nor for the property tax | to
be assessed at all.[8]

1   This is the conclusion of the statement giving the grounds for honouring Straton.
  Clearly he gave assistance to an Athenian embassy on its way to the Great King. The
  occasion is disputed: see Moysey.
2   Straton was king of Sidon *c.* 376–*c.* 360. A vassal of the King of Persia, he took part
  in the so-called Satraps' Revolt as a result of his association with Tachos of Egypt
  (Diod. 15.9.1ff.; St Jerome, *Ad Jovinianum* 1.45; Xen. *Ages.* 2.30). He was renowned for
  his luxury (Athenaeus 12.531a–e).
3   For this formula and its relevance to the date of this document see Austin.
4   See no. 35 n. 12.
5   This is the first known case of an exchange of diplomatic tokens, designed to
  guarantee the authenticity of communications between two parties.
6   Menexenos is mentioned (below) in no. 55 line 8 (treaty between Athens and Ceos,
  362) as the author of an earlier decree concerning the people of Iulis on Ceos.
7   See no. 54 n. 4.
8   These were some of the regular obligations of the metics (see Glossary) at Athens.
  Aliens were normally allowed to reside at Athens for any length of time only if they
  registered as metics. This rider dispenses with this requirement in the case of
  Sidonian merchants.

**41   Recommendation that Corcyra, Acarnania and Cephallenia
enter the Athenian Confederacy. Athens, 375.** Four fragments of a
marble stele, Ionic letters (inconsistent use of e or ei for ei, o or ou for
ou), stoichedon (except line 1, which has larger letters to form a
heading).

IG II² 96; *Tod 126, pp. 82–6; *SV* 2.262, pp. 217–18. Cf. Xen. *Hell.* 5.4.64; Isoc. 15.109;
Diod. 15.36.5; Nepos, *Timotheus* 2.1.

41 Adoption of new members of the Athenian Confederacy

Marshall, *Confederacy* 63; R. Sealey, *Phoenix* 11 (1957) 99; A.G. Woodhead, *Phoenix* 16 (1962) 259–60; G.L. Cawkwell, *Historia* 12 (1963) 84–95, esp. 91 n. 61; J. Buckler, *GRBS* 12 (1971) 354 n. 6; Cargill, *League* 68–74, 99–105.

Philokles[1] [-- was secretary]. | *In* [the archonship] of Hippodama[s (375/4), when Antiochis held the] *s|econd prytany*, [for which Phylakos --[2] of Oino|e][3] was secretary. Resolved [by the Boule and the People].
5 Kr[it|li]os made the motion: With regard to what is *reported* [in the] *Boule* by the ambassad|ors of the Corcyreans[4] and the [Acarnanians] *and* the Cepha[l]|lenians, commendation shall be given to *the* [ambassadors of the Corc]yreans an|d the Acarnanians and the Cephal[lenians, because
10 they are] good me|n toward the People of [Athens and the] allies ‖ now, as (they have been) in the *past*. [In order that] there may be accomplished | what they request, (the Boule) shall introduce [them before the] People, and the *opinio|n* of the *Boule* shall be added, [that it is the opinion] of the Boule | that [the] names of the cities that [have come] shall be inscribed on | the common stele of the [allies by the]
15 secretar‖y of the Boule,[5] and that [the oaths] shall be administered to the cities | that have come by the Boule [and the generals and] *th|e* knights and that the *allies* [shall in like manner swear the] *oa|th*. When this has been accomplished [the People shall choose], *in accord|ance with* whatever is resolved by the common (council) [of the allies, men] *to*
20 *ad‖minister* the oaths *to* [the cities and these[6]] shall be *re|gistered* on the [common] *stele*, [where the] *al|lies* have been inscribed. [And delegates[7]] *shall be sent* | by each of the cities to the *council* [of the allie|s], according
25 to the resolutions of the allies [and of the People of Athen]‖s. Concerning the Acarnanians *there shall be consultation*[8] [in common wit|h A]ischylos and Euarchos and Euru[-14- | -15-] and Rhusiad[es --]

1 The letter omega is extant on the stone immediately after the name 'Philokles'. This is the first letter of either his patronymic or, more likely, his demotic.
2 Phylakos' patronymic belongs in this space.
3 This restoration is assured by the prescript of a decree passed in the same prytany, *IG* II[2] 99. It creates the problem that two different secretaries are named on this stele. Since at this time the secretary held office for one prytany only, so that there were ten secretaries in each administrative year, the solution may well be that the motion was passed when Phylakos was secretary, but inscribed later. In the 360s the system was changed and one man was chosen by lot to be secretary for the whole year.
4 The old view that an epitaph from the Ceramicus (*IG* II[2] 5224), recording the burial at Athenian expense of two Corcyrean ambassadors who died at Athens, relates to this negotiation has been proved wrong by U. Knigge, *AA* 1972, 591–605.
5 The 'common stele of the allies' is presumably *IG* II[2] 43 (no. 35). On that stele are found 'the Acarnanians' (line 106) and 'of the Cephallenians: Pronnoi' (lines 107–8). The Corcyreans are not extant on the stone (see no. 35 n. 17), though a treaty was undoubtedly concluded (cf. no. 42). Likewise, although we have the

fragmentary remains of a treaty between the Athenians and the Cephallenians (*IG* II² 98), only Pronnoi of the four cities of Cephallenia is listed.
6 It is not clear whether the men or the oaths are meant. In fact, neither the men nor the oaths are on no. 35.
7 On the question how many delegates each state sent to the council see Cargill, *League* 113–14.
8 We do not know what special negotiations were required in the case of the Acarnanians nor anything about the men listed here.

42   Alliance of Athens and Corcyra.¹ Athens, 375 *or* 374/3 *or* 371.

Marble stele, surmounted by a relief representing a woman (Corcyra or Hera?) standing and talking to a seated male (Zeus, Demos, Asclepius or Kekrops?), behind whom stands Athena, Ionic letters (except o=ou in lines 4, 9, 25), stoichedon.

IG II² 97; Tod 127, pp. 86–8; *SV 2.263, pp. 218–20; Pouilloux, *Choix* 28, pp. 105–7.

For the bibliography see no. 41 and add Cargill, *League* 109–11, 120.

Alliance of the Corcyreans and the Athenians for | all time. If anyone comes for the purpose of (making) war in|to the land of the Corcyreans or against the Pe|ople of Corcyra,² assistance shall be given by the
5   Athenians in f|ull strength, in accordance with the demands of the Cor|cyreans, to the best of (their) ability. And if anyone comes again|st the People of Athens or against the land | of the Athenians for the purpose of (making) war, either by land | or by sea, assistance shall
10 be given by the Corcyreans in f|ull strength, to the best of (their) ability, in accordance with the de|mands of the Athenians. As for war and pe|ace, it shall not be permitted to the Corcyreans to mak|e (either) without the Athenians and [the] majority of the al|lies. In other
15 respects too they shall act in accordance with the re||solutions of the allies. The oath. *vv* | I shall give assistance to the People of Corcyra in full st|rength, to the best of (my) ability, if anyone comes for the purpose of (making) w|ar, either by land or by sea, against the l|and of
20 the Corcyreans, in accordance with the deman||ds of the Corcyreans. Concerning war and p|eace I shall act in accordance with whatever the majority of the a|llies resolve, and in other respects I shall act in accord-ance with the | resolutions of the allies. (That) this (is) true (I swear) by
25 | Zeus and Apollo and Demeter. If I keep || my oath, may I have many benefits, but if | [not], (may I have) the opposite. *vv* | [I shall give assist-ance] to the People of [Ath]ens in full stren|gth [to the best of (my)] *ability*, if anyone [comes for the purpose of (making) w|ar, either by] *land*
30 or by sea *against* [the || land of the Athen]ians, in accordance with the

demand|*s* of the [Atheni]ans. Concerning war *and pea*|*ce* [I shall act in accordance with] *whatever* the A[th]enia[n]s and [the] *m*|*ajority* [of the] *allies* resolve, *and in other respects I shall* | *act* [in accordance with the resol-
35 utions] of the Athen[i]ans and *the* ‖ [allies]. (That) *this* (is) [true] (I swear) by Zeus *and* | [Apollo and De]met[er]. If I keep my oa|th, [may I have many] *benefits*, but, if not, (may I have) [the o|pposite].[3]

1 This treaty has usually been considered as the logical sequel to no. 41, marking the entry of Corcyra into the Athenian Confederacy. But the absence of the Corcyreans from the list of allies in no. 35 is used by Cargill as an argument for the view that Corcyra never did join the Confederacy. For his reconstruction suggesting why this was so see *League* 69–74. He believes that the alliance translated here was a non-league alliance of 374 or 373, possibly inscribed in 371.
2 I.e. the alliance was made with the democratic faction, which was under pressure from the oligarchs supported by Sparta (cf. Xen. *Hell.* 6.2.4 and Diod. 15.46.1–3, 47.1–7).
3 The Corcyrean oath contains several Doric forms, though it is not consistently Doric.

43 Athenian alliance with Amyntas III. Athens, 375/4 *or* 373/2.[1]
Two fragments of a marble stele, Ionic letters (except o=ou thirteen times), stoichedon (but line 7 has one extra letter).

IG II² 102; *Tod 129, pp. 90–2; *SV* 2.264, pp. 220–1.

D.J. Mosley, *RSA* 2 (1972) 10; Ellis, *Philip II* 42–3; Cawkwell, *Philip* 25; Hammond-Griffith 172–80 (Hammond).

[--] *men to* [administer t|he] *oaths* to Amy[ntas and Alexandros a|nd] to take care of [the inscription and] | *the* stele, in order to [give effect to
5 what] *has been* ‖ *voted* by the People. Commendation shall be given to [Amynt|as] and the ambassadors who have come [fr|om] him, Ptolemaio[s] and Antenor and [-]|son. Commendation shall also be
10 given to the ambassadors | who were sent *by* the People to M[ac]‖edonia about *the alliance*. There shall be given | to the ambassadors who were chosen, for | (their) *travelling expenses*, 20 *drachmas* each by the treasur|er of the People. *Invitation shall be issued* (to come) for hospitality to the |
15 ambassadors [from Am]yntas and to those *who were s*‖*ent* [by the People] (to come) for dinner to | [the Prytaneion] *tomorrow. vv* | [--]² *Hipparchs.* |
20 [--]kles of Erchi(a). | [--Democh]ares³ of Paia(nia). ‖ [--Amynta]s, son of Arrhidaios. | [--Alexand]ros, son of Amyntas.⁴

1 The treaty is thought to have been occasioned by the expedition of either Chabrias (375) or Timotheos (373).

2   The list of Athenian ambassadors is arranged in two columns, the second of which
has the heading 'Hipparchs'.
3   Probably the son of Demon (III). See Davies, *Families* 3737.
4   The names of Amyntas and Alexandros are written in larger letters.

44   The peace of 375/4.

Didymus, *Demosthenes* col. 7.62–71 (on Dem. 10.34) (Philochorus, *FGrHist* 328F151).[1]
Cf. Xen. *Hell.* 6.2.1; Diod. 15.38; Isoc. *Antidosis* 109; Nepos, *Timotheus* 2.

Jacoby, *FGrHist* 3b.Suppl. 1.522–6; G.L. Cawkwell, *Historia* 12 (1963) 84–95; Ryder,
Eirene 58; J. Buckler, *GRBS* 12 (1971) 353–61.

It could be | (that it is) another peace initiated by the King, (one) which
65 | the Athenians gladly accepted, that is being re‖called at this point by
Demosthenes. Concerning this peace (it is) once again | Philochorus
who has a discussion, (saying) that it was very similar | to that of the
Laconian Antalkidas, (and that) they ac|cepted (it), because they were
exhausted by (the cost of) maintaining mercenary troops | and had
70   been worn down by the war for a long ti‖me. (This was the occasion)
when the altar of Eirene (Peace) was | built.[2]

1   Cf. nos. 12 and 23. Dem. 10.34 is translated under no. 12.
2   The fourth century saw the initiation of the practice of establishing cults of per-
sonifications of abstract concepts. The cult statue beside this altar was the work of
Kephisodotos. It depicted Peace with the child Wealth in her arms. For a photograph of this statue see Wickersham and Verbrugghe, *The Fourth Century* (Toronto
1972) 51.

45   Athenian law concerning the Certifier of silver coinage.
Athens, 375/4. Complete marble stele, Ionic letters (but o=ou, except
in lines 20–3, 41–2, 47 and 51), stoichedon (except lines 1–2).

*R.S. Stroud, *Hesperia* 43 (1974) 157–61.

Stroud, *Hesperia* 43 (1974) 161–88; A. Giovannini, *GRBS* 16 (1975) 191–5; F. Sokolowski,
BCH 100 (1976) 511–16; P. Gauthier, *RPh* 52 (1978) 32–5; T.V. Buttrey in *Greek Numisma-
tics and Archaeology*, ed. O. Mørkholm and N.M. Waggoner (Wetteren 1979) 33–45 and
Quaderni Ticinesi 10 (1981) 71–94; F. Bourriot, *ZPE* 50 (1983) 275–82; H. Wankel, *ZPE* 52
(1983) 69–74 and *ZPE* 53 (1983) 94; T.R. Martin, *Acta of the VIIIth International Congress of
Greek and Latin Epigraphy* (forthcoming).

Resolved by the Nomothetai,[1] when Hippo[damas] | was archon (375/
4). Nikophon made the motion: | Attic silver coinage shall be accepted
5   (as legal tender) [-- | --][2] silver and has the public *stamp*.[3] [The] ‖ public
Certifier,[4] sitting *among* [the] t|ables,[5] is to test (the coins) in accordance

with these criteria every *day* [except] | when there is a (public) payment
of cash,[6] then (he is to test) in [the] *Bouleut|erion*. If anyone brings for-
10   ward [--][7] | having the same stamp as the Atti[c --][8] || (the public
Certifier) is to give (it) back to the one who brought (it) forward.[9] But
if it is [bronze] beneath (the silver) | or lead beneath or base,[10] he is to
cut (it) across [-- | --][11] and it is to be sacred to the Mother of the Gods
and he is to *depos|it* (it) with the Boule. If the *Certifier* does not sit | or
15   does not test according to the law, let [him] be beaten || by the Syllogeis
of the People[12] fifty strokes *with the whi|p*. If anyone does not accept
whatever silver coinage [the] *Certifi|er* tests (and approves),[12a] let him be
deprived of whatever he *is selling on tha|t* day. Denunciations[13] shall be
made for offences in the *grain-market*[14] [before] | the Sitophylakes; for
20   offences in the agora and [in the] *re||st* of the city before the Syllogeis of
the People; for offences [in the] | market and the Pei[r]aeus before the
Epimelet|ai of the market, with the exception of offences in the grain-
market; for offences [in the] *grain-|market*[15] before the Sitophylakes.[16]
Of these *denunciations*, [all] *th|ose* that are below ten drachmas *are to be*
25   within the competence of [the] m||agistrates to decide, but those above
ten [drachmas] | are to be brought (by the magistrates) before the law-
court. The *Thesmothetai* are to p|rovide a *court* for them, assigning (it) by
lot, wh|enever they request (one), or are to be liable to a fine of [?]
drachmas. [The] | one who made the denunciation is to have half (the
value of the merchandise) as his share, if (he) secures a conviction
30   [--].[17] || If the seller is a slave, male or female, let [him] | be beaten fifty
strokes with the whip by [the magistrate|s] to whom the various
(denunciations) have been assigned. If one of *the magistrat|es* does not
act in accordance with what has been written, *let him be brought*[18] | before
the Boule by anyone of the Athenians who wishes, (from those) who
35   [are permitted]. || If he is found guilty, let him be removed from *offi|ce*
and let him be fined in addition by the Boule up to [500 drachmas]. In
| order that there may be in the Peiraeus also a Certifier [for the] *ship-
|owners* and the merchants and [all] the others, | let one be appointed by
40   the Boule from the public slaves, if [--][19] || or let one be bought; as for
the cost (of purchasing a Certifier), the Apodektai are to *disburs|e* (it).
The Epimeletai of the market are to see to it *th|at* he sits beside the stele
of Poseido[n][20] *an|d* let them apply the law (in his case) just as has in the
case of the city-*Cer|tifier* been stated, according to the same criteria. Let
45   there be inscribed on a *stel||e* of marble[21] (the text) of this law and let
(one copy) be placed in the *ci|ty* among the (bankers') tables, (another)
in the Peiraeus be|side the stele of Posei[d]on. The secretary | of the
Boule is to report the cost to the Pol[etai]. | The Poletai are to bring
50   (the cost) before the Boule.[22] P||ayment shall be made to the Certifier
in the *mar|ket*, in the archonship of Hippodamas (i.e. for this year), from

the time when *he is ap|pointed*; let the Apodektai make the disbursement, (the amount being) the same as for *the* Certifier in the city. But for the future | his payment shall come from the same source as for the *mint-*
55   *work||ers*. If there is any decree that has been inscribed anywhere on a stele (that is) *contrary to* t|his law, let it be destroyed by the secretary of the *Boule*.[23]

1   For discussion of this unique prescript see Stroud 162–3. The board of the Nomothetai had been in existence since at least 403/2 (Andocides 1.83–4), but, before the discovery of this inscription, its activities were not in evidence until 353/2.
2   Stroud restores 'when it is shown (to be) silver'.
3   The word used here (charakter) technically refers to the punch die that produced the design on the reverse of the coin. But the meaning can hardly be so specific in this context.
4   Though private banks were known to employ slaves as money-testers in the fourth century, the earliest evidence before this for a public slave was from the years 306–304.
5   Tables of bankers and money-changers, possibly situated in the north-west corner of the Agora, near the Stoa of Hermes. See Stroud 167.
6   Payments of public revenue were regularly received by the Apodektai in the Council-house (Bouleuterion). On these occasions the Certifier would be needed there.
7   Stroud suggests 'foreign silver currency'.
8   'if it is good' (Stroud, Buttrey); 'in accordance with the law' (Sokolowski); 'having examined (it)' (Wankel); 'as its device' (Martin; sim. Bourriot).
9   Stroud thinks this means that the coinage was accepted and its circulation was obligatory. A different view is held by Giovannini and Buttrey, who believe that the coinage was acceptable but not obligatory legal tender. Buttrey then interprets the beginning of the next sentence to read 'but if (someone brings forward a coin that is [bronze] ... '
10   Three classes of coins are to be rejected: (1) bronze or (2) lead cores covered with silver leaf, and (3) coins struck in a base (e.g. silver/copper) alloy.
11   'Immediately' (Stroud); sim. Wankel, though with a different reading.
12   The Syllogeis of the People, first mentioned here, were a board of thirty, whose primary purpose appears to have been punitive. For the evidence see Stroud 178–9.
12a Buttrey argues that the Greek form (dokimasei) by itself means 'approved'.
13   For the procedure involved in making a denunciation (*phasis*) see A.R.W. Harrison, *The Law of Athens: Procedure* (Oxford 1971) 218–21.
14   In the city.
15   In the Peiraeus.
16   For what is known about the two boards of Sitophylakes (grain-guards) and the Epimeletai (supervisors) of the market see Stroud 180–1.
17   Stroud suggests the restoration 'the purchaser' as the subject of the verb 'secures a conviction'.
18   Stroud. 'Let a charge of impeachment be laid' (Gauthier); thus already M.H. Hansen, *Eisangelia* (Odense 1975) 28.
19   Stroud suggests, *exempli gratia*, 'if there is one'.
20   There is no other reference to the existence or whereabouts of this stele.

21   For the use of the singular to refer to more than one copy there is a parallel in *IG* II² 125.17–19.
22   There is no other evidence for the Poletai as contractors of the cost of stelai in the fourth century. See Stroud 183 and, for the officials who did contract and pay for stelai in the fourth century, W.B. Dinsmoor, *AJA* 36 (1932) 158–9.
23   A law (nomos) had greater authority than any decree (psephisma), whether of the Boule or the People (Andocides 1.87).

46   Epigram commemorating the Theban victory at Leuctra. Thebes, 371. Limestone base, mixed dialect, elegiac couplets (lines 4–9), one line for each verse.

IG VII 2462; *Tod 130, pp. 92–4. Cf. Pausanias 4.32.5, 9.13.6; Xen. *Hell.* 6.4.7–14; Diod. 15.53.1–56.4; Polyaenus, *Strategemata* 2.3.8.

D.J. Mosley, *REG* 85 (1972) 312–18 (background to the battle); G.L. Cawkwell, *CQ* 22 (1972) 254–74 (the relation of the battle to the career of Epameinondas); H. Beister, *Chiron* 3 (1973) 65–84 (specifically on the epigram); Bury-Meiggs 367–83 (the hegemony of Thebes); Buckler, *Hegemony* 46–69 (Leuctra), 131.

Xenokrates,[1] | Theopompos, | Mnasilaos. |
5   When the Spartan spear held sway,[2] then it fell /‖ to Xenokrates' lot to carry the trophy in honour of Zeus,[3] /| fearing neither the army from Eurotas nor the Laconian /| shield. 'Thebans (are) superior in battle' //| proclaims the trophy[4] at Leuctra that announces the victory won by the spear,[5] /| nor did we run second to Epameinondas.[6] /|

1   Xenokrates was a Boeotarch at the time (Paus. 9.13.6).
2   That is, before the battle at Leuctra.
3   On the evidence of Pausanias (4.32.5) Xenokrates was chosen by lot before the battle to carry into battle some armour, though not, as Pausanias says, the shield of the Messenian hero Aristomenes (see Beister 77–81), to serve as a trophy indicating that Zeus had already given the victory to Thebes. He presumably selected Theopompos and Mnasilaos to help him in this task (Beister 75).
4   Most likely the trophy that Xenokrates had carried into battle was set up after the battle as a sign of victory.
5   Or 'the trophy that brings victory in war', suggested but rejected by Beister 81–2.
6   Not to be 'interpreted as a veiled protest against the undue glorification of that general' (Tod, p. 93), but simply as a reflection of the fact that the trophy-bearer and his assistants marched in the forefront of the Theban army (Beister 75).

47   Extract from an Athenian naval record[1] (lines 83–111). Athens, 371–70 *or* 366/5. Marble stele (inscribed in two columns[2]), Ionic letters (except o or ou=ou erratically), stoichedon (though the number of letters to a line decreases from 65 in line 83 to 63 in line 110; lines 111ff. are more closely inscribed with *c.* 80 letters to a line).

47 Extract from an Athenian naval record

IG II² 1609.

R. Sealey, *Phoenix* 11 (1957) 95–9; J.S. Morrison and R.T. Williams, *Greek Oared Ships* (Cambridge 1968) *passim* (esp. pp. 244–309); J.K. Davies, *Historia* 18 (1969) 309–33; L. Casson, *Ships and Seamanship in the Ancient World* (Princeton 1971) *passim* (esp. pp. 224–67).

[--]. Soizousa (Saviour):[3] trierarchs,[4] Apollodoros of Achar(nai),[5] Timokrates [of Kri(oa).[6] These] | have a complete set of wooden equipment[7] that Archestratos of Alopek(e) contributed:[8] of *hanging equipment*
85 || (they have) a sail that Stephanos of Euonymon contributed, white sidescreens,[9] *two* anchors [that Pasio]|n of Achar(nai)[10] contributed, sidescreens of hide and a hypoblema and a katablema[11] that Phil[-6- of Ach]|arnai returned, ropes[12] that Pasion of Achar(nai) returned. During our term of office *this* ship [--] | light ropes, a sail Na[-7-] contributed. *v* (These) triremes sailed out under Eukte[mon of Lou]|sia and Euthios of Souni(on), the cleruchy-commanders.[13] *v* Doris (Doric
90 Maid): trierarchs, Apollodoros of Achar(nai), [Timokrat]||es of Kri[oa]. Of the wooden equipment *this* ship has two ladders,[14] two poles,[15] two supports.[16] *v* He[gemonia?] (Leadership?): t|rierarchs, Philinos of Lamp(trai), Demomeles of Paia(nia).[17] These took no equipment (i.e. from the state) during *our term of office*. *v* [Mou]|sike (Arts): trierarchs, Phanostratos of Kephi(sia), Dorotheos of Eleusis. These [took] *no* equipment | during our term of office. *v* Nike (Victory): (the) work of (the shipwright) Pistokrates. One of the new ships. Trierarchs, Deinias of Erchi(a), [Leochares] | of Palle(ne). These are in possession of no equipment during our term of office. *v* Hegemonia (Leadership): one of
95 the new ships, Lysikr[ates'] *wor*||*k*.[18] Trierarch, Chabrias of Aixo(ne).[19] (He has) 200 oar-timbers and in place of (these) oar-timbers he must *return* a | complete set of oars.[20] *v* Eudoxia (Good Repute): trierarch, Kallippos of Aixo(ne).[21] He has hanging *equipment* [and] w|ooden (equipment), a full set (of both). This ship was given to the tithe-collectors.[22] *v* Bakche (Bacchante): one of the new ships, [the work] of Hierophon. | Trierarch, Aristaichmos of Chollei(dai). He has a full set of hanging equipment, and of the *wooden*, | 200 *oar-timbers*. In place of these he must return a full set. (He also has) a large mast.[23] *v*
100 Naukratis:[24] one of [the] *ne*||*w ships*, the work of Xenokles. Trierarchs, Timotheos of Anaph(lystos),[25] Theoxenos of Euo(nymon). These have [of the] h|anging (equipment) a sail, a hypoblema, a katablema, light ropes, 4 anchor-cables; of the *wood*|*en* (equipment); 200 oar-timbers; in place of these they must return a full set. *v* Eudia (Fairweather). One of the new ships, [Aristo]|kles' work. Trierarchs, Charikleides of Myrrhi(nous), Kallistratos of Aphid(na).[26] These *have* t|he hanging equipment in full and the wooden, except for the emergency mast; in

105   place of the complete set (of oars) ‖ he[27] took 200 oar-timbers, on condition that he return a complete set. *v* Amemptos (Blameless):
trierarchs, Philippos of Ko[lo](nos), [Poly]‖kles[28] of Anagy(rous).
These have a complete set of hanging equipment; of the wooden
(equipment) (they have) a *large* mast, a larg|e *yardarm*, ladders, 200
oar-timbers. In place of the oar-timbers a complete set (of oars) [must]
be returned by *th|em*. These[29] have returned the hanging equipment,
except for the heavy ropes and the undergirds;[30] of the *wood|en* (equip-
ment) they have returned a complete set of oars. *v* Rhodonia (Rose-
bed): trie(rarchs), Kleotimides of Atene, Kephalion of Aph[id](na).
110   [These] o‖we a complete set of hanging equipment; of the wooden
(they owe) a large yardarm, ladders. [The] *res|t* must be returned by
Timotheos of Achar(nai), Theodoros of Meli(te). *v*

1   This document is one of a very important series of inscriptions that contained the
yearly accounts of the superintendents of the shipyards in the Peiraeus. They
survive in a more or less fragmentary state and cover the period 377/6 to 323/2.
Most of them were found in the Peiraeus in 1834 during the excavation of a late
Roman or Byzantine drain.
2   Column 1 is almost entirely lost. The extract is taken from column 2, which is
largely preserved.
3   The name is feminine, as the names of Greek ships always are. On the types of
names the Athenians gave their warships see Casson 344–60.
4   On trierarchs and the trierarchy see the Glossary and B. Jordan, *The Athenian Navy
in the Classical Period* (Berkeley and Los Angeles 1975) 61–93, 134–7.
5   The deme names are often abbreviated in this document. Apollodoros was the son
of the banker Pasion. He appears in several Demosthenic orations and possibly
authored some. Dem. 50 details his naval experience.
6   A political associate of the Atthidographer Androtion (cf. no. 68). See Demosthenes 24 and Davies, *Families* 13772.
7   A complete set of wooden equipment comprised a set of 170 oars (often with a few
added for breakage), 2 steering oars, 2 ladders, a main mast and yardarm, frequently a smaller emergency mast and yard, and 3 poles. See Casson 265.
8   For an explanation of this formula, which occurs frequently in this inscription but
rarely in other naval records, see Davies 318ff.
9   Each trireme had four of these, two of canvas and two of hide. They were designed
to protect the rowers from the weather and the missiles of the enemy. See Casson
249 n. 99.
10   The banker. See Davies, *Families* 11672.
11   Both the hypoblema and the katablema were screens or awnings of a type, but
their precise use is unknown. Down to 325 a trireme carried one of each. See
Casson 250.
12   These ropes (schoinia) were heavy lines for moorage and anchor cables. They were
probably 11.5 or 15 cm in circumference. They were different from the lighter
ropes (topeia) used for the running and standing rigging. See Casson 250 n. 101.
13   Presumably the ships under their command were going out to found a cleruchy,
maybe that of 366/5 on the island of Samos. Cf. no. 77.
14   These were used for landing, one at each side of the stern. See Casson 251 n. 104.

15   The normal complement was three, one longer and two shorter. They were used for taking soundings and fending off. See Casson 251 and n. 105.
16   These were perhaps supports for the emergency mast (Casson 237 n. 59). But see Morrison and Williams (239), who think they were stakes for supporting the ship when drawn up on land.
17   These trierarchs had been in charge of Euporia (Plenty) earlier in the record (line 62). For a suggested explanation why they and Apollodoros and Timokrates (see lines 83 and 90) should have changed ships in the course of the year see Davies 321–2, 330–1.
18   It was not unknown to have more than one ship of the same name in the fleet at the same time. In that case the ships were frequently identified by the name of the builder. See Casson 350–1.
19   See Davies, *Families* 15086. For other references to this famous Athenian general see the Index.
20   Since there were 170 rowers, a complete set of oars should comprise 170 oars. In these naval records it is very frequent to find trierarchs receiving 200 oar-timbers from the state, but required to return only 170 oars. Presumably the trierarch had the responsibility for shaping the oars and was given a leeway for error.
21   See Davies, *Families* 8065.
22   Possibly this ship had been captured.
23   The main mast, as opposed to the smaller emergency mast.
24   The name of a Greek trading colony in Egypt.
25   Son of Konon. See Davies, *Families* 13700. For other references to Timotheos consult the Index.
26   See Davies, *Families* 8157. For other references to this Athenian politician consult the Index.
27   The verb changes to the singular.
28   Polykles is likely to be the opponent of Apollodoros in Dem. 50.
29   A qualification inserted by the superintendents to indicate that Philippos and Polykles had returned part of what they had received before the end of the year.
30   A trireme carried four of these strong cables, which could be run horizontally from stem to stern below the gunwale and were designed to protect the hull when it was under excessive pressure. See Casson 91–2.

48   Boeotia honours a Carthaginian. Thebes, 369/8 *or* 362 *or* 361.
Fragment of a marble stele (now lost), Boeotian dialect (with some Ionic spelling), non-stoichedon.

IG VII 2407.

F.C. Thomes, *Egemonia beotica e potenza marittima nella politica di Epaminonda* (Turin 1952) 24–30; Roesch, *Thespies* 75–7, 101; J. Wiseman, *Klio* 51 (1969) 196 n. 2, 197 n. 2, 199 n. 2; Bury-Meiggs 366–83.

God, (Good) fortune. When [Thi]ote[l]|es[1] was archon.[2] Resolved | by
5   the People: a proxenos | of the Boeotians and a ben‖efactor shall be Nobas, Axi|oubos' son,[3] the Carthaginian; and | he shall have (as regards) property and hom|e the right of possession, and freedom

10   from taxation, | and personal inviolability both *by land* || and by sea, both
during wa|rtime and when a state of *peace* exists.[4] | The Boeotarchs
were: Ti[mon], | Aiton[d]as,[5] [Th]ion, [M]e[n|o]n,[6] Hippi[a]s,
15   [E]umari[d]as, || P[at]r[o]n.

1 '[Thi]ote[l]es' (Dittenberger in *IG* VII); '[Di]ote[l]es' (all recent editors).
2 This is the first mention of an archon of the Boeotian federation.
3 The transcription of this document that has survived was made in the eighteenth
   century by the English scholar Pococke. It contains many errors, most of which can
   be corrected by comparison with contemporary documents. The names, however,
   prove more difficult, especially the name of the honorand. Translated here is the
   form found in the transcription, but the emendation 'Hannibal, son of Hasdrubal,'
   has won many adherents, despite the philological objections raised by Dittenberger.
4 The standard formula in Boeotian proxeny-decrees. See Roesch 101, and D.
   Knoepfler, *BCH* 102 (1978) 375–93.
5 'Daitondas' (Wilhelm (*ap. IG* VII)).
6 'Melon' (Wilhelm). Cf. Xen. *Hell.* 5.4.2.

49   The Thessalians honour Pelopidas. Delphi, 369/8[1] or 364/3.[2]
Statue base, elegiac couplets (lines 1–4), stoichedon.

A. Wilhelm, *Wiener Jahreshefte* 33 (1941) 38. Cf. Plut. *Pelop.* 32.5–34.7; Nepos, *Pelop.* 5.5.

Wilhelm, *Wiener Jahreshefte* 33 (1941) 35–45; Buckler, *Hegemony* 180 and 311 n. 53.

[*Destroyer*] *of Sparta,* [who came as our helper], /| with praise, with *trust,*
[with a statue we crown you]. /| Very often [after this may it be possible
for you other trophies too] /| to set up, [glorious leader] of the
5   Boeo[tians]. //|| (This statue of) Pelopidas, son of Hip[pokles, the
Theban], | *was dedicated* by the Thessalians [to Apollo Pythios].
| Lysippos, son of Lys[--, the Sikyonian, was the sculptor].

1 I.e. after his first expedition into Thessaly, when he reformed the Thessalian
   League. For the chronology see Buckler 245–9.
2 I.e. after his death in the battle of Cynoscephalae.

50   Institution of the Pezhetairoi. 369–7 *or c.* 350.[1]

A. Scholiast to Demosthenes 2.17 (Theopompus, *FGrHist* 115F348). **B.** Harpocration,
Lexicon s.v. Pezhetairoi (Anaximenes, *FGrHist* 72F4).

A.B. Bosworth, *CQ* 23 (1973) 245–53; R.D. Milns, *Alexandre le Grand* (Fondation Hardt,
Entretiens 22, 1975) 87–101; Hammond-Griffith 705–13 (Griffith).

A. Demosthenes 2.17

Those in his entourage, mercenaries and Pezhetairoi (Infantry Companions), who have the reputation of being remarkably well trained in military matters, are no better than any others, as I hear from one who has been in that very land (Macedonia), a man who is in no way capable of telling a lie.

SCHOLION
Theopompus says that the biggest and the strongest, chosen from amongst all the Macedonians, formed a bodyguard for the king and were called Pezhetairoi (Infantry Companions).

B. Harpocration, *Lexicon s.v.* Pezhetairoi

Demosthenes in *Philippics*. Anaximenes in the first book of the *Philippika* speaking about Alexandros says: Next, after he had accustomed those of highest honour to ride on horseback, he called them 'Companions', and, after he had divided the majority and the infantry into companies and squadrons and the other commands, he named them Infantry Companions (Pezhetairoi), so that each of the two (classes), by participating in the royal companionship, might continue to be very loyal.

1 Other dates suggested – in the reign of Alexandros I (Philhellene), *c.* 495–51, or in the reign of Archelaos, *c.* 413–399 – are beyond the scope of this volume.

51   The Arcadian League honours the Athenian Phylarchos. Tegea, between 368 and 361.[1] Marble stele, surmounted by a relief of Fortune holding a helm in her left hand and with her right touching a trophy, Attic dialect, non-stoichedon (now lost).

IG V (2) 1 (with a line drawing); *Tod 132, pp. 98–102. Cf. Xen. *Hell.* 6.5.1–7, 5.27; Diodorus 15.57–94.

Larsen, *States* 180–95; J. Wiseman, *Klio* 51 (1969) 177–99; J. Roy, *Historia* 20 (1971) 569–99 (esp. 571) and *Historia* 23 (1974) 505–7.

God: Fortune. | Resolved by the Council of the | Arcadians and by the
5 | Ten Thousand.[2] Phylarchos,[3] || son of Lysikrates, the Athenian, | shall be a proxenos and benefactor | of all Arcadians, | himself and his family.
10 | The following were the Damiorgoi:[4] ||

1 The date of this inscription is disputed. See Roy 505–7 and Tod, pp. 100–2.

2 The assembly of the League. Membership was most likely based upon a property
   qualification, probably the ability to provide weapons. The Ten Thousand are
   mentioned in contemporary sources first by Xenophon, *Hellenika* 7.2.38, and last
   by Aeschines 2.79. See Busolt-Swoboda, *Griechische Staatskunde* (Munich 1920–6)
   406–9, and Larsen.
3 Nothing is known of this man.
4 There follows a list of 50 damiorgoi (probably a presiding committee of the Council)
   from ten cities. The cities are listed in the following order (I indicate the number of
   damiorgoi in parentheses after each): Tegea (5), Maenalia (3), Lepreum (2),
   Megalopolis (10), Mantinea (5), Cynuria (5), Orchomenus (5), Cletor (5), Heraea
   (5), Thelphusa (5).

52   Alliance between Athens and Dionysios I of Syracuse. Athens, 368/7. Marble stele, Ionic letters (but o=ou occasionally), stoichedon (lines 23 and 27 have one less letter).

IG II² 105 and 523+; *Tod 136, pp. 107–9; *SV* 2.280, pp. 236–8. Cf. Xen. *Hell.* 7.1.28;
Diod. 15.74.

D. Lewis, *ABSA* 49 (1954) 37–8; J. Wiseman, *Klio* 51 (1969) 180–4; J. Roy, *Historia* 20
(1971) 591; Rhodes, *Boule* 70 n. 6, 81 n. 1, 226.

[In the] archonship of [Nausigen]es (368/7), [when Aianti|s held the
seventh] *prytany*, [Moschos of Kydathen|aion]¹ *was secretary*, [on the
thirty-second²| (day) of the] *prytany*. [Of the Proedroi, the one who put
5   (the motion) to the ‖ vote was -6-]s, son of Daippos, [of Marath(on).
Resolved by the Pe|ople. Pan]d[ios]³ made the motion: [With good]
fortune [for the Athen|ians] *let it be resolved* by the *People*: [Commendation
shall be given to D|ionysi]o[s], the [ruler] of Sicil[y,⁴ because he is] | a
10 good [man] toward the [People of Athens ‖ and] their allies. *He shall be*
[an ally, him|self] *and* his descendants, [of the People of Athen|s] for all
time [on the following terms: If anyone | comes] *against* the land of the
A[thenians for the purpose of (making) wa|r either] by land or by sea,
15 [assistance shall be given by Dio‖nysios] and [his] descendants, [in
accordance with] | the demands of the Athenia[ns, both by land and
| by] sea in full [strength to the best of (their) abil|ity. And] if anyone
comes against [Dionysios or his d|escendants] or any of the territory
20 over which [Dionysios] *rules* [for the purpose ‖ of (making) war] either
by land or by [sea, assistance shall be giv|en] by the [Athe]nians, in
accordance with [their demands, bot|h by] land and by sea [in full
strength | to the best of] (their) ability. [And it shall not be permitted
for] an attack [to be m|ade] by D[io]nysios or [his descendants
25 ‖ against] the territory of the A[thenians with hostile in|tent,⁵ either] by
land or by [sea. Nor] | shall it be permitted for an *attack* [to be made] by

the [Atheni]a[n]s [against | Diony]si[o]s or [his] *descendants* [or | any of
30 the territory over which] Dionysios *rules* [with hostile intent either b‖y
land] or by sea. (The oath) [shall be administered, the | oath] concern-
ing the *alliance*, [by the ambass|adors] *who* [have come] from Dionysi[os,
and it shall be sworn | by the] Boule and the [generals and t|he] hip-
35 parchs and the [taxiarchs. The oath shall be sworn] ‖ by [Dio]nysios
and the [magistrates and the | Council] of the Syracus[ans and the
generals a|nd the] *trierarchs. The oath that is sworn* (shall be) [the custom-
ary o|ath] for each party. The [oaths shall be administered] (to the
Syracusans) | by the ambassadors of the [Atheni]ans [who] *are sailing to*
40 ‖ [Sicil]y. [This] *decree* shall be inscribed | [by the] *secretary* of the [Boule
on a marble] stele | [and set up on the Acropolis], and [for] its [in|scrip-
tion the treasurer of the] *People* [shall give 30 drachmas]. *vacat*

1 The text translated here is that printed in Tod and commonly accepted. It is based
upon the prescript of *IG* II² 106, a decree honouring Koroibos of Sparta that also was
passed in the archonship of Nausigenes. It does, however, create the possibility of
a conflict with Diod. 15.74 (see Wiseman 182). Furthermore, all the supplements
(tribe in prytany, number of the prytany, name and demotic of secretary) have been
challenged by Lewis and must be regarded as very uncertain.
2 The first recorded appearance of this formula. See Rhodes, *Boule* 226.
3 A Pandios was the proposer of honours for Dionysios and his sons in the last prytany
of the archonship of Lysistratos (369/8). But the supplement here is not certain.
4 This is the standard title given to Dionysios I in all extant Attic decrees concerning
him. Cf. no. 20. It is also found in the honorary decree of 368 (*IG* II² 103) mentioned
in n. 3.
5 For this formula cf. Thuc. 5.18.4.

53 Athens honours Mytilene. Athens, 367. Four fragments of a
marble stele, Ionic letters, stoichedon (lines 3–6 and 35 ff., otherwise
non-stoichedon; lines 1–6 are in larger letters).

IG II² 107; *Tod 131, pp. 95–8.

Marshall, *Confederacy* 84; Ryder, *Eirene* 77–8; Cargill, *League* 144–5; G.L. Cawkwell, *JHS*
101 (1981) 53.

Gods. | Concerning the [Myt]ileneans. | [Nausig]enes was archon
(368/7), Aiantis[1] held | the prytany, Moschos[2] of Kydathenaion was
5 ‖ secretary, Aristyllos of Erchi|a presided. *vacat* | Resolved by the Boule
and the People | *vv*, [Dio]pha[ntos][3] made the motion: Concerning the
matters that the ambassadors who have come from Lesbos re|port, *be it
voted* by the Boule that they (the ambassadors) be introduced before the
10 Pe‖*ople* by *the Proedroi*, whoever are chosen by lot to be Proedroi, at the
firs|t assembly, and that the opinion of the Boule be communicated to

[the] *Peop|le*: that it is resolved by the Boule, since the Mytileneans [are good] men | to the People of Athens both *now* and in the [previous t|ime], that commendation shall be given to the People of Mytilene *for*

15   their excellence ‖ [towards the People] of Athens, and that they shall have (the right of) approach, [if there is any|thing they need], to the Boule or the People *first* after the sacrifices. | *Commendation shall also be given* to Hiero[i]tas because he is a good man to the | People of Athens and the (People) of Mytilene. Inscription shall be made of thi|s decree

20   by the secretary of the *Boule* on a marble stele ‖ [and] set up on the Acropolis. Inscription shall also be made, o|n [the] same stele, of the decree that the People passed in response to the ambassadors | of the [My]tilen[ea]ns (who came) with [Hie]roit[as]. *For* the inscript|ion [of the] *stele* the treasurer of the People [shall give] to the secretary of t|he *Boule* 20 drachmas. Commendation shall be given to the ambassadors

25   who ‖ *were sent* to Mytilene and invitation shall be issued (to them) for dinner at | [the] Prytaneion for tomorrow. Invitation shall also be issued to the Proedro|i of the Mytileneans for hospitality at the Prytan[e]ion for tomorr|ow. Invitation shall also be issued to the Proedroi of the Methymneans | and of the [A]ntissans and of the

30   Eresians and of the Pyrrhans[4] for *hospitality* ‖ [at] the Prytaneion for tomorrow. Autolykos[5] made the motion:[6] (Let) all the | rest (be) as (proposed) by the Boule, and commendation shall be given to the ambassadors | *who* were sent to Lesbos, T[i]monothos and Autolyk|[os] and A[r]istopeithes, and invitation shall be issued to them for dinner

35   a|t the Prytaneion for tomorrow. *vacat* ‖ [In] the archonship of [Ly]sis-tratos (369/8); resolved by the | [Boule] and the People. Kallistratos[7] [made | the motion]: Commendation shall be given to the People of Myt[il|ene] because they nobly and enthusiastically joined *in pro|secut-*

40   *ing* the war, just conclud‖ed,[8] and *reply shall be made* to the ambassadors, [wh|o have come], that the Athenians fought the war [fo|r the freedom] of the Greeks. And [sin|ce the Lacedaemon]ians were making war [on

45   th|e Greeks in contravention of] the oaths and the [agree‖ments, both they themselves] gave assistance and the [res|t of their allies] were called upon by them to give [the] assistance | *they owed* to the Athenians, (and they did so)[ab|iding by] the oaths, against those who *trans|gressed*

50   *the* treaty,[9] and they think it right [--- ‖ ---][10]

---

1   We know from *IG* II[2] 106 that Aiantis held the seventh prytany in this year. The inscription is therefore to be dated to the spring of 367.

2   Moschos, son of Thestios, was treasurer of Athena in the following year (*IG* II[2] 1428.6).

3   Probably Diophantos of Sphettos, who was a prominent politician in this period. Cf. Isaeus 3.22 and Demosthenes 19.86; 19.297 and 20.137.

4   These are the five cities of Lesbos.

5   Possibly the man who was spokesman for the Areopagus in 346 (Aeschines 1.81–3) and who was later indicted by Lykourgos for having sent his family to safety outside Attica in the emergency that followed the battle of Chaeronea (Lyc. 1.53; Harpocration *s.v.* Autolykos).

6   The purpose of this rider is in dispute. See the discussion in Rhodes, *Boule* 279 notes. Cf. no. 5, n. 3.

7   Most likely to be identified with Kallistratos of Aphidna, on whom see R. Sealey, *Historia* 5 (1956) 178–203. This motion is the decree referred to in lines 20ff.

8   A reference to the hostilities of 378–371.

9   Tod (p. 98) thinks that the 'tardily rendered' Athenian thanks for Mytilenean help in the war were designed to allay allied suspicions of Athens' intentions. But it is more likely that Marshall is correct in thinking that it was Athens' alliance with Sparta that required justification. Cf. Ryder and Cargill.

10 Disjointed fragments of several more lines can be read.

54   Seizure of the Attic Spondophoroi[1] by a member state of the Actolian League. Athens, 367. Two fragments of a marble stele, Ionic letters (o=ou occasionally), stoichedon (except lines 1–3, which form a heading).

E. Schweigert, *Hesperia* 8 (1939) 5 7 (with a photograph on p. 6); *Tod 137, pp. 110–12. Cf. Aeschines 2.133, 138.

Schweigert, *Hesperia* 8 (1939) 8–12; G.L. Cawkwell, *REG* 73 (1960) 430–1; Larsen, *Government* 69–71 and *States* 78–80, 195ff.; A.B. Bosworth, *AJAH* 1 (1976) 165.

Gods. | [Demo]philos, son of Theoros, from Kephale | was secretary.
5   *vacat* | [Resolved] by the Boule and the People. Oineis[2] || *held the prytany*,
Demophilos, son of Theoros, from Kephale | *was secretary*, Phi[li]ppos[3]
of Semachidai *pr|esided,* [P]olyzelos *was archon* (367/6), Kephisodotos[4]
ma|de the motion: Since, after the league of the Aetolians had accept|ed the
10 sacred truce[5] for the Mysteries of Dem||[eter] of Eleusis and of Kore,
tho|se who *proclaimed* the truce, (members) of the Eumolpid|[ai and
Ke]rykes, have been held in chains by the T[r]ichoneians, (namely)
Pro|[phetes] and Epigenes, contrary to the laws *c|ommon* to the Greeks,
15 there shall be chosen by the *Bo||ule* right away a herald out of the Athe-
nians *at* | *large, who* is to go to the League | [of the Aeto]l[ians and
demand that the] men be *rel|eased* [--][6]

1   Heralds who travelled throughout Greece proclaiming the sacred truce for all panhellenic festivals, in this case the Greater Eleusinian Mysteries. The Spondophoroi for this festival were chosen from the clans of the Eumolpidai and Kerykes, who also held the ancestral priesthoods at the Mysteries.

2   Oineis held the third prytany in this year (Schweigert 10).

3   Probably the man who proposed the despatch of Athenian cleruchs to Potidaea in 361. Cf. no. 58.

4   For Kephisodotos see Xen. *Hell.* 6.3.2, 7.1.12ff.; Aristotle, *Rhet.* 3.10, and no. 40.
5   The sacred truce lasted for 55 days in the spring (for the Lesser Mysteries) and
     again in the autumn (for the Greater Mysteries). Cf. *IG* I^2 6.57–67, 76–89 = Fornara
     75(B).
6   There is not enough of fragment B preserved to permit an intelligible translation.

55   Treaty between Athens and Ceos. Athens, 362. Marble stele,
Ionic script (o=ou, e=ei occasionally), stoichedon (except line 1,
which forms a heading).

IG II^2 111+; Tod 142, pp. 125–32; *SV* 2.289, pp. 246–50.

Marshall, *Confederacy* 45–50; P. Cloché, *La politique étrangère d'Athènes* (Paris 1934) 128–9;
Accame, *Lega* 126, 184, 240; H.T. Wade-Gery, *Essays in Greek History* (Oxford 1958) 190
n. 2; D.M. Lewis, *ABSA* 57 (1962) 1–4; Cargill, *League* 134–40.

Gods. | In the archonship of Charikleides (363/2). Aiantis held the
prytany, Niko|stratos[1] of Pallene was secretary, Philittios of Boutadai
5 | presided. Resolved by the Boule and the People. Aristophon[2] || made
the motion: Since the Iulietae[3] whom the Athenians restored re|veal
that the city of the Iulietae owes the city | of the Athenians the three
talents from the money calcul|ated in accordance with the decree of the
People of Athens that Menexeno|s[4] moved, be it resolved by the People
10   that the Iulietae pay the Atheni||ans this money in the month
Skirophorion[5] that is | in the archonship of Charikleides. But if they do
not pay at the t|ime appointed, let (the money) be exacted from them
by those chose|n by the People to exact monies due fro|m the
Islanders, (exacting it) in whatever way they know, and let help in
15 || exacting (the money) be given them by the generals of the Iulietae,
Eche|timos and Nikoleo[s] and S[a]tyros and Glaukon and
Herak|leides. In order that both the oaths and the treaty that were
conclu|ded by the general Chabrias and sworn (by him) to the Ceans
on behalf of the Atheni|ans and the Ceans who were restored by the
20   [A]thenians may be valid, let them be ins||cribed by the generals of the
[Iu]lietae, the ones who are instructed in the | decree to help in exacting
the money, on a stele of mar|ble and set up in the sanctuary of Apollo
the Pythian, just | as they are inscribed at Karthaia. They shall be
inscribed | also by the secretary of the Boule on a stele in the same way
25   and || set up on the Acropolis. For the inscription there shall be given
by the t|reasurer of the People 20 drachmas from the decree fu|nd.[6]
Since those of the Iulietae who transgressed the oa|ths and the treaty
and made war against the Peo|ple of Athens and the Ce[a]ns and the
30   other allie||s and, though condemned to death, returned to | Ceos, (since

they) both cast out the stelae, on which were inscribe|d the treaty with
the Athenians and the names of those who trans|gressed the oaths and
the treaty, and (of) the friends of the A|thenians, whom the People had
35   restored, they killed some, and others ‖ they condemned to death and
confiscated their property contrary to | the oaths and the alliance, (these
latter actions in the cases) of Satyrides and Timoxenos an|d Miltiades,
because they were the accusers of Antipa[t]ros when the Boule of the
Athen|ians condemned him to death for killing the proxe|nos of the
40   Athenians, A[-]aision, contrary to the decrees of the Pe|ople of Athens,
and for contravening the oaths and the allia|nce – (for all these actions)
these men shall be banished from Ceos and Athens and their property
| shall become the public property of the People of Iulis. Registration
shall be made | of their names right away in the presence of the People
45   with the s|ecretary by the generals of the Iulietae who are now presen‖t
in Athens. If [any of those] (whose names) have been registered argu|e
that they do not belong to this *group*, it shall be permitted for them,
once guarant|ors have been provided to the generals of the Iulietae
within th|irty days, to *undergo* trials in accordance with the oaths and
the | alliance in Ceos and at Athens, the city of *final judgement*.[7]
50   S‖atyrides and Timo[xenos and] M[iltia]des shall depart t|o Ceos to
their own property. *Commendation shall be given* to those of the Iulietae
who have come, | Demetrios, Herakle[ide]s, E[cheti]mo[s],
K[al]liphantos. Commend|ation shall also be given to Satyr[ides] and
[Tim]o[xeno]s and Miltiades. | Commendation shall also be given to
55   the city of the Ka[r]thaians and to Aglokri‖tos, and invitation shall be
issued to them for *hospitality* [at] the Prytaneion for | tomorrow. *vv* The
following are the treaty made and the oaths sworn by the Athenian
generals t|o the cities on Ceos and by the allies: *v* I shall not bear a
grudge against the Ceans for any of the past events nor shall I kill of the
60   C‖eans anyone nor make an exile of anyone of those who abide by the
oath|s [and] this treaty, but into the alliance I shall *ad|mit* (them) *just like*
the other allies. If anyone causes a revolution | [on Ceos] contrary to
the oaths and the treaty, I shall not permit it, eith|er [by device] or by
65   stratagem of any sort, so far as I am able. If anyone ‖ [does not wish] to
live on Ceos, I shall allow him wherever he wants amongst th|e [allied]
cities to live and enjoy the fruits of his own property. These oaths | I
shall abide by, (I swear) [by] Zeus, by Athena, by Poseidon, by | [Dem-
eter. If I keep my oath], I shall have many blessings; if I am false to the
oat|h, (I shall have many) [evils. *v* The oaths and] treaty of the cities on
70   Ceos t‖o [the Athenians and the allies] and those Ceans who were
restored by the Ath[e|nians: *v* I shall be an ally to the Athenians and]
the allies and I shall no|t [revolt from the Athenians and] *the* allies
either on my own | [initiative or in obedience to another, so far as I am]

able. Private lawsuits and | [public indictments against Athenians I
75 shall make] all appealable (to Athens) *in* ‖ *accordance with* [the treaty, all
those that are over] one hundred drachmas. If | [anyone dares to wrong
those of the Ceans] *who have been restored* or the Athenian|[s or any of the
allies contrary to the oaths and] the alliance, | [I shall not permit it
either by device or by stratagem] of any sort, [but] I shall give assis-
tan|ce [in full strength to the best of (my) ability. These oaths] I shall
80 abide by, (I swear) b‖y [Zeus, by Athena, by Poseidon, by D]emeter. *If
I keep* | *my oath*, [I shall have many blessings, if I am false to the oath], (I
shall have many) *evils. vv* | [The following are the oaths sworn by those
of the Ceans who were restored by the Athenians. *v* I shall not bear a
grud|ge -- | ---]

1 Nikostratos is known to have been secretary for three prytanies during the archonship of Charikleides: that of Akamantis, the second (*IG* II^2 109); that of Oineis, the
   sixth (*IG* II^2 110); and that of Aiantis in this document. He is, in fact, the first
   attested secretary to hold office for a whole year instead of one prytany. The date
   for the change is between 368/7 and 363/2. See on this Rhodes, *Boule* 134f.
2 For Aristophon, son of Aristophanes, of Azenia see Davies, *Families* 2108; Tod 128
   and G.L. Cawkwell, *OCD s.v.* Aristophon. He was especially interested in Ceos.
3 The people of Iulis, one of the four cities on the island of Ceos, the others being
   Karthaia, Koressos and Poiessa. For their relationship to Athens at this period see
   Tod, p. 130, and Cargill, *League* 134–40, 169.
4 The proposer of the rider to no. 44.
5 The last month in the civil year.
6 For this fund see Rhodes, *Boule* 101 and n.3.
7 On the meaning of this difficult phrase (*ekkletos polis*) see Wade-Gery. There is a
   good discussion in Cargill 136ff.

56 Alliance of Athens, Arcadia, Achaea, Elis and Phlius. Athens, 362/1.
Two fragments of a marble stele (surmounted by a relief of Zeus
enthroned, with thunderbolt, approached by a female figure, probably
Peloponnesus, while Athena stands behind), Ionic letters (o=ou
occasionally), stoichedon (except line 1, which forms a heading).

IG II^2 112; *Tod 144, pp. 134–8; *SV* 2.290, pp. 250–2.

Ryder, *Eirene* 88; J. Roy, *Historia* 20 (1971) 587; Cargill, *League* 78; S. Dušanić, *MDAI (A)*
94 (1979) 128ff.

In the archonship of Molon (362/1). | Alliance[1] of the Athenians and
Arcadians[2] and Achaeans and El|eans and Phliasians. Resolved by the
Boule and the Peo|ple. Oineis held the prytany, Agatharchos, son of
5 Agatharchos, of Oë ‖ was secretary, Xanthippos of Hermos presided,
Pe|riandros[3] made the motion: The herald shall vow right a|way to
Olympian Zeus and Athena Polia|s and Demeter and Kore and the

Twelve G|ods and the August Goddesses (Erinyes), if benefit accrue to
10   the A[the]||nian People from their resolution concerning the alliance,
that a *sac|rifice* and procession shall be made,[4] when [these things] are
accomplished | in accordance with the resolution of the People. These
vows were made, [aft|er] the allies[5] had introduced a resolution to *the*
15   [Boul|e] that the alliance be accepted on the terms *proclaimed* || by the
[Ar]cadians and the Achaeans and the Eleans and the Phli[asians, an|d
the] Boule had made a probouleuma to the same effect, that it be
resolved [by the P|eople] that with good fortune [for the People] there
shall be an alliance [for | all] time between [the People] of Athen[s and
their all|ies and the A]rcad[ians and the Achaeans and the Eleans and
20   the Phli|asians. -- || --- | --- | --- | --- | -] on [this] stele. [If anyone comes
25   against Atti||ca] or [overthrows] the People [of Athens or a tyranny] | *is
established* or an *oligarchy*,[6] [assistance shall be given by the Arcadians
and the Achae|ans] and the Eleans *and* [the Phliasians to the Athenians
in full] *s|trength* in accordance with [the demands of the Athenians to
the best of (their)] *a|bility*. And if [anyone comes against these states
or] || overthrows [the] People [of Phlius[7] or if the constitutio|n][8] of the
30   Achaeans or the [Arcadians or the Eleans is overthrown or] | altered or
[any people] *are exiled*, [assistance shall be given by the Athenians to]
t|hese in full *strength*, [in accordance with the demands of those who
are] | w|ronged, to the *best* [of (their) ability. The chief command shall
35   be held] || by each in his own territory.[9] [If anything else is deemed right
by all] | the states *to be added*, [whatever is decided] *shall be* [valid without
breach of the oath].[10] | The oath shall be sworn [by the highest
authorities in each of the states of the Pelo]||ponnesians,[11] [and of the
Athenians by the generals and] t|*he* taxiarchs [and the hipparchs and
40   the] *phylar||chs*[12] and the [knights -- | ---]

1   On the chronology of this alliance (after the battle of Mantinea) see Roy 593–4.
2   Not the whole Arcadian League, but the part led by Mantinea. For the cause of the
     break between Mantinea and Tegea see Xen. *Hell.* 7.4.33ff. and Roy 586–8.
3   The son of Polyaratos of Cholargos. For the history of this significant fourth-
     century family see Davies, *Families* 11907.
4   For this vow compare the contemporary document, no. 58.
5   The members of the Second Athenian Confederacy, cf. no. 35.
6   For the clauses guaranteeing existing constitutions cf. no. 59.
7   The constitution of Phlius was democratic (Xen. *Hell.* 5.3.16).
8   Oligarchies existed in Achaea and Elis (Xen. *Hell.* 7.1.43, 4.15) and most likely in
     Mantinea. See Roy 587–8.
9   Restored by Foucart (*ap.* Tod, p. 136) on the basis of Xen. *Hell.* 7.5.3.
10   This formula is restored by Foucart on the basis of Thuc. 5.23.6.
11   Restored by Foucart on the basis of Xen. *Hell.* 6.5.3.
12   For these officials see the Glossary.

57   Greece and the Revolt of the Satraps. Argos, 362/1[1] *or* 344 *or* between 338 and 334. Fragment of a marble stele (now lost, but surviving in two transcriptions[2]),Attic dialect, perhaps stoichedon.

IG IV 556; *Tod 145, pp. 138–41; *SV* 2.292, pp. 253–5. Cf. Diod. 15.76.3, 89.1, 90f.; Polybius 4.33.8f.; Plut. *Ages.* 35.3f.

A. Momigliano, *RFIC* 62 (1934) 494ff.; R.P. Austin,*JHS* 64 (1944) 98–100; P. Meloni, *RSI* 63 (1951) 5–27; Ryder, *Eirene* 140–4; M.J. Osborne, *ABSA* 66 (1971) 319–20; Bury-Meiggs 384.

[--- | --] *by those participating* in the common [peace.[3] It shall be made | clear to the one] who has come [from] the Satraps[4] that the [Hellenes] *by | sending embassies* to one another have resolved their [differences and

5   achieved ‖ a] common peace, in order that having put an end to [their interstate] *war|fare* they may each make their own cities as great as possible [and prosper|ous] and may remain useful to their friends [and strong]. | They are not aware that the King has any war against [them. If] *th|erefore* he keeps quiet and does not set the He[llenes] against each

10   other [and does not, (in the case of) the] ‖ peace that we [now] have, attempt [to dissolve (it) by any device] | at all or by stratagem, we too shall be [at peace with the] K|ing. But if he makes war against any of those [who share the treaty with us or] | makes *trouble* for any of them with a view to the dissolution of [this] peace, [either in | person] against

15   the Hellenes who [have made] this [peace], ‖ or (through) someone else from his territory, [we shall defend ourselves jointly] | *all* (of us) in a manner worthy of the *peace* that we now have [and of our pre|vious achieve]ments. *vacat*[5]

1   An earlier date (371) has been suggested by Momigliano.
2   One by Fourmont, first published by A. Boeckh as *CIG* 1118; the other by Pouqueville, *Voyage de la Grèce*[2] 5.205. Of these Fourmont's is universally considered superior and it forms the basis of all modern texts. Restorations have been made by M. Fraenkel, *RhM* 56 (1901) 233ff., and A. Wilhelm, *RhM* 56 (1901) 571ff., whose text formed the basis of Tod's.
3   This and the reference in line 5 are the first appearances on stone of the term 'Common Peace'. See Ryder 142. Which peace is meant is much in dispute. See Ryder 143–4.
4   These satraps are usually considered to be those in revolt from Artaxerxes II.
5   Fourmont transcribed only lines 1–16. Pouqueville's transcription shows the presence of another line of this inscription (not read by Fourmont) after line 16, followed by a space separating this document from the first two lines of a different inscription that follows. This inscription appears to be in the Doric dialect and is concerned with the settlement of territorial disputes. Its relationship to the one above is not clear.

58   Athens sends cleruchs to Potidaea. Athens, 361.

58   Athens sends cleruchs to Potidaea. Athens, 361. Two fragments of a marble stele, Ionic letters (but o=ou), stoichedon (except line 1, which forms a heading).

IG II² 114; *Tod 146, pp. 141–3. Cf. Isoc. 15.108, 113; Dinarchus 1.15; Diod. 15.81.6, 16.8.5.

R. Sealey, *Phoenix* 11 (1957) 108; G.E.M. de Ste Croix, *CR* 13 (1963) 112; J.A. Alexander, *Potidaea* (Athens, Georgia 1962) 87–8; Cargill, *League* 148f.

[In] the archonship of Molon (362/1), when Erechtheis (held) the ninth[1] (prytany). | Resolved by the Boule and the People. Erechtheis *held the prytan|y*, Agatharchos, son of Agatharchos, of Oë was secretary, [-- | -]s from Kerameis presided, Phil[ippo]s made the motion:[2] [Con-
5   cerning the matters that] ‖ are reported by those who have come at public expense [from] the men *from* [Potida|e]a, let it be voted by the People: The [herald] *shall vow*[3] *r|ight* away to the Twelve *Gods* [and the August] *God|desses* (Erinyes) and to Herakles, if *benefit accrue* [to the Athenians] *for send|ing* the cleruchs to Pot[idaea, just as they are
10   requ‖ested] by those who have come [at public expense from the men from Potida|ea, that a sacrifice and procession shall be made, in accordance with | the resolution of the People --]

1   Early summer 361.
2   Cf. no. 54.
3   For this vow and the formula used cf. no. 56.

59   Alliance between Athens and Thessaly. Athens, 361/60.

59   Alliance between Athens and Thessaly. Athens, 361/60. Marble stele (with relief representing a mounted warrior), Ionic letters (but o normally =ou), stoichedon (except lines 1–4, which form a heading).

IG II² 116; Tod 147, pp. 143–7; *SV* 2.293, pp. 255–8.

Westlake, *Thessaly* 154–5; Larsen, *States* 24; Cargill, *League* 79.

Gods. | In the archonship of Nikophemos (361/60). | Alliance of the
5   Athenians and | Thessalians for all time. ‖ Resolved by the Boule and the People. Leontis held the prytan|y, Chair[i]on, son of Charinau[t]os, of Phaleron was secretary, Ar|chippos from Amph[i]trope presided. On the twelfth (day) of the pr|ytany, E[x]ekestides[1] made the motion: *Concerning* the matters that are reported by the a|mbassadors of the
10   Thessalia[ns], let it be voted by the People: Acceptance shall be ‖ given to the alliance, with good fortune, just as it is requeste|d by the Thessalian[s]. They shall have alliance with the A|thenians for all time. And

the Athen|ian allies shall all be allies of the Thessalia[ns] and those | of
the [Th]essalians (shall be allies) of the A[the]nians. The oath shall be
15   sworn on the A[the]nian side by the gen‖erals and the Boule and the
hipparchs and the knight|s, (and they shall swear) the following oath: I
shall give assistance in full strength to the best of (my) ab|ility, if
anyone comes against the League of the Thessalians for the purpose of
(making) w|ar, or overthrows the archon[2] whom the Thessalians have
20   elected, or | establishes a tyranny in Thessaly. They shall swear the ‖
customary oath. In order that the Thessalians may swear the oath to
the c|ity, the People shall choose five men from the Athenians | at large
to go to Thessal[y] and administer the | oath to Agelao[s][3] the archon
and the polemarchs and | the hipparchs and the knights and the
25   *hieromnemons*[4] ‖ and all the other magistrates who on behalf of the
League of the The|ssalians hold office, (and they shall administer) the
following oath: I shall give assistance in full stre|ngth to the best of
(my) ability, if anyone comes against the city of the Ath|[en]ians for the
purpose of (making) war or overthrows the People of Athen|[s]. And the
oath shall be sworn also by the ambassadors of the Thessalians before
30   ‖ the Boule, those (ambassadors) who *are present* in Athens, (and they
shall swear) the same oat|h. *It shall* not *be permitted* for the war against
Alexandros[5] t|o be brought to an end [either] by the Thessalians with-
out (the agreement) of the Atheni[ans] or by the A|[then]ians *without*
(the agreement) [of the] Archon and the League [of the Thess|alians].
Commendation shall be given to Agelaos the archon [and to the
35   L‖eague] of the Thes[sal]ians, because they *performed* well and eagerly
[all | matters], concerning which [the] city *made request* to them. *Commen-
dation shall be given* | [also] to *those who have come* as *ambassadors* of the
[Th]essalians and in|vitation shall be issued to them [for] hospitality at
[the Pr]yta[ne]ion [for] tomorr|ow. *The* stele relating to Al[exa]nd[r]os
40   *shall be destroyed* by the ‖ *treasurers* of the Goddess, (that is) [the one] *about
the* alliance.[6] To the ambass|adors the *treasurer* of the *People* shall give for
their travelling expenses *v* 20 drach|mas each. This alliance shall be
inscribed by the | secretary of the *Boule* on a marble *stele* [and] set up on
45   the Acropolis. For *the inscription* of the *stele* shall be give‖n by the
treasurer of the People 20[7] *v drachmas*. And it shall be on record that
[Th]e[ai]t|etos[8] of Erchia has given the best advice and has done what-
| ever good he could for the People of A[then]s *and* for the
The|ssal[i]ans. *vacat.*

1   Cf. no. 34 n. 3.
2   For the substitution of 'archon' for 'tagos' as the title of the leading magistrate of
     the Thessalian League see Larsen.
3   Probably a Pharsalian of the prominent Daochid family (Tod, p. 146).
4   Most likely the two Thessalian representatives to the Amphictyonic Council (Tod,
     p. 145).

5   Alexandros of Pherae. For the history of Thessaly under him see Westlake 126–59.
6   Alexandros had entered into alliance with Athens in 368/7. Cf. Diod. 15.71.3; Dem.
     23.120; Plut. *Pelopidas* 31.6.
7   30 (Tod).
8   Nothing more is known of this man or the services he performed.

60   Contributions for the rebuilding of the temple at Delphi. Delphi, 360. Thirty fragments of a marble stele. Phocian dialect, beautifully inscribed, stoichedon.

Fouilles de Delphes 3 (5) (Paris 1932) 3, pp. 39–44 and Plate II; *Tod 140, pp. 119–23. Cf. Xen. *Hell.* 6.4.2. Cf. no. 84.

M. Sordi, *BCH* 81 (1957) 38–75; Parke-Wormell 1.213–16, 239–40; J. Pouilloux, *REA* 64 (1962) 300–13.

In the archonship of Ais[chylos] (361/60),[1] | during the spring session (that was the) thir|teenth, the following c|ities made contributions of
5   the obol[2] || for the second time.[3] *vv* | Mega[r]i[an]s: Andron,[4] drachmas | three thousand, four hundred | forty-four. | Troezenians, drachmas
10   three hun||dred thirty-four, | brought by Ph[e]gon. | Kyphar[ran]s: Kombos, drachmas | one hundred seventy. | *vacat* In the following way
15   cities and individuals || *contributed the eparchai*[5] in this session. | Nax[ians], drachmas three hundred | fifty, brought by | Telesikrates,
20   son of Timokleides, | (and) Aristodemos, son of Aisimos. || Strombon of Naxos, drachmas two. | Demainetos of Naxos, Attic | drachmas ten. (Value) of this | in Aeginetan (money) drachmas seven.[6] | Telesikrates
25   of Naxos, || drachmas two. | Aristodemos of Naxos, | drachmas two.
30 | Messenians: Lysi[x]eno[s], | Phillis, K[-5-, Eu]ry[bi]os, || drachmas *seventy*. | Sosibios of Pharsalus, | one drachma. | Andokos of
35   Lacedaemon, | drachmas two. || Lygdamis of Tragilos, | drachmas six, obols four. | The people of Naucratis from Egypt, | brought by
40   Pythagoras, drachmas | three hundred fifty. || Endamos of Syracuse, | drachmas thirty. | Saraukos of Arcadia, drachmas two. | Kottabos of
45   Arcadia, drachmas three. | Eurydike[7] of Larisa, || drachmas two. | Aischylis of Selinus, | drachmas two. | Epicharmos of Arcadia, a drachma.
50 | Kleino of Phlius, || obols three. | Echenike of Phlius, | an obol (and) a
55   half-obol. | Kleonike of Phlius, | an obol (and) a half-obol. || Philostratis of Lacedaemon, | obols three. | Kleogenes, in Attic (money), | drachmas
60   four. (Value) of this | in Aeginetan (money), drachmas two, || obols four. | Peisios, in Attic (money), drachmas | four. (Value) of this in Aeginetan (money), | drachmas two, obols four. | Kteson, in Attic
65   (money), drachmas || four. (Value) of this in Aeginetan (money),

| drachmas two, obols four. | Theodoros of Athens,[8] | the actor,
70   drachmas | seventy. || Euteles, drachmas two. | Hegemon, obols three.
| Damothemis Euphaneus | of Phaselis, drachmas seven. | Ariston, a
75   drachma. || Pankon of Thebes, a drachma. | Timeas of Apollonia,
80 | drachmas seventy. | Thrasyboulos of Thespiae, | one drachma. || [The
People of] Apollon[ia], | bushels (medimnoi) of barley, | on the Pheido-
85   nian system, | three thousand.[9] For the|se the equivalent in bush||els of
the Delphian weight | was one thousand eight hundred | seventy-five.[10]
90 | The value of this was | drachmas three thousand, || five hundred
eigh|ty-seven, three | obols (and) a half-obol.[11] | This was transported
95   at their | own expense to || Delphi to the | coast by the | People of
Apollonia. | The transporters of the grain were | Ainesidamos of Delphi,
100 || Aristokleides | of Apollonia. | The total of the receipt, | during this
105 session, | in (the archonship of) A[i]schylos (was) drachmas || eight
thousand | five hundred | thirty, an obol, | (and) a half-obol.

1   This is one of a series of such lists, the best preserved of which are this list (spring
360) and the following (autumn 360) of the archonship of Mnasimachos. For the
date see Pouilloux.
2   A per-capita exaction of one obol on all the cities of the Amphictyony. See J.
Pouilloux, *BCH* 73 (1949) 177–200.
3   A second levy, begun in the eleventh session (in the archonship of Antichares,
362/1).
4   The envoy who brought the contribution.
5   Voluntary contributions of cities outside the Amphictyony.
6   The Delphians were on the Aeginetan standard and payments in Attic currency
are converted at the rate of 7 Aeginetan drachmas to 10 Attic. For smaller amounts
2 Aeginetan drachmas are the equivalent of 3 Attic.
7   It is interesting to note that six women made individual contributions: Eurydike;
Aischylis (line 46); Kleino (line 49); Echenike (line 51); Kleonike (line 53); Philo-
stratis (line 55).
8   The famous Athenian tragic actor. Cf. Dem. 19.246–7; Aristotle, *Rhet.*
3.2.1404b 1888, and see A.W. Pickard-Cambridge, *The Dramatic Festivals of Athens*[2]
(Oxford 1968) 100, 119, 132, 168.
9   For this gift cf. Plutarch, *De Pythiae oraculis* 16.
10   Thus one Pheidonian bushel = 0.625 of a Delphic bushel.
11   Thus one bushel of barley cost 1.924 drachmas (Aeginetan = approx. 3 Attic
drachmas). Wheat was usually reckoned to cost twice as much as barley.

61   Treaty between Philip II and Athens. 359/8 *or* 357.

A. Harpocration, *Lexicon* (as epitomized in the *Suda*) *s.v.* What is the meaning of the
statement in Demosthenes' *Philippics*? (Dem. 2.6). **B.** Scholion to Demosthenes 2.6. Cf.
Dem. 23.121; Diod. 16.4.1.

SV 2.298, pp. 266–8; G.E.M. de Ste Croix, *CQ* 13 (1963) 110–19; Ellis, *Philip II* 48–52;
Cawkwell, *Philip* 75; Hammond-Griffith 237–42 (Griffith).

Demosthenes 2.6

For I, too, men of Athens, should most certainly consider Philip an admirable man and one to be feared, if I found that he had increased in power through just action. But now, as I observe and consider (the situation), I find that it was through our simple-mindedness in the first place, when certain people drove away the Olynthians who were wanting to speak with you from this place, that he won (us) to his side, by saying that he would hand over Amphipolis and by fabricating that well-known secret that was much talked about once, . . .

A. Harpocration

What is the meaning of the statement in Demosthenes' *Philippics*, 'and that well-known secret that was much talked about once'? Theopompus has clarified this in the 31st book,[1] for he says: 'and he/it[2] sends Antiphon and Charidemos[3] as ambassadors to Philip to negotiate even about friendship. And when they were in his presence they attempted to persuade him to co-operate with the Athenians in secret, in order that they might get Amphipolis, while promising (him) Pydna. The Athenian ambassadors did not make any report to the People, because they wished to conceal from the Pydnaeans that they were intending to give them up, but handled the matter in secret with the Boule.

B. Scholion to Demosthenes 2.6

Why in secret? In order that neither the Potidaeans nor the Pydnaeans might be apprised (of their action) and so be on their guard. But Theopompus says that it concerned only Pydna and Philip, the purpose being that he might give Amphipolis to the Athenians and might receive from them Pydna, since it was his. And (it was) secret, so that the Pydnaeans might not be apprised and so be on their guard. For they did not want to be under Philip.

1   31st Harpocration (*Suda*); 1st (A. Schaefer); 1st or 3rd (Jacoby). See de Ste Croix 113 n. 1 and 117 n. 4.
2   The subject is not given. Suggestions include 'the Boule', 'the People', or 'the proposer of the motion'. See de Ste Croix 117–18, Hammond-Griffith 240 n.1.
3   On the possibility of identifying these ambassadors see de Ste Croix 113.

62   Philip II's relations with Thessaly. 358/7–353/2.

A. Justin, *Epitoma* 7.6.6–10. **B.** Harpocration, *Lexicon s.v.* Kineas (Theopompus, *FGrHist* 115F35). **C.** Stephanus of Byzantium, *Ethnika s.v.* Chalke (Theopompus, *FGrHist* 115F34 and 48). **D.** Scholion to Demosthenes 1.22. **E.** Justin, *Epitoma* 8.2.1. **F.** Polyaenus, *Strategemata* 2.38.2. Cf. Diod. 16.14.1–2, 35.1–6; Isocrates 5.20; Athenaeus 13.557b–d; no. 87.

Westlake, *Thessaly* 160–82; *SV* 2.315, pp. 290–1; C. Erhardt, *CQ* 17 (1967) 296–301; G.T. Griffith, *CQ* 20 (1970) 67–80; Ellis, *Philip II* 77–80; Cawkwell, *Philip* 58–66 (with a map p. 59); Hammond-Griffith 267–81 (Griffith); T.R. Martin, *CP* 76 (1981) 188–201; *idem*, *HSCP* 86 (1982) 55–78.

A. Justin, *Epitoma* 7.6.6–10

His (*sc.* Philip's) first contest was with the Athenians . . . After them he transferred the war to the Illyrians and killed many thousands of the enemy. He captured the very famous city of Larissa.[1] Thence he made a sudden attack on Thessaly, not out of a desire for plunder, but because he was very eager to add the strength of the Thessalian cavalry to his own army . . . As these affairs were progressing successfully, he married Olympias, daughter of Neoptolemos, king of the Molossians . . .

B. Harpocration, *Lexicon s.v.* Kineas (Theopompus F35)

It is agreed also on the part of the historians that Kineas[2] was one of those who betrayed Thessalian affairs to Philip, and especially by Theopompus in (his) first (book), at the point where he is recounting the history of the man.[3]

C. Stephanus of Byzantium, *Ethnika s.v.* Chalke (Theopompus F34 and 48)

There is another Chalke, a city near Larissa. It is found also in the plural, Chalkai. Theopompus (in the) first (book) of the *Philippika*: 'and in the third[4] year he joined in the war, making his attacks from Chalkai near Larissa'.

D. Demosthenes 1.22

These (Thessalian affairs) were, of course, congenitally untrustworthy and have always been so for all men, and, as they were, just so are they now for him (Philip). For they (the Thessalians) have voted to demand Pagasae back from him and have prevented him from fortifying Magnesia. I have heard from some that they will not even allow him any longer to enjoy the profits from the harbours and the marketplaces. For (they say that) the Thessalian League's affairs ought to be administered from these funds and that Philip ought not to take them.

SCHOLION

Aleuas, a descendant of Herakles, became tyrant over the Thessalians.
After him his sons also, and so, being unable to endure the tyranny and
in perplexity what to do, they sent for Philip for alliance. Then he came
and threw the Aleuadae out of the tyranny. And the Thessalians,
acknowledging their gratitude to him for this, allowed him to enjoy the
revenues of Pagasae and the moneys from the harbours and marketplaces.

E. Justin, *Epitoma* 8.2.1–2

Against him (Onomarchos) the Thebans and the Thessalians chose as
leader, not one of their own citizens, lest they should not be able to
endure the power of the victor, but Philip, king of the Macedonians,
and of their own accord yielded to an outsider the domination that they
feared among their own people.

F. Polyaenus, *Strategemata* 2.38.2

Onomarchos, drawing up his men in battle order against the
Macedonians, kept a crescent-shaped mountain at his rear and, after
concealing on the peaks on either side rocks and rock-throwers, led his
force forward into the plain below. When the Macedonians came out to
meet them throwing javelins, the Phocians feigned flight (and
retreated) half-way up the mountain. As the Macedonians were press-
ing them hard with a spirited and rapid pursuit, the men from the peaks
shattered the Macedonian phalanx by throwing stones. Then Onomarchos gave the order to the Phocians to turn about and attack the
enemy. The Macedonians, attacked both by the soldiers in their rear
and by those from above who were throwing stones, with great difficulty
retired in flight. In this flight Philip, king of the Macedonians, is
reported to have said, 'I have not fled, but I have retired, as rams do, in
order that I may make a more vigorous attack next time'.

1   This is the order of the manuscripts. In most texts this sentence is transferred to the
    end of the sentence on Thessaly, immediately before the reference to Olympias.
    Alternatively, the name of the city may be corrupt.
2   Cf. Dem. 18.295; Polybius 18.14.1.
3   It is not clear whether of Philip or of Kineas.
4   This follows the emendation proposed by T.R. Martin, *HSCP* 86 (1982) 55–6.

63   Philip II captures Amphipolis. Amphipolis, 357. Marble stele, Ionic letters (but o normally =ou), Ionic dialect of the Euboean type, stoichedon.

SIG 194+; *Tod 150, pp. 149–51. Cf. Dem. 1.8; Diod. 16.8.2.

Ellis, *Philip II* 63–5; Cawkwell, *Philip* 73–5; Hammond-Griffith, 237–8, 351f. (Griffith).

Resolved by the People: Phi|lon and Stratokle|s[1] shall be exiled from
5   Amphipoli|s and the territory of the Amph||ipolitans for all ti|me, both
      themselves and their | children, and if in any place they are c|aught,
10   they shall be treated | as enemies and || they shall be killed with
      impunity. | Their property | shall be confiscated and the te|nth part
15   (shall be) dedicated to A|pollo and Str||ymon. The presi|dents shall
      inscribe their | names on a marble stele. | Regarding this decree, if
20   anyone | puts (it) to a vote for revocation, or if (anyone) har||bours these
      men by any ar|t or stratagem whatsoeve|r, let his property be | confis-
25   cated and let him himself | be exiled from Amphipolis || for all time.

1   One of the two ambassadors who had sought Athenian assistance against Philip.
     The other was Hierax. Cf. Dem. 1.8 and Harpocration, *Lexicon, s.v.* Hierax
     (Theopompus, *FGrHist* 115F42), ' . . . that Hierax was one of those sent by the
     Amphipolitans as ambassador to Athens, when they wanted to hand over both their
     city and its territory to the Athenians is stated by Theopompus in the third book of
     the *Philippika*'.

64   Treaty between Athens and three Thracian kings. Athens, 357.[1] Fragment of a marble stele, Ionic letters, stoichedon.

IG II^2 126+; Tod 151, pp. 151–4; *SV 2.303, pp. 271–3. Cf. Dem. 23.173.

P. Cloché, *RPh* 46 (1922) 5ff.; *Mélanges Glotz* 1 (Paris 1932) 215–26; Parke, *Soldiers* 125ff., 146ff. Cargill, *League* 90, 180; E. Badian, *Pulpudeva* 4 (1983) 54ff.

[--- | --- | --- | - concerning] *all those* cities [that have been inscribed on
5   the st||elai as] *paying* to Berisade[s or Amadokos or Kersebl|eptes[2] their]
      tribute and (that) [are tributary] to the Athen[ians | already], *if* [the
      cities] do not pay to the Athe[nians their | tribute], (it) *shall be exacted* by
      Berisades [and Amadokos and Ke|rseblept]es to the best of (their)
10   ability. *And* [if anywhere to Berisad||es or Amadok]os or Kersebleptes
      shall not [be paid the tr|ibute by the citie]s, it shall be exacted by the
      Athenian[s and by the magistr|ates who at the time] are in power [to
      the best of (their) abilit|y. The citie]s of the Greeks that are in [the
15   Chersones|e, who pay to B]erisades and Amadok[os and Kers||ebleptes

the] *tribute* that is ancestral and to the A[thenians t|he syntaxis], they
shall be *free* and autonomous, [be|ing allies to the A]thenians, in accord-
ance with their oath, and [to Beris|ades and Amadoko]s and Kerseb-
leptes. If [any of t|he cities] *revolts* from the Athenians, *assistance shall be*
20   *given* [by Beris||ades and Amadokos] and Kerseblept[es, in accordance
with the d|emands of the Athenians]. And if [--].[3]

1   For the date (summer or autumn 357) see Cloché, *Mélanges Glotz* 1.215 n. 1.
2   After the death of Kotys I in 360 or 359 the Odrysian kingdom was divided into three
    parts. Berisades ruled the western part, Amadokos the central part, perhaps from
    Maronea to the Hebrus, and Kersebleptes the eastern part. All three shared control
    of the Chersonese.
3   This is the beginning of the clause stating Athens' reciprocal obligations.

65   Alliance of Athens and Euboean cities. Athens, 357/6. Three
fragments of a marble stele, Ionic letters, stoichedon (lines 1–17).

IG II[2] 124+; Tod 153, pp. 157–61; *SV 2.304, pp. 273–5. Cf. Diod. 16.7.2; Dem. 8.74,
21.174, 22.14; Aesch. 3.85 and no. 66.

W.P. Wallace, *The Euboian League and its Coinage* (New York 1956) 11ff.; G.L. Cawkwell,
C&M 23 (1962) 37–9; P.A. Brunt, *CQ* 19 (1969) 247–8; G.L. Cawkwell, *Phoenix* 32 (1978)
45.

[-- this dec|ree shall be inscribed on the Acropolis by] *the secretary* [for
| the prytany.[1] The money shall be given] for the [stele by the trea|surer
from the funds] that are to be spent [on business related to decrees[2]
5   There shall be chos||en five men to go] to exact [the oa|ths from the
Carystians. The oaths shall be sworn] to them by the [general|s who are
at Athens and by the] *Boulē*. Commendation shall be given [to the
Peo|ple of Car]ystus and [the] *ambassadors* of the Carystians [and t|he]
representative (of the Carystians on the allied council) and invitation
10   shall be issued to them for hospitality at the Pry[tane||ion] for
tomorrow. Commendation shall also be given to M[e]non,[3] the general,
[a|nd] the ambassadors who were sent to Carystus and invitation shall
be issue|d for dinner at the Pryt[a]neion for tomorrow. Payment shall
be made to t|*hem* for their travelling expenses too by the treasurer of the
People, (the sum of) 20 drachmas from the funds | that are to be spent *by*
15   *the* People on business related to decrees. Payment shall be || made by the
treasurer of the People also to the *ambassadors* who went on emb|assy to
Eretria and Chal[c]is and to [Hesti]aea, (the sum of) 20 drachm|as to
each. Payment shall be made also to those who negotiated the alli|ance
by the treasurer of the People, (the sum of) 10 drachmas [to each.]
T|hese swore the oath: The Boule (that held office) in [the archonship

87

20   of] Agath[okles] (357/6); the g‖enerals [[[Cha]brias of [Ai]xo(ne)]][4] *v*
Cha[res of Angele,[5] *v* Iphikrates] of Rhamno(us)[6] *v*, | Menon of
Pota(mos), *v* Philochares of Rham[no(us)], | Exekestides of
Thorik(os),[7] *v* Alki[machos of Anagyr(a)],[8] | Diokles from Alopeke,[9]
vacat.

1   Cf. Arist. *Ath. Pol.* 54.3 and see Rhodes, *Boule* 134f.
2   See Rhodes, *Boule* 101f.
3   Cf. Dem. 36.53, [Dem.] 50.12.
4   An attempt was made to erase the name and demotic of Chabrias, but the last five
letters of his name and the -xo- of his demotic are still visible. Possibly he had been
deposed for his lack of success in the Hellespont (cf. Dem. 23.171f.) and did not take
the oath. But see Cawkwell, *C&M* (cit.) 38 n. 23. For his career see Davies, *Families*
15086; Parke, *Soldiers* 56f., 73ff., and W.K. Pritchett, *State* 2.72–7.
5   See Davies, *Families* 15292; Parke, *Soldiers* 74, 82, 122f., 144f., and Pritchett, *State*
2.77–85.
6   See Davies, *Families* 7737; Parke, *Soldiers* 50ff., 77ff., 105ff., 127, and Pritchett, *State*
2.62–72, 117–25.
7   Not the ambassador to Byzantium in 378/7 (cf. no. 34), but probably the proposer
of no. 59. See Davies, *Families* 4718.
8   General in Thrace in 364/3 (schol. Aesch. 2.31) and later against Philip (Harpocration, *s.v.* Alkimachos, on [Dem.] 47.50, 78).
9   See Dem. 21.174 and Davies, *Families* 3990.

66   Athens aids Eretria. Athens, 357/6.[1] Marble stele, Ionic letters,
stoichedon (but lines 12, 14, 15 and 20 each have one extra letter).

IG II² 125; *Tod 154, pp. 161–3.

For the bibliography, see no. 65.

[Resolved by the] People. Heges[i]pp[os made the motion:[2] In order
that for the | future] none of the allies [of the People of Athens | nor]
anyone [else], be he a foreigner or [a citizen, may wrong] | any [of the]
5   *allies*, setting out [from Attica or ‖ from] *any* [of the] allied cities,[3] [let it
be vote|d] by the People: Concerning those who *made war* [against] *t|he*
territory of the Eretrians, the Boule, *after making a probouleu|ma*,[4] shall
bring (it) before the People at [the first] *ass|embly*, in order that (those
people) may pay the penalty in accordance with [the treaty. If] ‖ anyone
10   in the future *makes war* [against Ere]‖tria or against any other of the
allied [cities, (be he one) of the Athe]|nians or of the allies of the
Atheni[ans, death] | shall be his penalty and his property [shall be]
confiscated [and] t|he goddess (shall have) the tithe.[5] And [his property]
15   *shall be* ‖ liable to seizure from all the cities [of the alliance. If] | any city
expropriates (this property), it shall owe (it) [to the common (treasury)

of] t|he allies. The [decree] shall be inscribed [on a stele of] ma|rble and set up on the Acrop[olis and in the agora][6] | and in the harbour (i.e.
20 Peiraeus). The [money shall be given for the] i||nscription by the treasurer *of the* [People. Commendation shall be given to] t|hose who gave assistance to E[retria -- and to the Ca]|rystians [-- the] *gen|eral*
25 [-- | --- || ---]

1 This decree is conjecturally associated in date with no. 65.
2 For this unusual prescript see Henry, *Prescripts* 33. For Hegesippos see G.L. Cawkwell, *OCD s.v.* and Davies, *Families* 6361 (C).
3 On the unusual circumstances presupposed in this clause see Brunt, *CQ* 19 (1969) 248 n. 1.
4 See Rhodes, *Boule* 68 and n. 2, 81 and n. 5.
5 This clause echoes the provisions of no. 35, lines 55–7.
6 This restoration follows Kirchner in *IG* II.

67   Alliance between Philip II and the Chalcidians. Near Olynthus, 357/6.

Bottom right-hand corner of a block of local limestone, Ionian dialect of the Euboic type in lines 1–11, Phocian dialect in lines 12–16, non-stoichedon.

D.M. Robinson, *TAPA* 65 (1934) 103–22 (with a facsimile, p. 104, and a photograph, pl. 1); Tod 158, pp. 171–4; *SV 2.308, pp. 279–81. Cf. Diod. 16.8.3; Dem. 2.7, 14; 6.20; 23.107f.; Libanius *Hypothesis to Dem.* 1.2

Ellis, *Philip II* 67–8; Hammond-Griffith 244–6 (Griffith).

[--- | --] *v*[1] I shall be an ally in accordance | with [the terms agreed. *v* From the Chalcidians] the oath shall be sworn to Phili[p] by the *magistrates* of the League[2] and t|he [ambassadors (?). To the Chalci]dians (the oath shall be sworn) by (Philip) himself and whomever else the Chalcidians
5 dema||nd. [They shall swear the oath guilelessly] and sincerely, by Zeus, Ge, Helios, Poseidon;[3] *if they keep* | *the oath, they shall have* [many benefits], if they break the oath, (they shall have) many misfortunes. The oath shall be sworn *as they sacri|fice* [the victims, by both sides]. These articles shall be inscribed on a *stele* and (so shall) the oracular response tha|t [was given by the God] *concerning* the alliance. The Chalcidi[ans] shall set up (a copy) in the temple | [of Artemis at Olynthus, Philip] *in* Dium in [the] temple of Zeus *the* Olympian, and at Delphi of
10 both the *re||sponse* [and the stele] there shall be set up *copies*.[4] (Any) of these articles may by common agreement in a *per|iod* [of three months (?)][5] be amended] in whatever way seems good to Philip and the [Chal]cidians.[6] *vv* | [The God responded[7] to the Chalcidians] *and* Philip that it was more desirable and *better* that friends and | [allies they should be in accordance with the] terms agreed. Sacrifices shall be made, and

good omens obtained, to Zeus the All-powerful and | [Highest, to Apollo the Protector], to Artemis Orthia, to Herm[es], and that good
15 fortune ‖ shall attend [the alliance vows shall be made], and at Pytho,[8] to [A]pollo, thank-offerings | [shall be paid, and] *public thanksgivings offered. vv* |

1   The text of the treaty is missing.
2   See Larsen, *Government* 42–3.
3   These four gods, representing the four elements, occur frequently in such oaths. Cf., for example, no. 70.
4   For a similar provision cf. Thuc. 5.18.10 (Olympia and Delphi), 5.47.11 (Olympia).
5   The tentative restoration offered by Segre, *RFIC* 63 (1935) 497ff. Robinson (117–18) proposed 'in the course of time'. Tod (p. 174) wanted to read 'common agreement *being rea|ched* [by both sides to make a change]'.
6   Cf. Thuc. 5.18.11, 5.47.12.
7   The involvement of Delphi is intriguing. Cf. Parke-Wormell 1.234 and Griffith. See also J. Fontenrose, *The Delphic Oracle* (Berkeley 1978) 250 (H19) with comments.
8   I.e. at Delphi.

68   Arkesine honours the Athenian governor Androtion. Arkesine on Amorgos, spring 356.[1] Stele of white marble, Ionic letters, stoichedon (except for four inserted iotas).

IG XII (7) 5; *Tod 152, pp. 154–7.

G. Radet, *BCH* 12 (1888) 224–8; F. Jacoby, *FGrHist* 3b.Suppl. 1.88; G.L. Cawkwell, *C&M* 23 (1962) 34–49; P. Harding, *Historia* 25 (1976) 194; Cargill, *League* 158–9.

Resolved by the Council and the People of | Arkesine: since Androtion[2] a good man | has been to the People of Ar|kesine, in that, wnen he
5 was governor of the city, no ‖ one of the citizens or of the foreigners who c|ame to the city was harmed by him, a|nd, when he lent money in time of need to the c|ity, he did not wish to take any interest, a|nd, when the
10 pay for the garrison was unavail‖able for the city, after advancing (it) from his own funds, a|t the end of the year, when he was repaid, n|o interest was exacted by him and the city | spent less money by twelve
15 mina|i each year as a result of his actio‖ns, and since those (of the citizens) who were prisoners of war in enemy hands, | whom he happened upon, were ransomed by him, a crown shall be bestowed upon | Androtion, son of Andron, the Athenian, a gol|den crown worth five
20 hundred drach|mas, for his excellence and justice and goodw‖ill to the People of Ark|esine, and he shall be inscribed as a proxenos an|d benefactor of the city of Arkesin|e, both himself and his descendants, and there shall be | for him exemption from all taxation. *vv* Since [there-
25 fore] ‖ it has been resolved *also by the* allies [- | -] likewise [- | ---]

1   The arguments for the date are as follows: the tone of the inscription, especially the mention of prisoners of war, suggests that at least part of Androtion's governorship fell during the period of the Social War, 357–355. But Androtion was in Athens, serving as a councillor, for the year 356/5, for it is a reasonable inference that it was in the year immediately following his councillorship that he was indicted under the *graphe paranomon* for his proposal to crown the outgoing council. This indictment, for which Demosthenes wrote one of the speeches (Dem. 22), took place in 355/4 (Dionysius of Halicarnassus, *To Ammaeus* 1.4; see Cawkwell 40–5). Therefore, this leaves only the year 357/6, and, since the honours seem to imply the end of his governorship, the spring of 356. It should be noted, however, that Androtion was governor of Arkesine for more than one year (cf. lines 11–13) and that, therefore, his governorship began before the Social War started.

2   For Androtion, politician and author of an *Atthis*, see Davies, *Families* 913; Jacoby, *FGrHist* 3b. Suppl. 1.85–106, and P. Harding, *Historia* 25 (1976) 186–200; *AJAH* 3 (1978) 179–83.

69   Andros garrisoned by the Athenians in the Social War. Athens, 356.

Marble stele, Ionic letters, stoichedon (except line 2, which is one letter short, and line 6, which has eleven extra letters, no doubt owing to some error on the part of the engraver).

IG II² 123; *Tod 156, pp. 165–7. Cf. Aeschines 1.107–8.

G.L. Cawkwell, *C&M* 23 (1961) 34–49; Cargill, *League* 155–6.

In the *archonship* of Agathokle[s (357/6), when] | Aigeis held the ninth prytany, | in which Diodotos, son of [D]iokles, from An[gel|e] was
5   secretary, on the eighth (day) of the *pry*||*tany*.[1] Of the Proedroi, the one who *put* (the motion) *to the vote* | (was) [Dio]ti[m]os of Oino(e).[2] Resolved by the Boule and the *People*. | [Hege]sandr[o]s[3] made the motion: In order that And[ro|s] *may be safe* for the People of Athe[n]s[4]
10   [an|d] for the People of Andros and that *there may b*||*e* for the garrison on A[ndro]s *pa*|*y* from the syntaxeis in accordance with the resolut|ions of the allies and so that there may not be a dissol|ution of the guard-force, a general shall be chosen *fr*|*om* those who have been elected, [and] *the*
15   *one c*||*hosen* shall be in charge [of Andros].[5] | From the *islands* shall be exacted | by Archedemos the money *that is owing* to t|he soldiers [on
20   Andros], | and it shall be handed over to the [governor || on] Andros, so that [the soldiers] | *may have* their pay [--]

1   About May 356.
2   For the prescript see Henry, *Prescripts* 25 and 27.
3   Brother of Hegesippos, son of Hegesias, of Sounion, the proposer of no. 66. See Davies, *Families* 6351(B).
4   For this phrase, cf. Xen. *Hell.* 7.4.4.
5   '[of them]' (Nachmanson); '[of it]' (Tod).

70   Athenian alliance with Ketriporis, Lyppeios and Grabos. Athens, midsummer 356. Three fragments of a marble stele (crowned by a relief representing a prancing horse), Ionic letters, stoichedon (except line 1, which forms a heading, and line 41, which has one extra letter).

IG II²; Tod 157, pp. 167–70; *SV 2.309, pp. 281–4. Cf. Diod. 16.22.3; Plut. *Alex.* 3.5; Dem. 1.13; Isocrates 5.21.

Ellis, *Philip II* 70–1; Cawkwell, *Philip* 41–2; Hammond-Griffith 246–54 (Griffith); Cargill, *League* 90; E. Badian, *Pulpudeva* 4 (1983) 56–7.

Secretary: Lysias, [son of] Lys[--]. | Alliance of the Athenians with Ketripor[is the Thracian and] h|is brothers[1] and with Lyppeios the [Paeonian[2] and with Gra]|bos the Illyrian.[3] In the archonship of
5   Elpines (356/5), [when Hippotho‖ntis] held the first prytany, on the eleventh [(day) of the prytany.[4] | Of the] *Proedroi* the one who put (the motion) to the vote (was) Mnesarch[os --. Resolved | by the] Boule and the People, Kallisthe[nes[5] made the motion: With good for|tune for the] *People* of Athens, *acceptance shall be given* [to the] *allianc|e* [on the terms that Mono]unios,[6] the brother [of Ketriporis], says that [his]
10   b‖*rother* has agreed to with the (envoy) [sent from the] | People [of Athen]s to Ketriporis and [his brothers and L]|yppei[os the Paeo]nian and Grabos [the Illyrian. The] *Pro|edroi*, [who have been chosen by lot] *to be Proedroi*, [at the first] *assemb|ly* shall introduce [to] the People
15   [Monounios, the brother] ‖ of Ketr[iporis, and Peisianax[7] and the embassies] t|hat have come [from Lyppeios and Grabos and -- | who has come] from Chares[8] [and shall communicate the opinion of the] *Boul|e* to the People, [that it seems good to the Boule that the alliance]
20 | be accepted, since [-- ‖ ---] | Chares [-- | --- | -] *for the purpose of* (making)
25   *war* [-- | --- ‖ --- | --] the *mone|y*. [Commendation shall be given to Ketriporis and his] *brothers* because *they are* [g|ood men toward] the [People of Athen]s. Commendation shall be given | [also to Monounios his brother,
30   who] *has come from* [Metripor‖is, on account of his excellence and goodwill, and] invitation shall be issued for hospitality at | [the Prytaneion for] *tomorrow. Commendation shall* also *be given* to Peisiana|[x and invitation shall be issued for dinner at the Prytan]eion for tomorro|w. [Invitation shall be issued for hospitality to the ambassadors who] *have come* from
35   t|*he* [other kings] *at* the P[r]y[t]aneion for tomorrow. And if ‖ [it is necessary to add anything to this] decree, the Boule shall have the authority.[9] *v* | (The following) [have been chosen as ambassadors]: Lysikrates *v* of Oin[o]e, *v* Antimachos, *v* | [- 12 Thra]son *v* of [Er]chia.[10] *vv* | [I swear by Zeus and Ge] and Helios and Posei[d]on and Athena and | [Ares that I shall be a friend] to Ketriporis and the brothers of

40 K‖[etriporis and] (I shall be) an ally, and I shall fight (together) with
Ketripor|[is in the war] against Philip without guile in full strength | [to
the best of (my) ability], and I shall not be first to terminate the war
with|out [Ketriporis] and his brothers, (that is) the (war) against Philip,
and | [the other places that] Philip *holds* I shall join in subjugating *along*

45 ‖ *with* [Ketriporis] and his brothers and (in particular) Krenides[11] *I shall
help to cap|ture* [along with Ketrip]o[ris] and his brothers, and I shall
give back the | [--- | ---]

1 Ketriporis and his brothers had become rulers of the western Thracian kingdom
  on the death of Berisades (*c.* 357), whose sons they probably were. Cf. no. 64 n. 2.
2 The successor to Agis, who died in 359/8 (Diod. 16.4.2).
3 Grabos became the most powerful Illyrian king after the death of Bardylis in 358.
  He was defeated by Parmenion very soon after this treaty was made (Plut. *Alex.*
  3.5). A fragment of a treaty of alliance between Grabos and the Chalcidians has
  been found at Olynthus. The unfinished state of the inscription and the fact that
  it had been thrown into a riverbed have suggested to some that the treaty was
  never ratified. The Olynthians found alliance with Philip more attractive (cf. no.
  67).
4 Midsummer 356. Diodorus (16.22.3) places the alliance in this archon year (without mentioning Athens), but puts it after the conclusion of the Social War. This
  error is a result of his ordering of his material.
5 For Kallisthenes see Dem. 19.86.
6 The name is conjectural.
7 The Athenian ambassador. For his family and its relationship to the leading
  aristocratic families of the fifth century see Davies, *Families* 9688 (IX) and Table 1.
8 Chares had been in Thrace in 357, negotiating the Athenian agreement with the
  Thracian kings (no. 64). Subsequently, if we can accept any part of Diodorus'
  account of the Social War, he had taken part in the battle of Chios (Diod. 16.7.3)
  and may by this time have been in the Hellespont (Diod. 16.21.3).
9 For this provision see Rhodes, *Boule* 82.
10 Cf. Aesch. 3.138 and see Davies, *Families* 7305 (with stemma).
11 Founded in 360/59 (Diod. 16.3.7), probably with the help of the Athenian politician Kallistratos of Aphidna (cf. Hammond-Griffith 235 (Griffith)). It was
  clearly in Philip's possession by this time (lines 45–6). Later Philip changed its
  name to Philippi (Diod. 16.8.6, though his date, 358/7, is clearly wrong; cf.
  Hammond-Griffith 246ff.).

71 End of the Social War. 355/4.

Scholion to Demosthenes 3.28. Cf. Diod. 16.22.2; Dem. 15.26, 18.234; Aesch. 2.70.

R. Sealey, *JHS* 75 (1955) 75ff.; G.L. Cawkwell, *C&M* 23 (1962) 34–40 and *JHS* 83 (1963)
48; Cargill, *League* 178–85.

Demosthenes 3.28

. . . and those whom during the war we acquired as allies, these (politicians) have lost in peace-time.

SCHOLION
In the Social War the Chians and Rhodians and Byzantines and some
others revolted from them. So, by fighting against them, they gained
back some, but others they could not; then they made peace on the
condition that they would allow all the allies (to be) autonomous. So he
(*sc.* Demosthenes) means by this statement that even those whom we
brought over to our side in the war we have lost on account of the peace.
Euboulos was responsible for the peace being the kind that it was, by
administering affairs as he did.

72   Chares in Asia. 355/4.

A. Scholion to Dem. 4.19. **B.** Scholion to Dem. 3.31. **C.** Pap. Erzherzog Rainer: *FGrHist*
105.4. Cf. Diod. 16.22.1–2, 34.1; Dem. 4.24; Plut. *Aratus* 16.3.

Parke, *Soldiers* 122–3; Pritchett, *State* 78–80.

A. Demosthenes 4.19

Do not speak to me of ten thousand or twenty thousand mercenaries or
those paper armies, but of one that will belong to the city and one that
will obey and follow the general you elect . . .

SCHOLION
When the King of the Persians sent orders to the coastal satraps to
disband their mercenary armies on account of their excessive cost, the
satraps discharged the soldiers, who were about ten thousand in
number. They went to Chares, the Athenian general, who had a force
of mercenaries and made him their leader. Artabazos, a Persian, who
was in revolt from the King and at war with him, sent (a message) to
Chares, inviting him to ship his army over into the King's territory.
When the soldiers put pressure on Chares, saying that if he did not
provide them with maintenance they would go away to one who was
offering (it), he (Chares) was constrained to ship the army over. He fell
in with a Persian force of twenty thousand, most of them mounted,
under the command of Tithraustes and defeated it in battle. And he
even wrote (a letter) to the Athenians about the ten thousand, saying
that he had won a victory that was the sister of Marathon. Some people
bade Chares by letter to hire other (mercenaries) too.

B. Demosthenes 3.31

. . . but you, the People, hamstrung and stripped of money and allies, have been reduced to the position of a servant and an appendage, pleased if these men (*sc.* the politicians) give you a share of the Theoric monies or provide a procession at the Boedromia . . .

SCHOLION
Boidia. This is a reference to Chares. For having crossed over with his mercenary force into Asia to Artabazos, he sacked Lampsacus and Sigeum and sent oxen to the Athenians, which they distributed by tribes. Boidia. Boedromia, is a variant reading. For they say that, when Chares sent the booty, it was (the time of) the festival of the Boedromia.[1]

C. *FGrHist* 105.4[2]

[--] he [*sc.* Chares) *was making* | *war* against the King and, invad|ing Phrygia, he was laying waste Tithraus|tes' territory, until there arrived from Athens the | embassy that forbade war to be waged by hi|m with the royal satraps. Then, | after making peace with Tithraust[e]s, | he went down to the coast to Artabazos, and [--]

1 The festival was held in Boedromion, the third month of the Attic year, therefore autumn 355. The scholiast presumably had 'Boidia' (= 'little oxen') rather than 'Boedromia' in his text of Demosthenes.
2 A fragment of a historical work or, more probably, of a commentary on a work of Demosthenes (the *First Philippic*?).

73   The siege of Methone. 355/4.

A. *IG* II[2] 130. Athens, 355. Fragment of a marble stele, Ionic letters, stoichedon (except line 1, which forms a heading). *Pečiřka, *Enktesis* 35–6. **B.** Didymus, *Demosthenes*, col. 12.40ff. (on Dem. 11.22) (Theopompus, *FGrHist* 115F52 = Marsyas the Macedonian, *FGrHist* 135–6F16 = Duris of Samos, *FGrHist* 76F36). Cf. Diod. 16.31.6, 16.34.4–5; Dem. 1.9, 4.35, 18.67; [Plut.] *Lives of the Ten Orators* (= *Moralia* 851A).

Ellis, *Philip II* 75–6; Cawkwell, *Philip* 37 and 192 n. 18; Hammond-Griffith 254–8 (Griffith).

A. *IG* II[2] 130

[Proxeny for So]chares,[1] son of Chares, from Apo[llonia. | In] the archonship of [Kalli]stratos (355/4), when | [Pandio]nis held the fifth
5   prytan|y,[2] [in which Pand]ios,[3] son of Sokles, from Oion was *sec‖retary.* On the third (day) of the prytany. *Of th*|*e Proedroi* the one who put (the motion) to the vote (was) Glaukete[s | -8-]n.[4] Resolved by the Boule

and [t|he People. A]ristopho[n][5] made the motion: Commendation
10   shall be gi|ven [to Sochare]s, son of Chares, from Apollonia ‖ [--]
because he was zealous to the [- | -] to do service and he sent hi|s own
[son] into Methone,[6] and | he [shall be] proxenos of the People of
15 | [Athen]s, both himself and his *descendants* ‖ [and] *he shall have* the
privilege of possession of a house.[7] [T|he] *secretary* of the *Boule* shall
inscri|be [on] a stele within ten *days* [on the Acr|opol]i[s] at the expense
of [S]ochar[es th|is decree --]

B. [Demosthenes] 11.22

(Consider what a disgrace it is) . . . if one who originates from
Macedonia is so fond of danger that, in order to make his empire
greater, he has been wounded in every part of his body while fighting
his enemies, (but the Athenians . . .).[8]

DIDYMUS, *DEMOSTHENES*, COL. 12, 40ff.
About the wounds that Philip suffered, we have given a complete
account, and on this occasion it must be abbreviated. In connection
with the siege of Methone he had his right eye struck out, when it was
hit by an arrow while he was overseeing the siege-weapons and the
so-called (tortoise) sheds. This accords with what Theopompus
recounts in the fourth (book) of his *Histories* about him (Philip), and
Marsyas the Macedonian says the same. But Duris of Samos (for he
had to *talk of marvels* even here) says that the name of the man who let
loose the [timely] spear against him was [A]ster (Shooting Star), even
though almost *all* those *who were on the campaign* with him say that he was
wounded by an arrow.

1   The former reading (Lachares) has been proved wrong by the new reading in line 18.
2   Close to the end of the year 355.
3   The name of the secretary is not known for certain and could well be [Raid]ios. Cf.
    Pečiřka 37.
4   On the possible identification of this man cf. W.B. Dinsmoor, *AJA* 36 (1932) 165 n.
    4, and Pečiřka 35–6.
5   Most likely the son of Aristophanes of Azenia.
6   This is usually taken to indicate that by the end of 355 Methone was either under
    siege or in danger of being besieged. But cf. Cawkwell 192 n. 18.
7   For this privilege see Pečiřka, *passim*.
8   Cf. Dem. 18.67.

74   Contributions to the Sacred War. Thebes, 354–352. Stone slab,
Ionic letters, Boeotian dialect, non-stoichedon.

IG VII 2418; Buck, *Dialects* 40, pp. 229–30; *Tod 160, pp. 177–9. Cf. Diod. 16.14.3–5,
16.23–31, 16.34.2; Aesch. 2.131, 3.148; Pausanias 9.6.4, 10.3.1.

75   Euboulos and the Theoric Fund

N.G.L. Hammond, *JHS* 57 (1937) 44–78; P. Roesch, *Thespies* 79, 87; Bury-Meiggs 420–4.

[The following] *contributed money* [for the war | that] was being f[[ought]]
by the Boeotians for [the Temple at Delphi] | against those who are
5   committing sacrilege against the Temple [of Apollo the | P]ythian. ‖ In
the archonship of Aristion (354/3) Alyzeans, [--].[1] | (The) envoys (were)
Charops, son of Dadon, Aristo[--]. | Anactorians,[2] thirty minae: (the)
envoys (were) [--], | son of Phormos, Arkos, son of Tereus. | Byzantines,[3]
10   Lampsacene *staters* of gold, ‖ eighty-four, At[tic] silver, *dra|chmas* sixteen.
The delegates (to the federal council)[4] of the Byzantines [brought] | the
money, (namely) Kerkinos, son of Heirotimos, Ag[--], | son of
Deloptichos, Dionysios, son of Heiraion. | Athenodoros, son of
15   Dionysios, the Tened[ian],[5] ‖ proxenos of the Boeotians, one thousand
drachmas. | In the archonship of Nikolaos (353/2), Aly[zeans], | another
thirty minae, *brought* | by the envoys of the Alyzeans, (namely)
20   Theo[--], | son of [A]lexandros, Dion, [son of] Poly[--]. ‖ In the archon-
ship of [A]geisinikos (352/1), the Byzantines *contri|buted* another five
hundred staters [of gol|d], on the Lampsacene standard, for the war
that *on behalf of* [the] | temple at Delphi was being fought by the
Boeotian[s]. | (The) delegates (who) brought (the money were) Sosis,
25   son of Karatichos, ‖ [P]armeniskos, son of Pyramos.

1   The sum is missing.
2   Anactorium, on the coast of Acarnania. The Acarnanians had joined the Second
     Athenian Confederacy by *c.* 375 (cf. no. 35 line 107) but had seceded after the battle
     of Leuctra (Xen. *Hell.* 6.5.23). Some Acarnanians fought with the Athenians at
     Chaeronea (cf. no. 100).
3   Byzantium had played an important part in the revolt that constituted the Social
     War. It had been associated with Thebes since the late 360s through the diplomacy
     of Epameinondas.
4   So Tod, p. 178.
5   Tenedos was loyal to Athens throughout this period and, therefore, the state could
     not officially contribute to a war in which Athens was on the other side. So
     Athenodoros' contribution is a private one. Note that he is a Boeotian proxenos.

75   Euboulos and the Theoric Fund.[1]   About 354.

A. Harpocration, *Lexicon s.v.* Theorika. **B.** Scholion to Dem. 1.1. **C.** Scholion to
Aeschines 3.24. **D.** Harpocration, *Lexicon s.v.* Euboulos (Theopompus, *FGrHist* 115F99).
Cf. Dem. 1.19f., 3.2, 10f., 31f., [59].4f.; Aesch. 3.25; Aristotle, *Ath. Pol.* 43.1.

A.H.M. Jones, *Athenian Democracy* 34; J.J. Buchanan, *Theorika* (New York 1962) 53–74;
G.L. Cawkwell, *JHS* 83 (1963) 53–61.

A. Harpocration, *Lexicon s.v.* Theorika

Demosthenes in the *Philippics*. Festival money was certain state money gathered from the city's revenues. This was previously kept for the needs of wartime and was called military money but later was transferred to public building-projects and disbursements, the initiator of which was Agyrrhios the demagogue. Philochorus (*FGrHist* 328F33) in the third[2] book of his *Atthis* says, 'The festival fund was first considered "the drachma for the seat in the theatre", whence it got its name', etc. Philinos,[3] in his speech against the statues of Sophocles and Euripides, speaking of Euboulos, says, 'It was called the festival fund (theorikon) because, when the Dionysia were imminent, Euboulos made a distribution (of funds) for the festival, so that all might take part in the festival and no one of the citizens might fail to attend through poverty'.

B. Demosthenes 1.1

I think, men of Athens, that you would choose in place of a large amount of money that it should become apparent that the future will turn out well for the City in the matters you are now considering.

SCHOLION TO DEM. 1.1 (EXCERPTED)
... The Athenians had funds reserved for military purposes (stratiotika), but just recently they have made these for festival use (theorika) ... It should be known that these public funds were originally transferred to festival use by Perikles ... who proposed that the City's revenues become festival money for all the citizens. Then when a certain Apollodoros[4] attempted to make them military again, Euboulos the politician, who was a demagogue, out of a desire to draw more of the people's goodwill to himself, proposed a law that ordained the death penalty for anyone who should attempt to change the festival money to military. Wherefore as many times as Demosthenes refers to these funds in his *Philippics*, he only advises that the law be repealed, but does not make a (formal) motion in writing (concerning it), for that was dangerous.

C. Aeschines 3.24

But that Demosthenes was truly subject to audit at the time when this man (Ktesiphon) introduced his motion, since he held the office of Commissioner for the Theoric Fund ... I shall now try to show from the public records ...

SCHOLION

The Athenians distributed festival money first at a drachma to each man on the motion of Perikles. Later they also distributed many funds simultaneously under the guise of the festival fund, some of which was distributed by Diophantos, some by Euboulos.

D. Harpocration, *Lexicon s.v.* Euboulos

That he was a most distinguished demagogue, both careful and hardworking, and that he provided and distributed to the Athenians much money, wherefore under his administration it happened that the city became very soft and lax,[5] (is recorded by) Theopompus in the tenth (book) of his *Philippika*.

1   This entry is designed to illustrate Euboulos' special relationship to the Theoric Fund. The origin of the fund itself is a separate question that extends beyond the scope of this volume, for not only the scholia to Dem. 1.1 (B) and Aesch. 3.24 (C), but also Plutarch, *Perikles* 9.1, attribute it to Perikles. Suffice it to note that Agyrrhios is also mentioned in this context (A), on whose involvement with the introduction of pay for attendance at the Assembly see Arist. *Ath. Pol.* 41.3, and that Justin (6.9.1) dates the introduction of payments for attendance at the festivals to sometime after the battle of Mantinea (362 BC).
2   Possibly to be emended to sixth. Cf. Jacoby, *FGrHist* 3b.Suppl. 1.319.
3   An orator, possibly of the time of Lykourgos (338–325/4 BC), for it was Lykourgos who proposed the setting up of statues of the three tragedians. Cf. [Plut.] *Lives of the Ten Orators* (= *Moralia* 811f.).
4   The son of Pasion the banker. See Davies, *Families* 11672.
5   Most authors adopt Demosthenes' attitude towards Euboulos' use of the Theoric Fund as having a deleterious effect upon Athenian morale.

76   Treaty between Philip II and Kersebleptes. 352/1.

A. Scholion to Aeschines 2.81. **B.** Harpocration *s.v.* Amadokos (Theopompus, *FGrHist* 115F101). Cf. Dem. 1.13. Also, as background, Dem. 23.14; Diod. 16.34.3; Athenaeus 12.532d–e.

SV 2.319, p. 294; Ellis, *Philip II* 80–1, 87–9; *CP* 72 (1977) 32–9; Cawkwell, *Philip* 80; Hammond-Griffith 281–5 (Griffith) (especially 282 n. 3); E. Badian, *Pulpudeva* 4 (1983) 61–2.

A. Aeschines 2.81

I saw (in 346) . . . the son of Kersebleptes living as a hostage at the court of Philip. And that is the way it is even now (in 343).

SCHOLION

The Byzantines and Perinthians and Amadokos the Thracian waged a war against Kersobleptes, the king of a part of Thrace, over some disputed territory. Philip, assisting them, made war against Kersobleptes and compelled (him) to release the disputed territory to those who claimed it and, after making a pact of friendship for himself,[1] secured the king on the throne, but he took the (king's) son from him as a hostage and carried him off to Macedonia.

B. Harpocration *s.v.* Amadokos

There are two of these, father and son, who[2] joined the war against Kersobleptes in order to become an ally with Philip.[3] Theopompus makes mention of both in the eleventh (book) of the *Philippika*.

1 The reading of the manuscripts. 'Having established their friendship' (Sauppe).
2 This relative pronoun is singular and, most likely, refers to the son.
3 'Went to fight as Philip's ally in the war against Cersobleptes' (Hammond-Griffith 282). The spelling Kersobleptes is standard in the literary sources, but Kersebleptes is the epigraphic form. Cf. no. 64.

77   Athenian cleruchs sent to Samos. 352/1.

Dionysius of Halicarnassus, *On Dinarchus* 13 (Philochorus, *FGrHist* 328F154). Cf. Dem. 15.9; Diod. 18.18.9; Strabo 14.1.18; no. 47.

G. Grote, *A History of Greece* (London 1862) 7.260 n. 2; J.K. Davies, *Historia* 18 (1969) 328–9; Bury-Meiggs 377–8; Cargill, *League* 148–9.

This speech (*sc.* Dinarchus' *Against Pedieus*) was made in the archonship of Aristodemos (352/1), as is clear from the speech itself. For the cleruchs who were despatched to Samos were despatched during this archonship,[1] as Philochorus records in his *Histories*.

1 This is a reference to the third group of Athenian settlers. The original settlement was made under Timotheos in 366/5 and may be that mentioned in no. 47, lines 88–9. Another is attested for the year 361/60 by a scholion to Aeschines 1.53: 'The Athenians sent out cleruchs to Samos in the archonship of Nikophemos (361/60)'. At the time of this third settlement the Samians were expelled from their island.

78   Resolution of the dispute over the Sacred *Orgas*[1] between Athens and Megara. 352/1–350/49.

A. *IG* II² 204.1–30, 49–57. Eleusis 352/1. Stele of Pentelic marble, Ionic letters,

stoichedon. *F. Sokolowski, *Lois sacrées des cités grecques* (Paris 1969) 32, pp. 60–3. **B.**
Didymus, *Demosthenes* (13) col. 13.40–58 (Philochorus, *FGrHist* 328F155). **C.** Didymus,
Demosthenes (13) col. 14.35–49 (Androtion, *FGrHist* 324F30). Cf. Dem. 13.32, 23.212 and
Fornara 122.

Jacoby, *FGrHist.* 3b.Suppl. 1.142–3; 529–31; P. Amandry, *La mantique apollinienne à
Delphes* (Paris 1950) 151–3; Parke-Wormell 1.227; W.R. Connor, *AJP* 83 (1962) 235–43;
G.L. Cawkwell, *REG* 82 (1969) 328–32; W.R. Connor, *REG* 83 (1970) 305–8; G.E.M. de
Ste Croix, *The Origins of the Peloponnesian War* (London 1972) Appendix 37, pp. 386–8; K.
Clinton, *The Sacred Officials of the Eleusinian Mysteries* (Transactions of the American
Philosophical Society 64.3, Philadelphia 1974) 17–18, 50.

A. *IG* II² 204

5   [--- | --- | --- | --- || -- there shall be chosen by the] *People* ten me|n [from
the Athenians at large right away, and five] from the Boule. | [Those
who have been chosen are to hold hearings in the Eleusi]nion in the
cit|y [concerning the disputed boundaries] of the Sacred Orgas, after
s|*wearing* [the customary oath that they will] not, either for favour or for
10   m||*alice*, [cast their vote, but (will vote) as] *justly* and as piously as
possible. Th|e [sittings shall be held continuously] from the sixteenth
of Poseideo|[n² until a judgement is reached], during the archonship of
Aristodemos (352/1). There shall be presen|t (at the sittings) [the] *king*
(i.e. the king archon) and the Hierophant and the Dadoucho|s³ [and
the Kerykes and] Eumolpidai and of the rest of the Athenians anyone
15   who w||*ants*, [in order that] as piously and justly as possible the
boun|daries [may be set]. *Care shall be taken* of the Sacres Orgas and the
othe|r [holy places], *all those*⁴ that are in Attica, from this day for |
[all time] *by those whom* the law ordains for each of them and by t|he
20   [Council] of the Areopagus and the general, the one who for th||e *guard-
ing* [of the] country has been elected and by the commanders of the |
patrol⁵ and the *demarchs* and the Boule that at the time is in offic|e and
by any of the other [Athe]nians who wants in whatsoever way | *they know
how.* v The secretary of the Boule *shall write* on two plates | of tin of like
25   and [similar] form, [on] the one: If it is more profitable and bet||ter for
the *People* [of Athens] that the king *rent out* the (parts) that are no|w
under cultivation [of the Sacred Orgas, the parts] *within* the boundaries,
for (the cost of) the b|uilding of the *porch* [and the repair] of the
sanctuary of the Two Goddess|es. And on the other tin plate: [If] it is
[more profitable and] *better* | for the People of Athens that those parts
30   [within] *the boundaries* that are now under cultivatio||n of the Sacred
Orgas be left untilled and consecrated [to the Two] *Goddesses.*⁶

50   ... Depending on whichever of the two inscriptions the || God *replies* that
it is more profitable [and] better for the People of Athen|s, *in accordance*

[with that] it shall be done, in order that as pious as possible may be the affairs regarding t|he Two Goddesses [and that never in the future] time may any impiety take | place [concerning the Sacred] *Orgas* [and] the other holy places in A|tt[ica. For the present] inscription shall be
55   made of this decree and the previous one, the one ‖ of Phi[l]o[k]rate[s[7]] regarding the] *holy places*, by the secretary of the Boule on | two *stelai* [of marble and set up], *one* at Eleusis beside the e|ntry [of the sanctuary, the other in the Ele]usinion in the city.[8]

B. Didymus, *Demosthenes*[9] col. 13.40–55

One could know that the time of the speech | (Dem. 13) was the archon-ship of Kallimachos (349/8), | who followed Apollodoros (350/49). Why? Because he makes | mention of the actions of the Athenians
45   against | the Megarians over the Sacred Orgas. This ‖ happened during the archonship of Apollodoros, | as Philochorus records, in the following | words: ‘The Athenians were at odds with the Megarians | over the delimitation of the | Sacred Orgas. They entered Megara with
50   E‖phialtes, who was general for the country, and mark|ed out the limits of the Sacred Orgas. With the agreement | of the Megarians the men who marked out the boundaries were Lakrateides, | the Hierophant, and Hieroklei|des, the dadouchos. And they consecrated the edge-lands,
55   around the Orgas, ‖ since the sanctuary (at Delphi) had responded: it (was) more | profitable and better (for them) if they left them untilled and if they did not cultivate them. | And they marked it off in a circle with stelai in accordance with the dec|ree of Philokrates.’

C. Didymus, *Demosthenes* col. 14.35–49

Androtion too has discoursed | about this Orgas | in the seventh (book) of his *Atthis*, in the following words: | ‘And the Athenians delimited the Orgas towards the Megarians | on account of the Two Goddesses
40   (lacuna) as they wan‖ted. For the Megarians agreed | that the men to mark out the boundaries should be the hierophant | Lakrateides and the dadouchos Hiero|kleides. And they abided by their delimitation. |
45   They also consecrated the edge-lands, such as were beside the ‖ Orgas, after consulting the | oracle and after the God had replied that it was more profitable and | better (for them) if they did not cultivate them. It was marked off in a circle | with marble stelai on the motion of | Philokrates.’

---

1   Territory between Athens and Megara, sacred to the Eleusinian Goddesses. In most of its history it was left untilled, but the original meaning of the word is ‘a well-watered, fertile piece of land’. Cf. Sokolowski 32 n. 1.

2   The sixth month of the civil year, approximately November/December.
3   Officials at the Eleusinian Mysteries. The Hierophant (revealer of the sacred rite) was the chief priest, the dadouchos (torch-bearer) was also very important. They came from the clans of the Eumolpidai and Kerykes respectively. See no. 54 n. 1.
4   Zieneh. 'Ancestral [sanctuaries]' (Foucart); '[Sacred] precincts' (Tsountas).
5   For the 'general for the country' see Arist. *Ath. Pol.* 61.1 (with P.J. Rhodes, *Commentary ad loc.*), and for the patrol *Ath. Pol.* 42.3f. and nos. 108 and 109.
6   The following lines, here omitted, describe the elaborate process whereby the two tin plates are to be placed at random, one in each of two hydriai. One hydria is to be of gold and one of silver. Thus they will be conveyed to Delphi and the God will simply be asked to choose between the vessels.
7   Possibly to be identified with Philokrates of Hagnous, after whom the Peace of Philokrates is named, and who was active as a politician at this period; but the name is common.
8   The decree continues for another 28 lines. These contain instructions for a sacrifice to Demeter and Kore, details regarding the funding of the cost of inscription and reimbursement of expenses for the various elected representatives and provision for the preparation of marble stelai that will be used to mark the boundaries of the consecrated land (cf. B and C). There follows a list of those chosen in accordance with the provision of lines 5–6 and finally the Boule is given the authority to make any necessary additions.
9   The two following passages are taken from Didymus' commentary on the thirteenth work in the Demosthenic corpus (*On Organization*), which he is concerned to date.

79   Treaty between Erythrae and Hermias of Atarneus. Erythrae, between 350 and 344 *or* 342. Stele of white marble, Ionic dialect, stoichedon.

SIG 229; Tod 165, pp. 188–90; *SV* 2.322, pp. 299–301; *H. Engelmann and R. Merkelbach, *Die Inschriften von Erythrai und Klazomenai* (Bonn 1972) 9, pp. 56–60 and pl. 2. Cf. no. 90.

D.E.W. Wormell, *YCS* 5 (1935) 57–92, esp. p. 70; Hammond-Griffith 518–22 (Griffith).

[-- whatever the Erythraeans deposit[1] | in] the territory of [He]rm[i]as and [his] c|ompanions[2] on account of war *shall be exempt* | *from tax* in its entirety and (so shall) whatever these *produc*|*e*,[3] with the exception of
5   anything that is sold. [For whatever] *has* || *been sold* the tax is to be a fiftieth. W|henever peace is concluded, (these goods) *shall be taken* | *away* in thirty days. [But if they are] *n*|*ot* taken away, the taxes are to be paid. (The Erythraeans) *shall dep*|*osit* (their goods) after making *due* procla-
10   mation. || It shall be (lawful) also for Hermias and his *comp*|*anions*, if they want *to deposit* anything,[4] | (to do so) on the same terms. The oath shall be sworn by the Ery[thraean]|s to Hermias and his companions. [The]
15   oa|th is to be as follows: I shall give assistance to Hermi[as and] h||is

companions both by land [and by] | sea in full strength *to* [the] best of (my) a|bility and *I shall fulfil* my other obligations [in accordance with] | the terms agreed. Responsibility shall rest with *t*|*he* generals. The oath
20   shall be administered by [messeng‖ers],[5] who have come from He[r]mias *and* [his] *c*|*ompanions*, along with the generals [-- | --], with duly performed sacrifices, [and the v|ictims] shall be provided by the
25   city. *In a similar way* | [both He]rmias and his companions [shall sw‖ear] through the agency of messengers that they will give assistance [to the Erythra|eans] both by land and by [se|a] *in full* strength to the best of (their) *ability* [a|nd] that they will fulfil [their] other obligations in accordance with [the] *terms a*|*greed*. The oath shall be sworn in the name
30   of the Gods *of o‖aths*, and these (terms) shall be written on a *stele of m*|*arble* and set up by the Erythrae[ans | in the] temple of Athena, by He[rmias | in] the temple of Atarneus.[6]

1 'If the Erythraeans deposit anything' (Tod; Bengtson (*SV*)).
2 Most likely close associates of Hermias in government (Tod, p. 189). The title is suggestive, considering the recorded ties between Hermias and Philip II of Macedon (Dem. 10.32): the institution of 'hetairoi' is best known from the court of Macedon.
3 I.e. offspring of slaves or animals.
4 I.e. in the territory of the Erythraeans.
5 Restored on the basis of line 25. The word is used here as a synonym for 'envoys'.
6 Legendary king of Mysia and eponymous hero of the city.

80   Alliance between Athens and Olynthus and Athenian aid to Olynthus. 349/8.

Dionysius of Halicarnassus, *To Ammaeus* 1.9.734f. (Philochorus, *FGrHist* 328F49–51). Cf. Dem. 1–3, *passim*; Diod. 16.52.9. Cf. no. 67.

Jacoby, *FGrHist* 3b.Suppl. 1.328–9; *SV* 2.323, pp. 301–2; G.L. Cawkwell, *CQ* 12 (1962) 122–40; J.M. Carter, *Historia* 20 (1971) 418–29; Ellis, *Philip II* 93–9; Cawkwell, *Philip* 82–90; Hammond-Griffith 315–28 (Griffith).

This (the Olynthian War) happened in the archonship of Kallimachos (349/8), as Philochorus makes clear in the sixth book of his *Atthis*, writing word for word as follows: 'Kallimachos from Pergase. In this man's archonship[1] the Athenians made an alliance with the Olynthians, who were being attacked by Philip and who had sent envoys to Athens (lacuna)[2] and they (the Athenians) sent help (in the form of) two thousand peltasts, the thirty triremes that were with Chares and eight that they helped to man themselves.' Then, after narrating the few intervening events, he writes this, 'About the same time, when the Chalcidians in Thrace were being hard pressed by the

war and had sent an embassy to Athens, the Athenians sent them
Charidemos, the general in the Hellespont, who with eighteen triremes
and four thousand peltasts and one hundred and fifty cavalry invaded
Pellene and Bottiaea with the Olynthians and laid waste the land.'
Then, concerning the third alliance, he writes this, 'When once again
the Olynthians had despatched ambassadors to Athens and were beg-
ging the Athenians not to look the other way while they were being
destroyed in war, but in addition to the force already present to send
them assistance that was not mercenary but composed of the Athenians
themselves, the People sent them a further seventeen triremes and two
thousand citizen hoplites and three hundred cavalry in horse transports and Chares as the general of the whole expedition.'

1   The formula used in the *Atthides* to indicate the first entry under a given archon-year.
    (Cf. no. 86 n. 3; no. 92 n. 1.)
2   Some manuscripts indicate a lacuna here, for which A. Schaefer (*ap.* Jacoby) has
    suggested 'on the motion of Demosthenes, while Herwerden (*ap.* Jacoby) adds 'and
    friendship' to 'alliance'.

81   Chalcidian refugees at Myrina in Lemnos.[1] Myrina, *c.* 348.
Marble stele, Ionic letters, stoichedon.

IG XII (8) 4. Cf. Dem. 9.26, 19.196f., 229, 305f., 309. Aesch. 2.153f.; Diod. 16.33.

A.B. West, *The History of the Chalcidic League* (Madison 1918) 130–5; M. Gude, *A History of
Olynthus* (Baltimore 1933) 37–9; Hammond-Griffith 324–5 (Griffith).

[--] since also the *Pe|ople* of Ath[en]s who are living in [Myr]ina[2] g|ave
land to the Chalcidians, they shall s|et up the stele concerning the
5   cura||tor and the herald shall proclaim during the Dio|nysia at the
competition for the tragedies that the Ch|alcidians who are living in
Myrina | crown with this crown t|he curator Theophilos,[3] son of
10   Meliton, || from Alopeke for his upright character an|d justice towards
the Chalci[d]|ians who are living in Myrina.

1   After the utter destruction of Olynthus and possibly as many as thirty-two other
    settlements in Chalcidice (cf. Dem. 9.26 and see West 131 n. 37 for an attempt to
    name some of these places) by Philip in 348, most of the inhabitants were either
    killed or sold into slavery, like those seen by Aeschines (Dem. 19.305–6). Some,
    however, escaped. It is usual in this context to cite *IG* II[2] 211 (Tod 166) for the
    presence of Olynthian refugees in Athens, but the inscription is too fragmentary
    and the name of the people requesting freedom from the resident aliens' tax is only
    a restoration (cf. Cargill, *League* 79–80). The present inscription, however, which is
    rarely mentioned, shows where some Chalcidians gained asylum.

2 As cleruchs.
3 Possibly the Theophilos called to testify by Lykophron in Hypereides 2.20.

82   Athens honours Spartokos, Pairisades and Apollonios. Athens, 346. Marble stele (surmounted by a relief showing Spartokos and Pairisades enthroned, Apollonios standing at the side), Ionic letters, stoichedon (except lines 1–2, which form a heading, and lines 3–7, which contain the prescript).

IG II² 212+; *Tod 167, pp. 193–8. Cf. Isocrates 17.57; Dem. 20.29f., 36f. Cf. no. 27.

E.H. Minns, *Scythians and Greeks* (Cambridge 1913) 574–6; M.I. Rostovtzeff, *CAH* 8.566–7; S.M. Burstein, *Historia* 27 (1978) 428–36. See also R. Werner, *Historia* 4 (1955) 412–44; V.F. Gajdukevič, *Das bosporanische Reich*, trans. G. Janke (Berlin 1971) 96f.

For Spartokos, Pairisades, | Apollonios, the sons of Leukon.[1] | *vacat.* In the archonship of Themistokles (347/6) | when Aigeis held the eighth
5   pryt‖any, in which Lysima[ch]os, son of Soside[m|os, of Acha]r[n]ai was secretary, The[o]|philos of [Hali]mous presided, | Androtion,[2] son of Andron, of Gargettos made the motion: Con|cerning the messages
10 sent by Spartokos and Pair[isa]d[e]‖s and (the matters that) the ambas-sadors who have come from them re|port, answer shall be made to them that the Pe|ople of Athens commend Spart[o]kos and Pai|risades because they are good men and because they pro|mise to the People of
15 A[th]ens that they will take c‖are of the export of wheat just as | their father used to and that they will lend assistance z|ealously in whatever matter the People *ask*, and report shall | be made to them by the *ambas-sadors* that, if these promises are k|ept, there will be nothing they will
20 fail to get from the People ‖ of Athens. And since they grant those privileges | to the Athenians that S[at]y[r]os and Leukon gr|anted, [Spart]o[k]os and Pairisades shall have the p|rivileges[3] that [the] *People* granted to Satyros and Leuko|n, and they are to be crowned with a
25 golden crown at the Great Panathen‖aia, to the value of one thousand drachmas, | each man. The crowns are to be commissioned[4] by t|he athlothetai[5] in the year preceding the Great Panathena|ia, in accord-ance with the decree of the People | previously voted for Leukon, and it
30 is to be pro‖claimed that the People of Athens crown | Spartokos and Pairisades, Leukon's | sons, for their excellence and goodwill towards t|he People of Athens. Since the cro|wns are dedicated to Athena
35 Polias, ‖ the athlothetai are to dedicate in the temple t|he crowns with the inscription: Spartokos *vv* | and Pairisades, sons of Leukon, dedi-cate|d (these) to Athena, after being crowned by the Peo|ple of Athens.
40 The money is to be given to th‖e athlothetai for the crowns by the |

People's treasurer from the funds that for matters decreed | by the People are apportioned. For the present it shall be permitted for (the money) to be pro|vided by the receivers for the crow|ns from the mili-
45   tary fund. Inscription shall ‖ be made of this decree by the secretary of the | Boule on a marble stele and set up ne|ar the (inscription) for Satyros and Leukon; for the in|scription there shall be given by the treasurer of the People thir|ty drachmas. Commendation shall be given
50   to the ambassadors ‖ Sosis and Theodosios because they are taking care of tho|se who come from Athens to Bosporos an|d invitation shall be issued to them for hospitality at the Prytane|ion for tomorrow. Concerning the money that is o|wed to the sons of Leukon, to ensure
55   that ‖ they get it back, this business shall be introduced by the Proedroi, | who are chosen by lot to be Proedroi, before the People [on the] | eighteenth day[6] immediately after the sacrifices, in order tha|t, having got the money back, they may not have a complaint [against the]
60 | People of Athens. The People shall grant the *public slave row*‖*ers*[7] who are requested by Spartokos and Pairis[ades] and t|*he* ambassadors shall make a list of the names [of the] | *public slave rowers* whom they take for the secretary [of th|e] Boule. Those whom they list shall be [on] | record
65   as doing what[ever] good *they are ab*‖*le* for the sons of Leukon. P[olyeukt]|os, son of Timokrates,[8] of Krioa made the motion: (Let) the [rest] (he) | as (proposed by) Androtion, and a crown shall be given [also to Apol]|lonios,[9] the son of Leukon, for the [same] reasons. |

1 For the heading or superscript see Henry, *Prescripts* 35. Spartokos and Pairisades ruled the Bosporos jointly with Leukon from 349 to his death in 347, then together until the death of Spartokos in 342.
2 For Androtion cf. no. 68.
3 Citizenship and freedom from taxation. Cf. Dem. 20.29f.
4 This honour is to be bestowed every four years at the Great Panathenaia, for the present infinitives in this whole section concerning the crowns denote repeated action (Tod, p. 196).
5 Commissioners for the games. For their duties see Aristotle, *Ath. Pol.* 60.1, 60.3.
6 The eighteenth of Elaphebolion, cf. Aesch. 2.61.
7 On these see B. Jordan, *The Athenian Navy in the Classical Period* (Berkeley and Los Angeles 1975) 240–59.
8 For Polyeuktos and his more famous father Timokrates see Davies, *Families* 13772 with bibliography.
9 Apollonios clearly did not share the throne with his brothers (compare the crowning relief).

83   Athens renews her alliance with Mytilene. Athens, 346. Marble stele, Ionic letters, stoichedon.

IG II[2] 213; Tod 168, pp. 198–9; *SV* 2.328, pp. 310–11. Cf. Dem. 13.8, 15.9; [Dem.] 40.37.

Marshall, *Confederacy* 119; Accame, *Lega* 199–200; Cargill, *League* 183.

In the archonship of Themistokles (347/6). [Resolved] | by the Boule
and the People, Aig[eis] *held the pry|tany*,[1] Lysimachos, son of
Sosidemos, of Acharn[ai][2] *was secre|tary*, Theophilos of Halimous *pre-*
5   *sid‖ed*. Stephanos,[3] son of Antidorides, of E[roiadai] | made the motion:
Concerning the matters raised by the *ambassadors* of t|he Mytileneans
and the treasurer [of the Para]|los[4] and the *message* that Phaidros[5] the
10   general *has sen|t*, be it resolved by the People that the *friendshi‖p* and
alliance continue to exist [for the] *Peo|ple* of Mytilene towards the *People*
| of Athens, (the one) that was *mutually* arranged | by the cities. And the
15   money from *the cont|ribution*[6] (that accrues) to the My[til]ene[a]ns [- ‖ ---
| ---][7]

1   This inscription belongs to the same prytany as no. 82 and on the same day, since
Theophilos is still chairman. See Rhodes, *Boule* 25.
2   See Davies, *Families* 9480.
3   The husband of Neaira. Cf. [Dem.] 49, *passim*.
4   One of the two state-galleys. Cf. Dem. 21.171; Aristotle, *Ath. Pol.* 61.7.
5   Cf. Aesch. 1.43 and Davies, *Families* 13964.
6   The *syntaxis*. Cf. no. 36. What exactly was to be done with the money is not certain,
but Tod (p. 199) believes it was to be used to pay the garrison troops.
7   The inscription continues for several lines but in too fragmentary a state for any
sense to be made of it.

**84   Extracts from the accounts of the Delphian Naopoioi.[1] Delphi,
346–344.** Six fragments of a limestone slab, Phocian dialect, Ionic
letters, stoichedon (with irregularities).

Fouilles de Delphes 3 (5) (Paris 1932) 23, pp. 105–15; *Tod 169 (lines 1–20, 102–39), pp.
200–5. Cf. no. 60.

N.G.L. Hammond, *JHS* 57 (1937) 62ff.; M. Sordi, *BCH* 81 (1957) 38–75; G. Roux, *RA* 1
(1966) 245–96 (especially 262–73); P. Marchetti, *BCH* Suppl. 4 (1977) 67–89; *BCH* 103
(1979) 151–63; G. Roux, *BCH* 103 (1979) 501–5.

(Col. 1)[2] From *the city* [of Delphi], | *from* (the money) *that was handed over*[3]
[by the Naopoioi] | who (held office) during [the] war,[4] [from] *drachm|as*
5   of Aeg[in]etan currency *three thousand fo‖ur hundred* four, [one obol], | we
received *drachmas* [of Aegin]|etan currency one thousand *eight hundred*
10   *sev|enty* seven, *obols* [five]. | From the city of Delph[i, from] ‖ (the money)
that was owing to the Naopoioi, f|rom drachmas of Ae[gi]netan cur-
rency seven|ty-four thousand s|ix hundred *seventy*, obol|s two, *one half-*
15   *obol*, we recei‖ved drachmas of Aeginetan currency one hun|dred five. *vv*

| Total of receipt in thi|s session: of Aeginetan currency dr|achmas one
20 thousand nine hundred eig‖hty-two, obols five. |

(Col. 2) [In the archonship of - -[5] expend|itures for the autumn] *session*.
105 | For laurel [for two] *days*, two obols, ‖ four coppers.[6] For guarding the
sh|eep, four obols, one half-o|bol. Cost of a reed, one drachma. | To the
110 cooks of the sacrificial victims, pay, | three drachmas, two obols. ‖ To
Eukrates for smoothing a stele | on which the Naopoioi (are listed), two
drachmas. | To Eukrates for removing the bases | (for the statues) of
Onomarchos and Philomelos[7] | and the statues outside the sanctuary,
115 ‖ eight drachmas, three obols. | To Kleon for carrying away the horses
| and the statues, and for the w|ater around the temple, for removing
120 (it), | seven drachmas. To Athanogeiton, ‖ the Boeotian, for the stones,
for completely | cleaning (them), the ones for the temple, | twenty
drachmas. To a herald, pay, | two drachmas. To Xenodoros the
125 archi|tect, pay, from one session ‖ to another, drachmas three hund|red
sixty. To a clerk, | pay, forty drachmas. | Athanogeiton, the Boeotian,
130 rec|eived (the contract) for the cutting (of stone) from Corinth ‖ (in
place) of the destroyed stones; for arch|itraves six, triglyphs four|teen,
coping-stones seven, (the contract was worth) drachm|as one thousand
135 thirty-six. To hi|m we gave, after the ten per cent[8] ‖ [was deducted],
drachmas nine hundre|d *thirty*-one. Agathony|[mos, the Corinthi]an,
received (the contract for) the | [transportation of the] quarried stone
from L[e|chaion to Kirra---] |

1 Commissioners, established in 367/6, responsible for the rebuilding of the temple.
2 Above line 1 are indications of letters that suggest a heading. Bourguet, *Fouilles* 3 (5)
   108 suggests: '[Receipts in Damoxenos' | archonship, spring session]'.
3 I.e. money that had been deposited with the state of Delphi for safe-keeping during
   the war.
4 The Third Sacred War, 356–346. For most of this period the Naopoioi did not meet.
   Their meetings began again in the archonship of Damoxenos, in the autumn
   session, 'when the peace was made' (*Fouilles* 3 (5) 19.71).
5 Tod, following older editors, here restores 'Thebagoras'. But this name is no longer
   accepted and the archon for this session is unknown. Cf. Marchetti.
6 Chalkoi, of which there were 12 to the obol.
7 The two Phocian generals who had plundered the sanctuary.
8 The sum withheld by the Naopoioi until the completion of the contract.

85   Revision of the citizen-lists at Athens. 346/5.

A. Harpocration, *Lexicon s.v.* Diapsephisis (Androtion, *FGrHist* 324F52; Philochorus,
FGrHist 328F52). **B.** Scholion to Aeschines 1.77. **C.** Libanius' argument to Dem. 57. Cf.
Aesch. 1.77–8, 86, 114, 2.182; Dem. 57, *passim*; Aristotle, *Ath. Pol.* 42.1; Dion. Hal. *On
Isaeus* 16f.

A. Diller, *TAPA* 63 (1932) 193–205; A.W. Gomme, *CP* 29 (1934) 123–40; A. Diller, *CP* 30 (1935) 302–11; Jacoby, *FGrHist* 3b.Suppl. 1.157–62, Suppl. 2.141–5; MacDowell, *Law* 67–70

A. Harpocration, *Lexicon s.v.* Diapsephisis

Specifically it (diapsephisis) applies to the scrutinies in the demes. which take place for each of the demesmen, (to find) whether he is in fact a citizen and a demesman or whether his name has been illegally inscribed in the list, since he is a foreigner: (so) Aeschines (in the speech) *Against Timarchos*. The most complete description of the revision,[1] how it took place in the archonship of Archias (346/5), (has been given) by Androtion in his *Atthis* and by Philochorus in the sixth (book) of his *Atthis*.

B. Aeschines 1.77

There have been revisions of lists in the demes and each one of us has submitted to a vote concerning his person, (regarding) who is truly an Athenian and who is not.

SCHOLION
A certain Demophilos introduced the motion that there should be a revision of the lists of the citizens in the demes, in order that the demesmen could vote about each of those registered, that he was (in fact) a citizen. (There was to be) no accusation or defence, but (the vote was to be cast) on the basis of personal knowledge, and the ballots of the demesmen were final.

C. Libanius' argument to Dem. 57

A law exists among the Athenians that there shall be an examination of all those inscribed on the lexiarchic lists,[2] (regarding) whether they are legitimate citizens or not. Those who were not born of a citizen-father and a citizen-mother shall have their names erased. The demesmen shall vote about everyone. Those who have been rejected and abide by the vote of the demesmen are to have their names erased and shall be metics. It is granted to anyone who wants (to make) appeal to the law-courts. If they are found guilty also by the court, they are to be sold (into slavery), but, if they are acquitted, they shall be citizens.

1   The words 'diapsephisis' or 'diapsephismos' simply mean a voting by ballot, but came to be used specifically for a revision of the citizen-lists.
2   Lists of adult males, kept by the demes, to establish eligibility for office.

86   Athens rejects the Great King's request for re-affirmation of friendship. Athens, 344/3.

Didymus, *Demosthenes* col. 8.8–23 (on Dem. 10.34[1]) (Anaximenes, *FGrHist* 72F28; Androtion, *FGrHist* 324F53 and Philochorus, *FGrHist* 328F157). Cf. Diod. 16.44.1.

Jacoby, *FGrHist* 3b.Suppl. 1.531–3; G.L. Cawkwell, *CQ* 13 (1963) 230ff.; P. Harding, *Historia* 25 (1976) 197–8; Ellis, *Philip II* 146–7; Hammond-Griffith 484–8 (Griffith).

In the archonship of Lykiskos (344/3), when Philip sent (an embassy) about peace, the Athenians gave audience to the ambassadors of the Great King also, but they conversed with them in a more arrogant manner than was fitting. For (they said) they would be at peace with A[rtaxerx]es, if he did not attack the Hellen[ic cities]. *These affairs are recounted* by Androtion, who also [--[2] Ana]ximenes. But it would be better to add [the account] of [Phi]lochorus. For under the heading '*the archonship* of Lykisk[os]' he puts down: 'In this man's archonship[3] when the Great King sent ambassadors to Athe[ns] and was requesting that his ancestral friendship (with the Athenians) continue (to exist), (the Athenians) *replied* [to the] ambassadors at Athens that [the] *friendship* would continue (to exist) for the King, if the King did not attack [the] Hellenic cities.'

1   For a translation of this passage of Demosthenes see no. 12.
2   Usually restored to read 'who also [at that time proposed the motion, and Ana]ximenes'. But see Harding.
3   The formula used in the *Atthides* to indicate the first entry under a given archon-year. Cf. no. 80 n.1, no. 92 n. 1.

87   Philip of Macedon reorganizes his government of Thessaly. 344–342.

A. Harpocration, *Lexicon s.v.* Tetrarchia (Theopompus, *FGrHist* 115F208). **B.** Harpocration, *Lexicon s.v.* Dekadarchia. Cf. Dem. 6.22, 9.26; Diod. 16.69.8.

Westlake, *Thessaly* 196–204; Larsen, *States* 12–26; Ellis, *Philip II* 137–43; Hammond-Griffith 523–44 (Griffith).

A. Harpocration, *Lexicon s.v.* Tetrarchia

Demosthenes in the *Philippics*. Since there were four parts of Thessaly, each part was called a 'Fourth', as Hellanicus says (*FGrHist* 4F52) in his *Thessalika*. He says that the 'Fourths' were named Thessaliotis, Phthiotis, Pelasgiotis (and) Hestiaiotis. And Aristotle in his *Constitution of the Thessalian League* says that Thessaly was divided into four parts in the time of Aleuas, the son of Pyrrhos . . . That Philip established governors over each of these parts has been made clear by others and especially by Theopompus in his 44th (book).

B. Harpocration, *Lexicon s.v.* **Dekadarchia**

. . . Philip, however, did not establish a dekadarchy[1] among the Thessalians, as is stated in the sixth *Philippic* of Demosthenes (6.22), but a tetrarchy. (See A above.)

1   A division of Thessaly into ten administrative areas.

88   Payment of Phocian fine to Delphi.[1] **Delphi, 343** *or* **342.** Three fragments of a marble slab, Phocian dialect, Ionic letters, stoichedon.

Fouilles de Delphes 3 (5) (Paris 1932) 14; *Tod 172A, pp. 209–14 (abridged). Cf. Diod. 16.56.5–7, 60.1–3; Dem. 19.64f., 81; Aesch. 2.142f.

Parke-Wormell 1.230; Ellis, *Philip II* 120–4; Cawkwell, *Philip* 107–8; P. Marchetti, *BCH* Suppl. 4 (1977) 67–89; Hammond-Griffith 450–6 (Griffith); H. Wankel, *ZPE* 42 (1981) 159–66.

12   In the administration of these men the Phoc[ians] paid, | in the spring
15   session, | thirty talents. ‖ (This was) the second instalment of the sacred mon|ey, (paid) in the archonship of Kl[e]on (344/3 or 343/2) | at Delphi, when the prytaneis[2] were | Echetimos, Herakleidas, Antagoras,
20 | Ariston, Philinos, Choirikos, ‖ Ameritos, Sodamos. | The following were the hieromnemons:[3] | Of the Thessalians Kottyphos (and) Kolosimmos.[4] | Of those from Philip[5] Eurylochos[6] | (and) Kleandros.
25   Of the Delphians[7] Damon ‖ (and) Mnasidamos. Of the Dorians, from Matro|polis Nikon, of the Argives Deino[me]|nes. Of the Ionians Timondas (and) Mnesilochos, | the Athenian. Of the Perrhaebians (and) Dolopians | Phaikos (and) Asandros. Of the [B]oeotians
30   ‖ Daitadas (and) Olympion. Of the Locrians | Pleistea[s][8] (and) Theomnastos. Of the Achaeans | Agasikratos (and) Pythodoros. | Of the Magnesians Philonautes (and) Epikratidas. | Of the Aenianians
35   Agelaos (and) Kleomenes. ‖ Of the Malians Antimachos of Heraclea[9] | (and) Demokrates of Lamia. |

1   This is the first of a number of documents that contain evidence for the payment by the Phocians of the fine imposed upon them in 346, at the end of the Third Sacred War. It covered in two columns of writing the first five instalments, the first of which was paid in the autumn session of 344 or 343, in the archonship of Kleon. Most of it

is in a poor state of preservation, with the exception of the passage translated. Payments continued until 322. The first eight payments were of 30 talents; by the eleventh the sum was 10 talents, at which level it probably remained. The total fine paid, therefore, was less than 500 talents. The old date for Kleon (343/2) has been revised to 344/3 by Marchetti. But see Wankel, doubting Marchetti's arrangement. Contemporary with these records of receipts at Delphi, a list of payments was published by the Phocians at Elateia and set up in the temple of Athena Cranaea. This has also survived in very fragmentary form.

2   The financial committee of the Delphian Council.
3   The following list of members of the Amphictyony is the earliest complete list extant. For the Amphictyony see *OCD s.v.* 'Amphictionies'.
4   See Tod, p. 212.
5   Philip, who is never entitled king in any contemporary document, acquired two seats on the Amphictyonic Council after the defeat of Phocis in 346. See Hammond-Griffith.
6   On Eurylochos see Tod, pp. 212–13.
7   The Delphians were now for the first time given seats on the Amphictyonic Council. Cf. Ellis 121.
8   Tod, p. 213.
9   Heraclea Trachinia.

89   Alliance of Athens with Achaea, Arcadia, Argos, Megalopolis and Messenia. 343/2.

A. Schol. to Aeschines 3.83. B. *IG* II^2 225. Athens, 342. Fragment of a marble stele, Ionic writing, non-stoichedon. *SV* 2.337, pp. 325–6.

P. Cloché, *La politique étrangère d'Athènes* (Paris 1934) 260; Ellis, *Philip II* 158.

A. Aeschines 3.83

And finally, by proposing a crown for those who went on embassy with Aristodemos to Thessaly and Magnesia contrary to the terms of the peace, he (Demosthenes) destroyed the peace and he prepared the way for the final disaster of war.

SCHOLION
In the archonship of Pythodotos (343/2) the Athenians . . . sent ambassadors to many parts of Hellas (to negotiate) about alliance . . . As a result, at that time the Achaeans, the Arcadians who sided with Mantinea, the Argives, the Megalopolitans and the Messenians became their allies.

B. *IG* II^2 225

[In the archonship of Pythodotos],[1] when Aigeis | [held the tenth

prytany], *on the fourth* (day) of the prytany. | [Resolved by the People: Archik]leides of Paiania | [presided, Kleostratos], son of
5   [Timo]sthenes, of Aigilia was || [secretary]. *vv* Alliance of the [Peo|ple of Athens --][2] of the Messenian[s and | ---]

1   *IG* II[2] 224 confirms most of the restoration of this prescript. This prescript is unusual
    in that the president's name appears before the secretary's and the name of the pro-
    poser is missing. But it is possible that it appeared in the missing part of the inscrip-
    tion. See Henry, *Prescripts* 44.
2   There is space here for another name in the genitive and the word 'and'.

90   The character and death of Hermias of Atarneus.[1] 342/1.

A. Didymus, *Demosthenes* (10.32?)[2] col. 4.59–col. 5.21 (Theopompus, *FGrHist* 115F291); *Jacoby, *FGrHist* 2b.598–9. **B.** Didymus, *Demosthenes* (10.32?) col. 5.66–col. 6.18 (Callisthenes, *FGrHist* 124F2); *Jacoby, *FGrHist* 2b.640. Cf. Dem. 10.32; Diod. 16.52.5; Diog. Laert. 5.1.3ff.; Athenaeus 15.696a–697b.

D.E.W. Wormell, *YCS* 5 (1935) 57–92; Hammond-Griffith 517–22 (Griffith).

A. Didymus, *Demosthenes* col. 4.59–col. 5.21[3]

For example [there are some who] emphasize the best in their account of the man (*sc.* Hermias), while others emphasize the worst. [The leading representative of the latter] is Theopompus, who in the ---ty-sixth[4] (book) of the History of Philip writes [as follows]: Hermias set out on [this] path, though he was a eunuch [and] *mutilated* in [appearance through] the process of cauterization and thirdly *had associated* for *unjust purposes* with [his] *master*[5] *when he was sick.*[6] He took [-- As]sos, his master's [fort, and] Atarneus and all the territory nearby, [and ruled][7] *in a most unjust* and base manner. He always *behaved* [most cruelly] both to [his friends and] others. For [one he killed] by poison, another *by the noose.* [He was not willing] *to protect* with his unpaid soldiery the territory, over which the Chians and the Mytilene[ans] had made *him* [overseer], despite their *requests.* He insulted very many Ionians. For, being a *bought slave* and one who sat at the money-changers' table and *was* [entirely] the product [of][8] disaster, he did not rest, [but assiduously] *hoarding treasure* while simultaneously [transgressing] propriety *he wronged* [most men], and of many *he attempted to get* [--], and amongst some [--] *he preferred to restore* constitutions *that were extreme.* And yet he did not escape scot-free nor did he prosper by making himself impious and base *to all men*, [but], *once* having been dragged up to the Great King's court [and] after [--] suffering patiently under the outrages to his body, *he ended* his *life on the cross.*

B. Didymus, *Demosthenes* **col. 5.66–col. 6.18**

What is more, Callisthen[es][9] too composed an [encomium][10] about
him (*sc.* Hermias), (in which) [he says] *especially the following*: 'Not only
[was he] *a man of this sort* [when he was free from] dangers, but also,
[when he came] close (to them), he [ever] continued to be the same.
And, [I suppose,] he gave the *greatest proof* of his courage in [his] very
last moments. For the barbarians, seeing (him) [carried off captive,] *were
full of admiration* for his courage, while the King, since *in the course of
conducting his examination*[11] he kept hearing [nothing] but the same
accounts [from his friends], being delighted at his courage and the
steadfastness of his ways, formed the intention of letting him off
entirely, in the belief that, if (Hermias) became his friend, he would be
most useful of all men. But when Bagoas[12] and Mentor[13] objected on
account of their envy and fear lest he, once released, become the leading (courtier) in their stead, he (the King) changed his mind again, but,
when he was about to pass judgement on him, he brought it about that
for his courage he (Hermias) did not share in the sufferings that were
usual at *his* (the King's) court. Now such moderation was *quite unexpected
from* an enemy *and particularly* [contrary to] the *way* of the barbarians.
[And he, therefore], as he was on the point *of dying summoned* Philis[tos
to] himself and [said nothing] other (than) *to enjoin* upon him *to send a
message* to his friends [and] companions, (reporting) that he had done
nothing *unworthy* of philosophy [or] unseemly.

1   The two passages translated below are taken from a long excursus on the death of
    Hermias of Atarneus in Didymus. Much of the material not translated can be
    found in Diogenes Laertius and Athenaeus, as cited, especially the *Hymn to Arete* by
    Aristotle, who was married to Pythias, Hermias' niece and adopted daughter.
2   The preamble to the excursus in Didymus is lost, so it is not known for certain
    which passage of Demosthenes he is commenting upon, but it is most likely 10.32.
3   This passage is in a very poor state of preservation. The restorations are by several
    scholars. Many are quite uncertain.
4   In Jacoby's view the space suggests the restoration 'forty-sixth', but the subject-
    matter belongs better in the 'thirty-sixth' book.
5   Euboulos.
6   For the restoration from 'mutilated . . . sick' Schubart restores '*Bithynian* by [birth ---]
    he was carried away [by Plat]o *to attendance at his teaching*.' All alternate restorations are
    taken from the *apparatus criticus* to *FGrHist*.
7   'He took . . . Atarneus and the territory nearby, [having done] *everything in a most
    unjust* . . . ' (Grenfell-Hunt).
8   Wendland.
9   The nephew of Aristotle, who, together with Aristotle, resided for a time at
    Atarneus and later went on Alexander's expedition as the official historian.
10 '[History]' (Diels-Schubart).
11 Cronert.

12   For Bagoas see no. 1(C).
13   For Mentor of Rhodes see no. 119 n. 8.

91   Alliance between Athens and Chalcis and the liberation of Oreus. 341.

A. Didymus, *Demosthenes* (18.79) col. 1.13f. (Philochorus, *FGrHist* 328F159).
B. Stephanus of Byzantium, *Ethnika s.v.* Oreus (Charax of Pergamum, *FGrHist* 103F19).
Cf. Dem. 9.57ff.; Aesch. 3.90ff.

SV 2.339, p. 328; G.L. Cawkwell, *CQ* 13 (1963) 210–13; P.A. Brunt, *CQ* 19 (1969) 251–65;
G.L. Cawkwell, *Phoenix* 32 (1978) 42–67; Hammond-Griffith 545–54 (Griffith).

A. Demosthenes 18.79

And first of all I proposed the embassy to the Peloponnese, when he
(Philip) was first attempting to slip into the Peloponnese; next, when
he was laying hands on Euboea, (I proposed) the embassy to Euboea;
then the expedition – no longer an embassy – to Oreus and the
(expedition) to Eretria, after he had established tyrants in those cities.

DIDYMUS, *DEMOSTHENES* COL. 1.13f.
[To these statements also the account in Philo]chorus bears witness.
For concerning the assistance *that went out* to [Oreus], under the head-
ing 'the archonship of Sos[i]ge[nes' (342/1), he says] *this*: 'The
Athenians *made* an alliance with the Chalcidians [and] together with
them liberated the people of Or[e]us during the month of
[Skirophor]ion, under the generalship of Kephisophon, and Phi[lis-
tid]es the tyrant died.'

B. Stephanus of Byzantium, *Ethnika s.v.* Oreus

Charax in the sixth (book) of his *Chronika*. 'The Athenians together
with the Chalcidians in Euboea and the Megarians made an expedition
against Oreus, killed the tyrant Philistides and liberated the people of
Oreus.'

92   Athenians under Phokion restore democracy to Eretria. 341.

Didymus, *Demosthenes* (18.79) col. 1.18ff. (Philochorus, *FGrHist* 328F160). *Jacoby,
FGrHist 3b. 144. Cf. Diod. 16.74.1 and no. 91.

Jacoby, *FGrHist* 3b.Suppl. 1.535–7; G.L. Cawkwell, *CQ* 13 (1963) 210–13; P.A. Brunt, *CQ* 19 (1969) 251–65; G.L. Cawkwell, *Phoenix* 32 (1978) 42–67; Hammond-Griffith 545–54 (Griffith).

Didymus, *Demosthenes* **(18.79) col. 1.18ff.**

Concerning (the assistance sent) to Eretria [once again] *the same author* (*sc.* Philochorus) says the following, under the heading 'the archonship of Nikomachos' (341/40): 'In this man's archonship[1] [the Ath]enians crossed over to Eretria under the leadership of Phokion [and], with a view to restoring the People, besieged Kleitarchos [who] had previously been the leader of the faction opposed to Ploutarchos[2] and his political rival, but had become tyrant, when he (Ploutarchos) was expelled. At this time the Athenians overcame him by siege and handed (control of) the city back to the People.[3]

1 Information listed under this rubric by the Atthidographers is usually taken to be the first event of the archonship (cf. no. 80 n. 1; no. 86 n. 3). Therefore, since the campaign against Philistides (no. 91) took place in the last month of the previous archonship, these two campaigns can be viewed as parts of a consistent Athenian policy in Euboea.
2 The former tyrant of Eretria, expelled by Phokion after the battle of Tamynae (349). Cf. Plut. *Phokion* 13.
3 A scholion on Aeschines 3.103 also records this campaign, but, since it adds no new information, it has not been translated here.

93 Foundation of the League of Greek states for defence against Philip II of Macedon. 340.

*[Plut.] *Lives of the Ten Orators* (= *Moralia* 851b). *SV* 2.343, pp. 331–2. Cf. Dem. 18.237; Aesch. 3.95f.

P.A. Brunt, *CQ* 19 (1969) 256ff.; H. Wankel, *Demosthenes: Rede für Ktesiphon über den Kranz* (Heidelberg 1976) 2.1050ff.; Cawkwell, *Philip* 133–5; Hammond-Griffith 549–51 (Griffith).

... And[1] because he brought into alliance with the People by persuasion and by his actions as benefactor and adviser, by means of which he persuaded (them), the Thebans, Euboeans, Corinthians, Megarians, Achaeans, Locrians, Byzantines and Messenians, and for the forces that he joined to the People and their allies, namely ten thousand foot soldiers and one thousand cavalry, and for (the) contribution of funds that by his efforts as ambassador he persuaded the allies to give for the war, (a contribution) of more than five hundred talents; ...

1   This extract is taken from a document in which Demochares, nephew of Demosthenes, requests that a bronze statue of Demosthenes be set up in the agora in
honour of Demosthenes, and that his descendants be maintained at public expense
in the Prytaneion and given the privilege of front seats in the theatre at public
festivals. The document dates from the second decade of the third century. It is the
first of three documents appended to the *Lives of the Ten Orators* and is generally
considered genuine. Cf. Plut. *Dem.* 30.5.

94   Athens honours Elaeus.[1] Athens, 340. Marble stele, Ionic letters, stoichedon.

IG II[2] 228; *Tod 174, pp. 218–19.

S. Casson, *Macedonia, Thrace and Illyria* (Oxford 1926) 210ff. (with a map on p. 211);
Hammond-Griffith 379–82 (Griffith).

In the archonship of Nikomachos (341/40), [when | P]andionis held the
seventh [prytan|y], on the twenty-ninth (day) of the pryt|any; of the
5   Proedroi (the one who) put (the motion) to the vot||e was Aristomachos
from Oion, Onesippo|s of Araphen was secretary. Resol|ved by the
People, Hippostratos, son of Etear|chides, of Pallene made the motion:
10   There shall be als|o for the Elaeusians the same privileges that || the
People have voted for the Chers[one]|sitai and the general Cha[res][2] |
shall take care of them in a *mann|er* that is identical, in order that,
possession being (guaranteed) for the [Ela]|eusians of their own prop-
15   erty, in a right and just || manner they may live with the Atheni[ans[3] in
the Ch]|ersonese. And invitation shall be issued to the [Ela]|eusians for
dinner[4] at [the Pry]|taneion for tomorrow.

1   Situated near the south tip of the Thracian Chersonese.
2   General in the Hellespont in this year.
3   The Athenian cleruchs.
4   An honour normally given to citizens.

95   Immediate causes of the outbreak of war between Athens and Philip II of Macedon. 340.

A. The attack on Perinthus and Byzantium. Dionysius of Halicarnassus, *To Ammaeus*
1.11.740f. (Philochorus, *FGrHist* 328F53–4). **B.** Philip's seizure of Athenian grain-ships.
Didymus, *Demosthenes* col. 10.34–11.5, on [Dem.] 11.1 (Theopompus, *FGrHist* 115F292;
Philochorus, *FGrHist* 328F162). **C.** The declaration of war. (1) Dionysius of Halicarnassus, *To Ammaeus* 1.11.741 (Philochorus, *FGrHist* 328F55a); (2) Didymus, *Demosthenes*
col. 1.67–2.2 (Philochorus, *FGrHist* 328F55b). Cf. [Dem.] 11 and 12, *passim*; Dem. 18.72,
87ff., 139, 240f.; Diod. 16.74.2–76.4 (siege of Perinthus and Byzantium), 16.77.2–3
(declaration of war).

Jacoby, *FGrHist* 3b.Suppl. 1.331, 537–9; Ellis, *Philip II* 175–85; Cawkwell, *Philip* 135–40; Hammond-Griffith 566–81 and Appendix 5 (Griffith); H. Wankel, *ZPE* 42 (1981) 159–66.

A. The attack on Perinthus and Byzantium.

DION. HAL. *TO AMMAEUS* 1.11.740f.

The causes through which they came to war, each one claiming the other was in the wrong, and the time at which they ended the peace, (these) are revealed in a detailed manner by Philochorus in the sixth book of his *Atthis*, but I shall mention only the most essential parts of his account. 'Theophrastos of Halai: In this man's archonship (340/39), Philip, after sailing up, at first attacked Perinthus, but meeting with no success (moved) from there to besiege Byzantium and brought up his siege-weapons.'

B. Philip's seizure of Athenian grain-ships.

[DEM.] 11.1

That Philip did not make peace, but rather kept on putting off the war has become clear to you all, men of Athens.

DIDYMUS, *DEMOSTHENES* COL. 10.34–11.5

The war of the Athenian[s] against the Macedonian was kindled [by] all Philip's other offences (relating to) the Athenians,[1] while he was pretending to be at peace, but especially his expedition against By[zan]tiu[m] and Perinthus (lacuna)[2] he was ambitious to bring over to his side for two reasons: to deprive the Athenians of their grain supply and (to ensure) that they (the Athenians) might not have coastal cities to provide bases for their fleet and places of refuge for the war against him. And (it was kindled) most when he perpetrated his most lawless act, by seizing the grain-merchants' ships that were at Hieron.[3] According to Philochorus (the ships) were two hundred and thirty (in number), according to Theopompus 180, and from these he gathered seven hundred talents.[4] Those things were done *the year before* in the archonship of Theophrastos who was archon after Nikomachos, as Philochorus in particular recounts in the following words: 'And Chares sailed away to a gathering of the royal generals, leaving warships at Hieron to see to the marshalling of the vessels from the Pontus. And Philip, observing that Chares was not present, at first attempted to send his warships to seize the transports, but, being unable to capture (them), he shipped his soldiers over to the other side against Hieron and became master of the transports. In total there were not less than two hundred and thirty vessels. And judging these to be prizes of war he broke them up and used the timbers for his siege-engines. In addition he came into possession of grain and hides and a great amount of money.'

C. The declaration of war

(1) DION. HAL. *TO AMMAEUS* 1.11.741
Next, after recounting all the charges Philip made against the Athenians by letter, he (Philochorus) goes on word for word as follows: 'When the People had heard the letter [and] Demosthenes had urged them to war and (himself) proposed the decree, they voted to destroy the stele that had been set up to record the peace and alliance with Philip, to man a fleet and to put themselves in all other respects on a wartime standing.'

(2) DIDYMUS, *DEMOSTHENES* COL. 1.67–2.2
Well [now], (as to the fact) that [it was in the time of Theophrasto]s, who held the archonship after Nikomachos, that [the stelai] *were destroyed*, it is *manifestly* sufficient (to quote) Phil[o]chorus, who writes as follows [in the course of his] sixth (book): 'When [the] People had heard [the letter], after Demosthenes had urged [them to] war and (himself) proposed the decree, *they voted* to destroy the stele that had been set up [to record the] peace *and* alliance with Philip, [to man] a fleet [and] *to put themselves* on a wartime standing.'

1 The text here is quite uncertain.
2 Blass restores in the lacuna '[stirred them up. These cities]'.
3 On the Thracian coast of the Propontis, near Perinthus.
4 This figure is possibly attributable to Theopompus.

96   The wooing of Thebes before the battle of Chaeronea. 340/39.

A. Dionysius of Halicarnassus, *To Ammaeus* 1.11.741f. (Philochorus, *FGrHist* 328F56a).
B. Didymus, *Demosthenes* (11.4) col. 11.37–51 (Philochorus, *FGrHist* 328F56b); *Jacoby, *FGrHist* 3b.115. Cf. Aesch. 3.140ff.; Dem. 18.168ff., 211; Diod. 16.84.2; Plut. *Demosthenes* 18.1.

Jacoby, *FGrHist* 3b.Suppl. 1.331–3; Ellis, *Philip II* 190–3; Cawkwell, *Philip* 140–4; Hammond-Griffith 585–95 (Griffith).

A. Dionysius of Halicarnassus, *To Ammaeus* 1.11.741f.

After describing these events that took place during Theophrastos' archonship, he (Philochorus) goes on to narrate the things that were done after the breaking of the peace in the year following during the archonship of Lysimachides (339/8). I shall mention only the most essential of these events also. 'Lysimachides of Acharnai: In this man's archonship they set aside the work related to the ship-sheds and the arsenal[1] because of the war against Philip and they voted that all funds be designated for military purposes, on the motion of Demosthenes. When Philip had seized Elateia and Kytinion and had sent[2] ambassadors from the Thessalians, the Aenianians, the Aetolians, the Dolopians and the Phthiotians to Thebes, and the Athenians about the same time had sent a delegation of ambassadors under Demosthenes (*sc.* to Thebes), they (the Thebans) voted to make alliance with the latter.'

B. [Dem.] 11.4

He is suspected by the Thebans because he holds Nicaea[3] with a garrison and has slipped into the Amphictyony . . .

DIDYMUS, *DEMOSTHENES* COL. 11.37–51
In the course of his sixth (book) Philoch[or]us says [that] Philip ordered it (*sc.* Nicaea) to be given back to the Lo[c]rians by the Thebans, as follows: 'When Phil[ip] *had seized* Elateia and Kytin[ion] and had sent[2] ambassadors from the The[ss]alians, the Aen[i]anians, the Aetolians, the Dolopians and the Phthiotians to Thebes and was demanding[2] that in accordance with the resolution of the Amphictyons they (the Thebans) give back to the Locrians Nicaea – a place that, though garrisoned by Philip, had been taken by the Thebans after they had expelled his garrison, when he was in Scythia – they (the Thebans) replied to those (ambassadors) that (they would send) an embassy to Philip to negotiate about all matters.'

1 The arsenal of Philon.
2 Keil (*ap. FGrHist* 3b.115) has suggested emending these three verbs to the plural form, which would make the Thessalians, etc. the subject.
3 A key fort by Thermopylae, long desired by the Thebans.

97 Athens honours the Tenedians. Athens, 340/39. Two fragments of a marble stele, Ionic letters, stoichedon (but lines 9 and 31, if rightly restored, have each one extra letter).

IG II^2 233; *Tod 175, pp. 219–23. Cf. Diod. 16.77.2.

Hammond-Griffith 579 (Griffith); Cargill, *League* 125–6, 185–6.

In *the archonship* of The[ophrastos (340/39), resolved by the People:
Ke]|kropi[s held the prytany]. *On the eighth* (day) [of the prytany]. Of
t|he Proedroi (the one who) put (the motion) to the vote (was) S[-16-
|-], the secretary was Aspetos, [son of Demostratos, of Kytheros,
5 || Ka]llikrates, son of Charopides, [of Lamptrai made the motion:[1]
Concern|ing] what the Tenedians report, [commendation shall be
given to the] *P|eople* of Tenedos [for their] *courage* [and goodwill]
| toward the People of A[thens and their] *alli|es*, both for their [assist-
10 ance] in the *past* [and for the assistance th||at] they have given [just
15 now -- |-] money [- |--- | (lacuna) --- |--- ||-] as much as [- |-] in the
archonship of Theophras[tos - |-] for the *assistance* [- |-] *everything*, let it
20 be resolved [by the People - |-] the [-] after Theophra[stos || the] *con-
tribution* that has been voted [- |-] and for the *current* [administration -
|- in] the year after [- |-][2] they shall restore to T[enedos.[3] - |-][4] these
25 things until they recover [- ||-.[5] During] this period *it shall* not *be permitted*
[for an exaction to be made] *e|ither* by a general or by anyone *at all*
[either of mon|ey] or of anything at all, nor to the *synedroi*[6] [shall it be
permitted] | to make an assessment[7] during *this* period, [until] *there is
30 re|covered* by the Tenedians *all* the money [that] *they len||t*, in order that
also for the future [time it may be known] | by the allies and anyone else
who [is well disposed to the] | People of Ath[e]ns that the People [of
Athens] *pay | heed* justly to those [of the] *alli|es who do* things that are
35 advantageous to the People [of Athens and] || to the allies. Commen-
dation shall be given [to the People of Te]|ned[o]s and [they] shall be
crowned [with a golden] *crow|n* worth one thousand drachmas [for their
excellence and] *goodwil|l* toward the People [of Athens and the] *all|ies*.
40 Commendation shall be given [to the synedros[8] of the Tenedia]||ns,
Ara[t]os, and [he shall be crowned with an olive] *crow|n. Commendation
shall also be given* [-- the] *s|ynedroi* [-- |---][9]

1 For this prescript see Henry, *Prescripts* 36.
2 Lines 11–24 are so badly preserved that they are hardly intelligible, though they are
   generally thought to refer to a loan made by Tenedos to Athens. See Tod, p. 221.
3 Or, 'shall restore them to T[enedos'.
4 Possibly to be restored '[They shall have] these things' (i.e. concessions or
   privileges).
5 Restored to read '[the money in tot||al]'.
6 The delegates to the Council of the Allies.
7 Or 'levy'. Cf. Cargill, *League* 125.
8 The delegate to the Council of the Allies.
9 Interpretation of this document is confused by the existence of another decree (*IG*
   II[2] 232) honouring Tenedos and its synedros, Aratos, together with his brothers and
   an unnamed Tenedian envoy. See Tod, pp. 222–3.

98   Epigram in honour of the Athenian dead at Chaeronea. Athens, 338. Fragment of a block of marble, Ionic letters, elegiac couplets, non-stoichedon. The lines of the inscription coincide with the lines of the poem.

IG II² 5226; *Tod 176, p. 223.

For the battle see Hammond-Griffith 596–603 (Griffith); H. Wankel, *ZPE* 21 (1976) 97–115.

[O] *Time*, [all-surveying deity] of all kinds of affairs for mortals,
[Be] *a messenger* to all men of our [sufferings],
[How striving to save the sacred land of Greece,
We died on the famed plains of the Boeotians.]¹

1   The restorations are based on the extant copy of this epigram in the Palatine Anthology 7.245. See *The Greek Anthology*, trans. W.R. Paton (Loeb Classical Library, Cambridge, Mass. 1970) 2.138–9.

99   Philip II's settlement in Greece: the 'League of Corinth'.¹ 338/7.

A. *IG* II² 236. Two fragments of a marble stele, Ionic letters, stoichedon (with irregularities), Athens. Tod 177, pp. 224–31; *SV* 3.403, pp. 3–7. B. Justin, *Epitoma* 9.5.1–6. Cf. Diod. 16.89.1–3; [Dem.] 17. *passim* (especially 6, 8, 10, 15, 16, 19); no. 138.

C. Roebuck, *CP* 93 (1948) 73–92; Ryder, *Eirene* 102–6, 150–62; Larsen, *Government* 47–65; T.T.B. Ryder, *CQ* 26 (1976) 85–7; Hammond-Griffith 623–46 (Griffith); Heisserer, *Alexander* 8–20 (with photographs of the fragments); M.T. Mitsos, *Arch. Eph.* 1900, 54–7.

A. *IG* II² 236

FRAGMENT A
[---² | Oath. I swear by Zeus, by Ge, by Helios, by Pose]idon, by
A[thena, | by Ares and by all Gods and Goddess]es. I shall abide [- | -³
5   and I shall not break the] treaty [- ‖ --⁴] nor *shall I bear* weapons [w|ith
harmful intent against any of those] who abide by t|he [oaths,⁵ either by
land] or by se|a; [and not a city nor a] *fort*⁶ shall I captu|re, [nor a harbour,
10   for the purpose of (making)] war, or any of those who ‖ *participate in the*
[peace],⁷ by any art | [or stratagem; nor] the kingdom of Ph|ilip and his]
descendants shall I overthrow, nor th|e [constitutions that were in exist-
ence] in each city, when they swore | *the* [oaths, concerning] *the* peace;
15   ‖ [nor shall I myself do anything] *contrary* to this | [treaty nor] shall I
allow *anyone else*⁸ so far as | (I have) [the power. And if anyone does

anything] in breach of | [the treaty, I shall give assistance] in accord-
ance with the *sum|mons* [of those who are wronged[9]] and I shall make
20   war upon th‖e one who *transgresses* [the common peace][10] in accordance
with | [whatever is resolved by the common] *council*[11] and (whatever)
the hegemo|n[12] [orders and] *I shall* [not] *desert the cause* -- | ---

FRAGMENT B

[--]: 5 | [---][13] Of the [Thes]salians: 10 [--]: 2 | [--] Of the [-]iotians:
5   1[14] ‖ [-- Of the Samothracians and[15]] Thasians: 2 | Of the [--]:[16] 2 Of
the Ambraciot[s: 1 | --] from Thrace and [--][17] Of the Phocians: 3 Of the
Locrians: 3 | [--][18] Of the [Oet]aeans and Malians and
10   ‖ [Aenianians -- and Ag]raeans[19] and Dolopians: 5 | [-- Pe]rrhae-
bians:[20] 2 [--- of Zacynthu]s[21] and Cephallenia: 3.

B. Justin, *Epitoma* 9.5.1–6

When affairs had been put in order in Greece, Philip bade envoys from
all the states to be called to Corinth to shape the condition of matters
at hand. There he established the law of universal peace for Greece on
the merits of the individual states and chose a council of all, as it were
one senate from them all. Only the Lacedaemonians spurned both the
king and the law, thinking it servitude not peace, since it was not to the
advantage of the states themselves, but was imposed by the victor.
Next the military levies of the individual states were assigned, whether
the king was to be helped by that force when someone was attacking or
whether war was to be declared under his leadership. For there was no
doubt that it was the empire of the Persians that was the object of these
preparations. The total of the military levies was 200,000 infantry and
15,000 cavalry.

1   After the battle of Chaeronea Philip concluded separate treaties with several
     states, especially the Athenians, with whom he contracted a peace and alliance
     (Diod. 16.87.3), on condition that their league be dissolved (Pausanias 1.25.3),
     though they kept their fleet, the islands of Samos (Diod. 18.56.7; Plut. *Alex.* 28.1),
     Lemnos, Imbros and Scyros (Aristotle, *Ath. Pol.* 61.6, 62.2) and gained Oropus
     (Pausanias 1.34.1). Next he settled affairs in the Peloponnese in a way that isolated
     Sparta. Then early in 337 he convoked a gathering of delegates from all over
     Greece at Corinth, which led to the establishment of what is now called the
     'League of Corinth'. See Hammond-Griffith 604–23 (Griffith).
2   The text of the treaty is lost.
3   Restorations include: '[by the alliance]' (Wilcken); '[by the peace]' (Schwahn);
     '[by the oaths] or [by the treaty]' (Calabi). These restorations and the others listed
     in the notes below are to be found in the *apparatus criticus* of *SV* 3, p. 5.
4   Restorations include: '[with Philip the Macedonian]' (Wilcken); '[made with
     Philip]' (Raue).

5   '*The* [peace]' (Köhler).
6   Wilhelm; '*place*' (Köhler).
7   '*Abide by the* [treaty]' (Raue).
8   '[I shall not do anything] *contrary* to the [treaty neither myself nor] shall I allow *anyone else*' (Köhler).
9   '[Of those who at the time request]' (Wilhelm); '[of the synedroi]' (Schwahn).
10 '[The common treaty]' (Schwahn); '[this treaty]' (Schehl); '[these oaths]' (Raue).
11 '[Whatever is enjoined upon] *me*' (Wilhelm).
12 For the alternate tradition that Philip was given the title 'general with absolute authority' see no. 1(C) col. 3.11. But see Hammond-Griffith 629–31.
13 '[Of the People of Corcyra: 2]' (Schwahn).
14 'Of the [Achaean Phth]iotians: 1' (Köhler); 'Of the [Elim]iotians: 1' (Wilhelm); '[Of the Achaean Phthiotians: 2] Of the *Islanders*: 1' (Schwahn).
15 '[Of the People of the Samothracians and]' (Schwahn); '[Of the Andrians: 2 Of the Parians and]' (Raue).
16 '[Of the Aetolians: 5] Of the [Acarnanians]' (Schwahn); '[Of the Naxians: 2] Of the [Acarnanians]' (Raue).
17 '[Of the cities] from Thrace and | [of the Chersonese:] *or* [The Chersonesitae] from Thrace and | [---]' (Wilhelm); '[Of the Chalcidians: 3] From Thrace and | [the Chersonese: 5]' (Schwahn); '[Of the Tenedians: 1 Of those] from Thrace and | [---]' (Raue); '[The Chersonesitae] from Thrace and | [the Cardians]' (Kahrstedt).
18 '[Of the Dorians and]' (Schwahn).
19 '[Of the Aemianians: 3 -- and Ag]raeans' (Wilhelm); '[Of the Aemianians and Ag]racans' (Schwahn); '[Of the Aetolians and Ag]raeans' (Raue).
20 '[Of the Athamanians and Per]rhaebians' (Schwahn); '[Of the Athamanians: 1 Per]rhaebians' (Raue).
21 '*Of the People* [of the Zacynthians]' (Schwahn); '[Of those from Zacynthu]s' (Raue).

100   Athens honours loyal Acarnanians. Athens, 337. Stele of Pentelic marble, Ionic letters, stoichedon (with irregularities in lines 35 and 37, and lines 38–40 short).

IG II^2 237+; *Tod 178, pp. 231–4. Cf. Diod. 17.3.3.

Pečiřka, *Enktesis* 49–51; Hammond-Griffith 613 (Griffith); M.J. Osborne, *ZPE* 42 (1981) 171–2.

[In] the archonship of [Chairon]das (338/7), [when Pandionis (held)] *the ten|th prytany*, in which Ph[---]^1 | *was secretary*, [on the 27th of] Tharge[lion],^{2} *on the th|ird* (day) of the prytany. Of the [Proedroi] (the
5   one who) put (the motion) to the vote (was) [-- || --] of Erchia. Resolved by the [People, Hege]sippos,^{3} [son of Hegesia|s], of [Souni]on made the motion: Concerning the matters reported by the A[carna]nians, [Pho|rmi]on and Karphinas, who have recently *arrived*, let it be resolved [by the] | People, since Phormion and Kar[phi]nas, being *ancestral|ly*
10 *friends* of the People of Athens, maintain [th||e] goodwill that their ancestors handed on to them toward [th|e] People of Athens, and just

recently, having given assistance with a (military) f|orce,[4] they ranged themselves beside the Athenian[s] in accordance with the g|eneral's orders, commendation shall be given to them for (their) excellence

15 | and each of them shall be crowned with a golden cro‖wn. Since Phor[m]ion,[5] Phormion's and Kar[ph]in[as'] | *grandfather*, was made *v* an Athenian by the People of Athens along | with his descendants, and (since) the decree, by which the gra|nt was made, has been inscribed (and set up) on the Acropolis, *there shall be* for Phor|[m]ion and

20 Karphi[nas] and their descendants confirmatio‖n *of the privilege* that the People *gave* to Phormion, their grand|father. *v* They *shall choose* the tribe and the deme and *phra|try* [to which] *they want* to belong. Commendation shall also be given to the | *other* [A]c[a]r[nanians] who gave assistance along with Phormio|[n] and [Ka]rph[inas and] they shall have, until

25 such time as they return hom‖e, [the right of possession of whatever] *houses* they wish, while they live at Athen|[s,[6] free from liability to the] *metics' tax*, and they shall pay penalties | [and exact them][7] *just like* Athenian[s], and as for capital levies, | [if any] *occur*, they shall pay (these) with the Athenians and | [care shall be taken] *of them* by the

30 Boule that is on any occasion in offic‖e and by the generals who on any occasion hold that office, in order that | [they may not] *be wronged.* *Inscription shall be made* of this decree on a st|ele of marble by the *secretary* of the Boule and it shall be set up | [on] the Acropolis. Inscription shall also be made of the names of the Acar|[nan]ians on the same *stele* (and)

35 beneath shall be written the citie‖s of Acarnan[ia to which] *each* [one] belongs. For the *in|scription* of the *stele* [there shall be given] by the treasurer of the People to the | [secretary] *of the* [Boule] *thirty* drachmas from the (money) | [that is spent] *by the People* on [decrees].[8]

       Phormion (was crowned)   Karphinas (was crowned)

40   By the People   By the People[9]

1   The secretary's name is restored by Stamires (*Hesperia* 26 (1957) 243) as Philippos, son of Antiphemos, of Eiresidai.
2   The first known case where both the name and day of the month is given in a prescript. The actual figures depend on restoration. Cf. Henry, *Prescripts* 38.
3   For Hegesippos cf. no. 66 n. 2.
4   Usually taken as a reference to an Acarnanian contingent at the battle of Chaeronea, although there is no reference to one in our literary sources.
5   It is possible that this Phormion was named after the famous Athenian general of that name, who was very popular in Acarnania. Cf. Thuc. 3.7.1.
6   As refugees.
7   I.e. have parity with Athenian citizens in the courts.
8   Following Tod's text. See Osborne for a redistribution of line 38 over three very short lines at the left hand edge, with the entries 'Phormion | By the People' and 'Karphinas | By the People' to their right.

9   The list of names of the other Acarnanians is lost. The names of Phormion and
Karphinas are inserted between crowns.

101   Athenian law against tyranny. Athens, 337/6. Marble stele (surmounted by a relief representing Democracy about to crown the People of Athens), Ionic letters, stoichedon.

B.D. Meritt, *Hesperia* 21 (1952) 355–9; *Pouilloux, *Choix* 32, pp. 121–4.

M. Ostwald, *TAPA* 86 (1955) 103–28; R. Sealey, *AJP* 79 (1958) 71–3; C. Mossé, *Eirene* 8 (1970) 71–8; MacDowell, *Law* 175–86.

In the archonship of Phrynichos (337/6), when Leontis (held) the n|inth
prytany, in which Chaerestratos, son of Ameinias, | of Acharnai was
secretary. Of the Proedroi (the one who) put (the motion) to the v|ote
5   (was) Menestratos of Aixone. Eukrates,[1] son of Aris‖totimos, of
Peiraeus made the motion: With good fortune for the P|eople of
Athens. Let it be resolved by the Nomothet|ai:[2] If anyone revolts
against the People for the purpose (of establishing) a tyranny | or joins
in setting up a tyranny, or the People | of Athens or the democracy at
10   Athens ‖ (if anyone) overthrows, (in the case of) the man who has com-
mitted any of these (crimes), whoever k|ills (him) shall be free from
prosecution. It shall not be permitted for (any) of the councill|ors of the
Council of the Areopagus, if an over|throw of the People has occurred
or of the democracy at Ath|ens, to go up onto the Areopagus or to sit
15   ‖ together in the Council or to deliberate, not | even about one matter.
And if anyone, (at a time) when the People or the democr|acy at Athens
has been overthrown, goes up, (anyone) of th|e councillors of the
Areopagus (that is), onto the Areop|agus or sits together in the Council
20   or deliberat‖es about anything, he shall lose his citizen-rights, both
himself and the offspring | of his body, and his property shall be confis-
cated | and the Goddess shall have the tithe. Inscription shall be made
of th|is law on two marble stelai by the s|ecretary of the Boule and they
25   shall be set up, the one by t‖he entry to the Areopagus that (leads) into
the co|uncil-chamber as one enters, the other in the assembl|y. For the
inscription of the stelai the treasurer | of the People shall give 20
drachmas from the money that on de|crees is spent by the People. *vv*
30   ‖ *vacat.*

1   Most likely the Eukrates who died in 322 along with Hypereides and other leaders
of the Athenian resistance to Macedon. Cf. Lucian, *Encomium on Demosthenes* 31.
2   A board of officials, to whom, in the fourth century, all proposals for new laws
(nomoi) or for alterations to existing laws had to be referred from the Assembly.
Their decision on the proposal was final. See MacDowell, *Law* 48–9. Cf. no. 45.

102 Renewal of the treaty between Macedon and the Greeks by Alexander the Great *or* Alliance between Alexander and Athens. Athens (336/5). Fragment of a marble stele, Ionic letters, stoichedon.

IG II² 329+; Tod 183, pp. 240–1; *SV* 3.403, pp. 7–10; *Heisserer, *Alexander* 4–8 (with a photograph, line drawing and epigraphic commentary). Cf. no. 99; Diod. 17.4.9; Arrian, *Anab.* 1.1.2; Plut. *Alex.* 14.1; [Dem.] 17, *passim*.

J.A.O. Larsen, *CP* 20 (1925) 316–17; Parke, *Soldiers* 186 n. 5, 223 n. 1; G.T. Griffith, *The Mercenaries of the Hellenistic World* (Cambridge 1935) 297ff.; Ryder, *Eirene* 156–7; W.K. Pritchett, *Ancient Greek Military Practices* (Berkeley and Los Angeles 1971) 1.21; Hammond-Griffith 626–30 (Griffith); Heisserer, *Alexander* 3–24.

5 [--- | --- | -] escort [-]¹ | shall provide grain [--] *shall pr‖ovide for* each man [-- | -] as many as *come*. But if [-- | -].² *Whence the grain* shall be acquired
10 [- | -] Alexander [- | -] to a hypaspist a drachma and to the [- | ‖ -] for each day. *Shall discharge* [-- | -]³ may use the force if any [--]⁴ | after giving grain for *ten* days *shall discharge* [the soldiers. --] *w|atch*⁵ shall set up at Pydna in the (temple) of Athe[na --] |

1 '[Shall take care of the] escort [of the grain]' (Heisserer).
2 '*Provision-money*' (Heisserer).
3 '[The summoning] *cities*' or '[All the states that participate in the] *peace*' (Heisserer).
4 'If any [ally has need of assistance for a longer time]' or 'If any [ally, having need of assistance for a longer time, sends for (it)]' (Heisserer).
5 '[These terms shall be inscribed on a marble stele by those appointed to the common] *watch* and shall be set up' (Wilhelm, followed by Tod, Schmitt (*SV*) and Heisserer).

103 Priene honours Antigonos Monophthalmos.¹ Priene, ?334. Marble stele, Ionic letters, unornamental script, non-stoichedon.

SIG 278; F. Hiller von Gaertringen, *Inschriften von Priene* (Berlin 1906) 2; *Tod 186, pp. 244–6.

Wehrli, *Antigone* 30.

[Resolved] by the *Council* [and the People, in the month | of Met]ageitnion, on the second (day), | when a *principal* meeting of the assembly was held, at a time when autonomy | was in existence for the Prienians,
5 in the presidency of Hippo[kra‖tes]: To Antigonos, son of Philippos, the Macedonian, | since he has been a benefactor and shown himself zealous | in the interests of the city of Priene, there shall be given | to him proxeny and citizenship and | the privilege of possession of land
10 and a house, and exemption from all taxation ‖ in all respects that relate to his household with the exception of the land, | and freedom to import

and export both in time of war | and in time of peace without violation
and without formal treaty, and acc|ess to the magistrates and the
People of Pri[e]|ne first after the sacrifices. These privileges shall be
15 || both his and his descendants'.

1   Antigonos was one of Philip's generals, who led the allied contingent in Alexander's
    expedition (Arrian 1.29.3). On his way to Gordium in the winter of 334/3 Alexander
    made Antigonos satrap of Phrygia (Arrian, *ibid.*). Antigonos is mentioned nowhere
    else in Arrian's *Anabasis*, though he clearly played a useful part in keeping Alexan-
    der's lines of communications open against Persian attacks (cf. Curtius 4.1.35).
    After Alexander's death he emerged as one of the most powerful 'Successors', along
    with his son Demetrios the Besieger. He died in 301 at the battle of Ipsus (see no.
    140).

**104   Delphi honours Aristotle and Kallisthenes. Delphi, between
334 and 331 *or* 327.**[1] Fragment of a marble stele, Ionic letters,
stoichedon (except for the second surviving line, if correctly restored).

SIG 275; *Tod 187, pp. 246–8. Cf. Diogenes Laertius 5.26; Plut. *Solon* 11.1.

Jacoby, *FGrHist* 124T23, *FGrHist* 2b. (Commentary) 414; A.B. Bosworth, *Historia* 19
(1970) 407–13.

[-][2] *compiled* [a tabl|e] of those who *from* [the archonship of Gylidas*[3]*] *had
| been victors* in the [Pythian Games] | and of those (by whom) from (the)
5   *beginning th||e* contest had been organ|ized,[4] commendation shall be
    given | to Aristotle and [K]|al[li]sthenes and (they) shall | be crowned.
10 *Dedication shall be m||ade* of the *table by th|e* treasurers [in the te|mple], *after
    it has been transcr|ibed* [onto stelai --] |

1   *SIG* 252.42f. (= *Fouilles de Delphes* 3(5)58.42f.) reads: 'To Deinomacho[s], for the
    inscription of the victors' list of the Pythian Games, on the orders | of the hieromne-
    mons, two minai.' This confirms that a victors' list was inscribed. The inscription is
    dated to the archonship of Kaphis (331/30 or 327/6).
2   The immediately preceding lines are restored *exempli gratia* by Homolle (*BCH* 22
    (1898) 260ff.) as follows: '[-- since Aristotle, son of Niko|machos, of Stageira | and
    Kallisthenes, son of D|amotimos, of Olynthu|s]'.
3   591/90. Cf. Fornara 16(D). Witkowsky (*ap.* Tod, p. 247) restores: 'of those who *in
    both had | been victors* . . . ' 'Both' could refer either to the musical and gymnastic
    contests or to the penteteric and annual Pythian Games.
4   Presumably the agonothetai.

**105   Alexander dedicates the temple of Athena Polias at Priene.
Priene, 334/3 *or* 330.** Marble block, Attic/Ionic dialectal forms, non-
stoichedon.

F. Hiller von Gaertringen, *Inschriften von Priene* (Berlin 1906) 156; Tod 184, pp. 241–2;
*Heisserer, *Alexander* 142–5 (with a photograph on p. 143).

E. Badian, *Ehrenberg Studies* 47; Heisserer, *Alexander* 156–8.

King Alexander | dedicated the temple | to Athena Polias.

106   Alexander's regulations for Priene and Naulochum. Priene, 334/3 *or* 330.

Sixteen fragments of marble from the south anta of the Temple of Athena Polias immediately below no. 103, large clear lettering with slight serifs, Koine, non-stoichedon.

F. Hiller von Gaertringen, *Inschriften von Priene* (Berlin 1906) 1; Tod 185, pp. 243–4;
*Heisserer, *Alexander* 145–56 (with a line drawing and photographs of the fragments).

E. Badian, *Ehrenberg Studies* 47–9; D. van Berchem, *MH* 27 (1970) 198–205; Heisserer,
Alexander 156–8.

From King Al[exand]er.[1] | Of those who in Naulochum[2] *are resid|ing*, all
5 who are [Prienian]s auto|nomous shall be and *free*, ‖ possessing the [land]
and the hous|es in *the* city, all (the houses), and the | countryside, *just like*
[the] Prieni[ans themselves. | --] in which *they want* [-].[3] | But the [-- of
10 the] Myrs[eloi][4] ‖ and P[edieis[5] the land and the neighbouring]
countryside | I judge to belong to me, and those who r|eside in the
villages ment|ioned shall pay the tribute. From the | contribution I
15 release the Prie‖nians' city and the garrison [- | --] shall introduce [- | ---
20 | -] the lawsuits [- | --] you ‖ [--] law court | [--] but us [- | --] you [-] |

1   These letters are spaced across the stele more widely apart than the rest of the text,
    so that they form a heading.
2   The site has not been identified, but Naulochum is usually considered to have been
    the harbour of Priene.
3   Other restorations punctuate after 'countryside' and read either: '[But] *all those who*
    [are not] Prieni[ans] *shall live* | [in the villages], in which *they* [themselves] *want*' (von
    Prott); or: '[But] the Prieni[ans amongst those who live in | the villages], in which
    they want, (shall be) [free from taxation]' (Hicks). For von Prott see Hiller; for Hicks
    see Heisserer 242.
4   The restoration here is quite hypothetical. For a discussion of the alternatives see
    Heisserer 156.
5   The Pedieis were a non-Greek tribe that lived in the lower Maeander valley.

107   Alexander's letter to the Chians. Chios, 334/3 *or* 332.

Stele of grey limestone, Ionic letters and dialect, non-stoichedon.

SIG 283+; Tod 192, pp. 263–7; *Heisserer, *Alexander* 79–83 (with a photograph p. 82).

Cf. Arrian, *Anab.* 1.17.10, 1.18.2, 2.1.1, 2.1.4, 3.2.3ff.; Curtius 3.1.19–20, 4.5.15ff., 4.8.12; Diod. 16.89, 91.2, 17.2.4, 5–6, 17.29.2.

E. Badian, *Ehrenberg Studies* 48–53; A.J. Heisserer, *Historia* 22 (1973) 191–204; H. Hauben, *AncSoc* 7 (1976) 82–6; Heisserer, *Alexander* 83–95.

In the presidency of Deisitheos, from King Ale[xande]r [to the] Chia[n] | People. | All those (who have been) in exile from Chios shall return home; the constitution (that) shall ex|ist in Chios (shall be) demo-
5   cratic. Law-writers shall be chosen to wr‖ite and correct the laws in order that nothing oppos|ed to the democracy or the return of the exiles may be (in them). Whatever has been co|rrected or written shall be referred to Alexander. | The Chians shall provide twenty manned triremes at their | own expense, and these (triremes) shall sail as long
10   as the rest of the flee‖t of the Hellenes sails with us. Of those who betrayed | the city to the barbarians, all those who have escaped shall have banishment imposed | upon them from all the cities that partici-pate in the pea|ce and shall be liable to seizure in accordance with the resolution of the Hellenes; all those | who were left behind shall be
15   brought back and judged in the Hel‖lenes' council. If there is any dis-pute between those who have re|turned and those in the city, those people (in disagreement) shall be judged on this matter in | our court. Until the Chians are reconciled, there shall be a garrison in their midst supplied by | Ale[x]ander the king, of a size that is adequate. Support | for this (garrison) shall be given by the Chians. *vv* |[1]

1   Four fragments of a 'Second letter of Alexander to the Chians' have been found, though two are now lost. For a line drawing, photograph, commentary and historical discussion of this fragmentary document see A.J. Heisserer, *Alexander* 96–111. Heisserer offers a tentative translation on p. 108.

108   Dedication of the ephebes of the tribe Kekropis. Athens, 334/3. Marble stele, Ionic letters, stoichedon.[1]

IG II² 1156; *O.W. Reinmuth, *The Ephebic Inscriptions of the Fourth Century B.C.* (Leiden 1971) 2, pp. 5–10. Cf. Aesch. 2.167; Aristotle, *Ath. Pol.* 42.2–5; and no. 109.

Ch. Pélékides, *Histoire de l'éphébie attique* (Paris 1962) 120–3; F.W. Mitchel, *Greece and Rome* 12 (1965) 189–204; esp. 197–8; O.W. Reinmuth, *Acta of the 5th Epigraphic Congress Cambridge 1967* (Oxford 1971) 47–51; O.W. Reinmuth, *The Ephebic Inscriptions of the Fourth Century B.C.* (Leiden 1971) 123–38; Mitchel, 'Athens' 37–9; P. Rhodes, *ZPE* 38 (1980) 191–201.

Kallikrates of Aixone made the motion: Since the ephebes of

Kekr[opi]│s during the archonship of [Kte]s[i]kles (334/3) are behaving in an orderly manner and are performing │ all the duties that are enjoined upon them by the laws and to their tribal *supervis*│*or*[2] are obedient, the one who was elected by the *People*, commendation shall be
30   giv║en to them and they shall be crowned with a golden crown worth [500] *drachmas* │ for their orderliness and discipline. Commendation shall also be given to their super│visor, Adeistos, son of Antimachos, of Athmonon and he shall be crowned with a golden │ crown worth 500 drachmas, because in a good and public-spirited manner he took care │ of the ephebes of the tribe Kekropis. Inscription shall be made of this
35   dec║ree on a marble stele and it shall be set up in the temple of Kekrops. │ Hegemachos, son of Chairemon, of Perithoidai made the motion: Since the ephebes │ of the tribe Kekropis, who were stationed at Eleusis,[3] in a good and public-spirited manner are t│aking care of the things that are enjoined upon them by the Boule and the People and in a well-d│isciplined manner are deporting themselves, commendation
40   shall be given to them for their orderliness ║ and for their discipline and they shall be crowned with a crown of an olive-branch, *each one* │ of them. Commendation shall also be given to their supervisor, Adeist[os], son of [Anti]│machos, of Athmonon and he shall be crowned with a crown of an olive branch, when │ he has undergone his review. Inscription shall be made of this decree on the *dedication* │ that the ephebes of
45   Kekropis are setting up. *vv* ║ Protias made the motion: Let it be voted by the demesmen, since in a good and pu│blic-spirited manner care is being taken of the guard at Eleusis by [Kekropi]│s' *ephebes* and by their supervisor, Adeistos, [son of An]ti[m]a[chos, of Athmo│non], commendation shall be given to them and each one of them shall be crowned [with an olive-branch │ crown]. Inscription shall be made of this decree
50   on the dedication [that] is ║ being set up by those who were ephebes of Kekropis during Ktesikle[s]' │ archonship. *vv* │ Euphronios made the motion: Let it be voted by the demesmen, since the [ephebes] │ who were registered during the archonship of Ktesikles are behaving in an orderly manner [and] │ are performing all the duties that are enjoined
55   upon them by the laws, and (since) the su║pervisor who was elected by the People reveals that they │ are obedient and are performing all other duties in a public-spirited manner, comm│endation shall be given to them and they shall be crowned with a golden crown worth 500 drachm│as for their orderliness and discipline. Commendation shall also be given to the │ supervisor of them, Adeistos, son of Antimachos,
60   of Athmonon, and he shall be cr║own(ed with a golden crown worth) 500 drachmas, because in a good and public-spirited manner he to│ok care of both the demesmen (and) all (the) others from Kekropis │ tribe. Inscription shall be made of this decree on the dedication that is being

| set up by the ephebes of Kekropis and their supervisor.[4] *vv* |
The tribe   The Boule   The Eleusinians   The Athmoneans

1   The inscription contains four honorific decrees passed respectively by the four
    bodies listed at its conclusion, in the order in which they are listed. The first twenty-
    five lines, which have not been translated, contained a list in two columns of the
    ephebes involved. There are thirty names partly or wholly preserved from seven
    demes. Fifteen lines are missing. Since four demes are not represented, there is
    room for their names and those of eleven more ephebes. That is, however, if all
    demes were represented, which was not always the case. Estimates of the total of
    ephebes range from 41 to 60. See Reinmuth, *Ephebic Inscriptions*, p. 7.
2   The Sophronistes. There were ten of these, one for each tribe, chosen by the People.
    See Arist. *Ath. Pol.* 42.2.
3   Aristotle (*Ath. Pol.* 42 3) mentions only Munychia and Akte as places where the
    ephebes did guard-duty, but this inscription and a similar decree for the ephebes of
    Hippothontis of the same year make it clear that they were also stationed at Eleusis
    at the beginning of the Sacred Way.
4   This inscription is the oldest ephebic dedication known to date and is often used as
    evidence for the date of institution of the ephebeia. Those who believe that the
    ephebeia was a Lykourgan institution often refer to a law of Epikrates, the evidence
    for which is Harpocration, *Lexicon s.v.* Epikrates, which reads: 'There is another
    Epikrates who is mentioned by Lycurgus in the (speech) *On Administration*, where he
    says that a bronze statue (of him) was set up on account of his law about the ephebes;
    and they say that he possessed a property worth six hundred talents.' Cf. Davies,
    Families 4909.

109   Oath of the Athenian ephebes.[1]

A. The stele from Acharnai.[2] Athens, 4th century. Marble stele (with a pediment on
which is represented a hoplite's defensive armour), Ionic letters, stoichedon (except
lines 1–4, which form a heading). Tod 204, pp. 303–6; *G. Daux, 'Deux stèles
d'Acharnes', in *Charisterion A. Orlandos* (Athens 1965) 1,78–84 (with a photograph facing
p. 80). **B.** Pollux, *Onomastikon* 8.105–6. **C.** Stobaeus, *Florilegium* 43.48. Cf. Dem. 19.303;
Lycurgus, *Against Leokrates* 76; Plut. *Alkibiades* 15.6; no. 108 (above) and Fornara 57, pp.
55–6.

C. Pélékidis, *Histoire de l'éphébie attique* (Paris 1962) 75–8, 113; O.W. Reinmuth, *The
Ephebic Inscriptions of the Fourth Century B.C.* (Leiden 1971) 136; N. Robertson, *Historical
Reflections* 3 (1976) 3–24; P. Siewert, *JHS* 97 (1977) 102–11.

A. The stele from Acharnai

Gods. | The priest of Ares[3] and Athena | Arcia,[4] Dion, son of Dion, of
5   Achar|nai made the dedication. || The ancestral oath of the ephebes,
    which must be sworn by t|he ephebes. *vv* I shall not disgrace the sacred
    wea|pons (that I bear) nor shall I desert the comrade at my side, wher-
    ever I s|tand in the line. And I shall fight in defence of things sacred and
    se|cular and I shall not hand down (to my descendants) a lessened

10   fatherla‖nd, but one that is increased in size and strength both as far as
      in me lies an|d with the assistance of all, and I shall be obedient to those
      who on any occasion are g|overning prudently and to the laws that | are
      established and any that in the future may be estab|lished prudently. If
15   anyone tries to destroy (them), I shall r‖esist both as far as in me lies
      and with the assistance of al|l, and I shall honour the sacred rites that
      are ancestral. The witnesses | (are) the Gods Aglauros, Hestia, Enyo,
      Enyalios, Ar|es and Athena Areia, Zeus, Thallo, Auxo, | Hegemone,
20   Herakles,[5] (and) the boundaries of my fatherland, the wheat, ‖ the
      barley, the vines, the olives, the figs.[6] *vv*

B. Pollux, *Onomastikon* 8.105–6

Men on patrol. The ephebes went around the countryside doing guard-
duty, practising, as it were, to be soldiers. And they entered the (state
of being) ephebes when they became eighteen years old, for two years
they were numbered among the patrolmen and on attaining their twentieth (year) they were registered on the lexiarchic list and swore in the
temple of Agraulos[7] the (following) oath: I shall not disgrace the
weapons nor shall I abandon the comrade at my side, with whom I
stand in line. I shall fight in defence of things sacred and secular, both
alone and in the company of many, and I shall hand down (to my
descendants) a fatherland that is not lessened, but I shall go to sea
[and] shall plough up all the land I received by inheritance. I shall
hearken to those who on any occasion are making decisions and I shall
obey the established laws and any other (laws) the People establish
prudently. And if anyone tries to destroy the laws, or does not obey
(them), I shall resist (him) and I shall fight in (their) defence, both
alone and with the assistance of all, and I shall honour the sacred rites
that are ancestral. The witnesses (are) the Gods Agraulos, Enyalios,
Ares, Zeus, Thallo, Auxo, Hegemone.

C. Stobaeus, *Florilegium* 43.48

Oath of the ephebes at Athens. I shall not disgrace the sacred weapons
(that I bear) nor shall I leave in the lurch the comrade at my side, with
whom I stand in line. I shall fight in defence of things sacred and secular
both alone and in the company of many. I shall hand down (to my
descendants) a fatherland that is not lessened, but greater in size and
strength than the one I received by inheritance. And I shall be obedient
to those who on any occasion are making decisions prudently and I
shall obey the laws that are established and any others that the People
establish in agreement. And if anyone tries to destroy the laws or does

not obey (them), I shall resist (him) and I shall fight in (their) defence, both alone and with the assistance of all. And I shall honour the sacred rites that are ancestral. The witnesses of these (oaths are) the Gods.

1   I have left this document undated because there are two separate questions involved, the date at which the oath was introduced and the date of the inscription (A), from which B and C are derived. The date of the introduction of the oath is, of course, closely associated with the institution of the ephebeia (no. 108), which some have traced back to the fifth century (see now the article by Siewert). The inscription belongs to the second half of the fourth century, but cannot be dated any more precisely. For these reasons I have placed this document next to 108.
2   Beneath this document, on the same stele, is the oath of the Athenians sworn before the battle of Plataea, Fornara 57.
3   The stele must have stood in the sanctuary of Ares at Acharnai.
4   Ares and Athena Areia are associated in several other inscriptions.
5   For the Gods invoked as witnesses see Tod 305–6 and Daux 83–4.
6   A distorted echo of this list of impersonal witnesses is found in Plut. *Alkibiades* 15.7f.
7   The same spelling is found in Plut. *Alkibiades* 15.7, but the inscriptions and most authors read Aglauros.

110   Philonides, courier and surveyor for Alexander. Olympia, after 334. Statue base of limestone, occasional Doric spelling, non-stoichedon.

SIG 303; *Tod 188, p. 249. Cf. Pausanias 6.16.5; Pliny, *NH* 2.181, 7.84.

J.G. Frazer, *Pausanias' Description of Greece* (London 1898) 4.48–9; Hamilton, *Alexander* 55; N.G.L. Hammond, *Alexander the Great* (London 1981) 28, 67, 97, 172, 177.

King Alex[ander's] | courier[1] and | surveyor[2] of Asia, | Philonides, son
5   of Zoites, a Cretan || from Chersonesus,[3] dedicated (this) | to Olympian Zeus.

1   Hemerodromes or hemerodromos means 'day-runner' or 'long-distance runner'. Cf. Herodotus 6.105, 9.12; Livy 31.24.
2   Bematistes means literally 'stepper' or 'route-measurer'. Cf. Athenaeus 10.442b; Pliny, *NH* 6.61, 6.69, 7.11; Diog. Laert. 2.4.17.
3   A town on the north coast of Crete, east of Cnossus.

111   Athens grants Citian merchants a plot of land for building a temple. Peiraeus, 333. Marble stele, fourth-century letter-forms, Ionic spelling (with inconsistencies), stoichedon.

IG II² 337+; *Tod 189, pp. 250–2.

Pečířka, *Enktesis* 59–61; Mitchel 'Athens' 32–3.

Gods. | In Nikokrates' archonsh|ip (333/2), when Aigeis (held) the
5   firs|t prytany.[1] Of the Proed‖roi (the one who) put (the motion) to the
vote (was) Theophilo|s of Phegous. Resolved by the B|oule, Antidotos,
son of Apollo|doros, of Sypalettos made the motio|n: Concerning the
10   request of the Cit‖ians regarding the foundation | of the temple to
Aphrodite,[2] | let it be resolved by the Boule that th|e Proedroi, whoever
15   are chosen by lo|t to be Proedroi, at the fi‖rst assembly shall introd|uce
them and transact the busi|ness, and that the opinion shall be com-
municat|ed, (the opinion) of the Boule, to the Pe|ople that it seems
20   good to the Boule ‖ that the People, when they have heard from the
| Citians about the found|ation of the temple and from any other | of the
25   Athenians who wishe|s, shall decide whatever to th‖em seems to be
best.[3] | In Nikokrates' archonsh|ip, when Pandionis (held) the s|econd
prytany. Of the | Proedroi (the one who) put (the motion) to the vote
30   (was) Pha‖nostratos of Philaidai. Reso|lved by the People. Lykourgos,
son of L|ykophron, of Boutadai[4] made the mot|ion: Concerning the
matters that the merchants (that is, the) C|itians have decided to make
35   a lawful su‖pplication in requesting from the P|eople the privilege of
possession of a plot on | which to build a temple of Aphr|odite, let it be
40   resolved by the Peop|le that there shall be given to the merchants ‖ from
Citium the privilege of possession of a pl|ot on which to build the
| temple of Aphrodite, just | as also by the Egyptians the | temple of Isis
45   has been buil‖t.[5]

1   The absence of the secretary's name and of any directions at the end of the decree
for its inscription suggests that it was not set up by the state, but by the Citians at
their own expense. Cf. Tod, p. 251, and Henry, *Prescripts* 43.
2   Aphrodite was early associated with Cyprus. Cf. Hesiod, *Theogony* 188–200. The
Citians most likely worshipped her as Heavenly Aphrodite. Cf. Plato, *Symposium*
180de.
3   This is the end of the first part of the inscription, which, in essence, represents a
referral of the decision by the Boule to the Assembly. The decision of the People
follows.
4   The famous orator, politician and financier, who guided Athens through the years
immediately following the battle of Chaeronea. See Mitchel, *passim* and especially
11–13; Davies, *Families* 9251.
5   Tod accepts as a possibility the suggestion that Lykourgos' grandfather was 'instru-
mental in the founding of the temple of Isis'. But see Pečiřka 60–1.

**112   Six documents relating to the tyrants of Eresus. Eresus, *c.* 332
(A–B), 324/3 (C), 323/2 *or* 319 (D), 306/5 (E) and 301/0 (F).** Two
fragments of two separate marble stelai; Aeolic dialect (with some
Koine), Ionic letters, stoichedon (fr. 1), stoichedon, with irregularities
arising largely from the observance of syllabic division (fr. 2).

IG XII 2.526; Welles, *RCHP* 2, pp. 12–14; Tod 191, pp. 253–63; *Heisserer, *Alexander* 27–58. Cf. [Dem.] 17.7; Diod. 16.91.2, 17.7.8, 18.56.1–8; Arrian, *Anab.* 1.11.6, 1.17.10–12, 1.18.2, 2.1.5, 3.2.4, 3.2.7; Curtius 4.5.19; and cf. nos. 107 and 113.

E. Badian, *Ehrenberg Studies* 41–53; Hamilton, *Alexander* 75; Heisserer, *Alexander* 58–78 (bibliography on pp. 239–40).

A. Fragment 1.[1] The trial of Eurysilaos

vacat | he *stripped* (the citizens) of their weapons [and] | he excluded
5   (them) from the *ci*|*ty* en masse; their | wives and *their* || daughters he
    seized, | imprisoned on the acropo|lis, and he exacted | two thousand
10 and three | hundred staters; the || city and the temples he pi|llaged with
    his | pirates and burned down, | and (he) burned along with them | the
15 bodies of the citizens. || He shall be tried | by a secret vote *in accord*|*ance*
20 with the edict of the | King Alexand[er] | and the laws. [And if] ||there is
    voted [again|st] him the death penalty, after a counter-|proposal (for
    punishment) has been put forward by Eury[si|l]aos,[2] the second
25 *judge*|*ment* shall be made by || show of hands, (to indicate) in what | way
    he ought | to die. There shall be obtained | in addition advocates by the
30 | city, ten (in number), who, || after swearing an oath to Appol[l|o]
    Lykeios, all together shall act | as advocates [for the city as] | *well* as *they
    are able* [-- | ---]

B. Fragment 2 (front face). The trial of Agonippos

[-- those] *who had been besieged* | [on the] *acropolis* he [--][3] and from the
    ci|*tizens* he exacted twenty thousand staters, [and] | he repeatedly plun-
5   dered *the* Greeks with his raids, and the altars he razed || to the ground,
    (the altars) of Zeus [Ph]ilippi[os]; and after a war had been inst|ituted
    by him against Alexander and the Greeks, | he stripped the citizens of
    their weapons, exc|luded (them) from the city en masse, and, after
    their wiv|es and their daughters had been seized by him and
10 imprisoned || on the acropolis, three thousand and two hundred | staters
    he exacted (from them); the city and the temples | he pillaged with his
    pirates and burned down, and | (he) burned along with them the bodies
15 [of the] citizens; and fi|nally he went to Alexander and gave || a false
    account and slandered the citizens. They shall try | him under oath by
    secret vote regarding | (whether to put him to) death. And if the death
    penalty is voted, after a counter-p|roposal (for punishment) has been
    put forward by Agonippos, the second vote | shall be made, (to indicate)
20 in what way he ought to di|e. If, after Agonippos has been convicted by
    the court, | anyone tries to restore any of the family of Agonippos or
    makes a motion or proposal | about (their) return or about the restor-

ation of their property, ac|cursed shall be that man both himself and
his family, | and in all other respects let him be liable to the law [that]
25   (is aimed at anyone) by whom the stele ‖ is destroyed, (the stele) that
concerns the tyrants and their descend|ants. And a solemn vow shall be
made in the assembly *imm|ediately*, that the man who in making his
judgement also brings assistance to the city | and to justice shall prosper,
but that to those who contrary to just|ice cast their vote the opposite of
30   this (shall happen). ‖ A decision was reached. (There were) eight
hundred and eighty-three (voters). Out of | these, seven acquitted, the
rest condemn|ed. *vv*

C. Fragment 2 (front face). Decision of the People regarding the descendants of former tyrants

Decided by the People. Concerning the matters that are reported by
the ambassadors, | the ones who were sent to Alexander, and (in
35   response to whom) Ale‖xander sent back his edict, since there have
co|me to him the former tyrants' descend|ants, (namely) both
Heroidas, son of Tertikon, the son of Heraios, and [A]|gesimenes, son of
Hermesidas, and since they have proclaim|ed to Alexander that they
40   are ready for a trial ‖ to be undergone (by them) before the People
concerning the accusations that have been made, | with good fortune
let it be resolved by the People: Since [-- | ---]

FRAGMENT 2 (RIGHT SIDE). CONTINUATION OF ABOVE
[--[4] the man who] *justly be|haves* and brings assistan|ce [to the] city and to
5   the | *laws* by a just (vote) shall pr‖osper, both themselves[5] | [and] their
descendants, but to the man who | contrary to the laws and | to justice
10   make their judge|ment[6] the opposite (shall happen). (This) o‖ath shall
be sworn by the citizens | who are making the judgement. | 'Truly I shall
judge the [suit] | in all respects that by the *l|aws* are encompassed in
15   accordance with the *l‖aws*, and in all other respects *making every* | *effort*
(to judge) as well and | as justly as possible, and I shall impose a
pen|alty, if I condemn (anyone), in a right | and just manner. This is the
20   way I shall act, ‖ (I swear) truly by Zeus and Helios.' |

D. Fragment 2 (right side). Letter of Philippos III (Arrhidaios)

(From) Philippos.[7] Against the exil|es the judgements that have been
25   ma|de by Alexander ‖ are to be valid and | those whom he condemned
to exile are to be in e|xile; liable to extradition, | however, they are not
to be. |

E. Fragment 2 (right side). Letter of Antigonos (Monophthalmos)

30   The Prytanis (was) Melidoros, ‖ King Antigonos | to the Council of the
Eresians | and to the People, Greetings. | There came up to u|s from you
35   ambass‖adors and they conversed (with us), | saying that by the People,
| after they had received from u|s the letter that we wr|ote on behalf of
40   Agonip‖[p]os' sons, a decree *had* | *been passed*, which they read | *to us* and
that they *had* | *been sent* [-- | ---].[8]

FRAGMENT 2 (REVERSE). CONTINUATION OF ABOVE[9]
[--- | --] Alexan[der-] | *you come upon* [--] Farewell. |

F. Fragment 2 (reverse). Decree of the People

5   *Decided* [by the People. -- the] *Council* proposed after deliberation [- ‖ -]
or changed the resolution [-- (as regards) the] men who *have been* | *elected, all*
the things [--] against the tyran|ts,[10] *both those* who have *lived* in the city
and the *descend*|*ants* [of these men], they[11] are *producing* and the docu-
10   ments | *they are introducing* into the assembly. And since pre‖viously by
King Alexander an edict was des|patched (in which) he ordered the
[Er]esians to hold trials about both | [Ag]onippos and Eu[rys]il[a]os
(to decide) what they ought to suffer, [the | People] *obeyed* the edict
(and) a court | was *established* in accordance with the laws and that
15   (court) judged that Agoni[p‖p]os and Eurysil[ao]s should die, and that
the descen|dants of these men *should be* liable to the law on the | stele
and that their possessions should be sold in accordance | with the law.
And when Alexander had also sent a letter a|bout the descendants of
20   Apoll[od]oro[s] and his brother‖s Hermon and Heraios, who pre-
viously were tyran|ts of the city, and their descendants, (saying that) a
decision | should be made by the People (regarding) whether it seemed
good that the return from exile | of these men (be allowed) or not, the
People in obedience to the edict | convened a court for them in accord-
25   ance with the *l*‖*aw* and the edict of King Alexande[r], | [and that] (court)
decided, after speeches had been made on both sides, that the *l*|*aw*
against the tyrants should be valid and | that they should be banished
from the *city*. (Since these decisions were made in the past,) let it be
resolved by the People | that there shall remain valid against the
30   tyrants, both those ‖ who have lived in the city and the descendants of
the|se men, both the law regarding the tyrants that has been inscri|bed
on the old stele and the edic|ts of the kings against these men and the
35   de|crees that were previously written by our ances‖tors and the judge-
ments that were voted against the tyrants. [If,] | however, in contra-
vention of this decision one of the tyrants is caught, [either] | one of

those who has lived in the city or one of the descendants of the|se men, setting foot on the territory of the Eresians, [- | -] the People shall take
40   council and [-- || --- | ---]

1   For the order in which the fragments are arranged see the diagram in Heisserer 33.
2   I.e. regarding the way in which he is to be put to death.
3   Suggested restorations are 'walled up in the acropolis' (Paton) and 'he rebuilt the acropolis' (Dittenberger). For a detailed discussion of the remains on the stone see Heisserer 52–3, who himself ends up with a verb form of 'no ascertainable meaning'.
4   For the missing part of this formula cf. 'The Trial of Agonippos' lines 26–7.
5   The pronoun is in the plural, despite the singular verbs that precede.
6   The verb changes to the plural.
7   The name is set in the centre of the line to form a heading.
8   Welles continues: 'both the [decisions of the courts to make known ---]'.
9   For the arguments in support of this conclusion see Heisserer 55–6.
10   These badly preserved lines have been restored by Paton in *IG* XII to read: 'Concerning the matters that the] *Council* proposed after deliberation [or that the *Council* resolved or changed by resolution and the] men who *have been* | *elected all* the things [written] against the tyran|ts . . .' For the difficulties in this restoration see Heisserer 56.
11   I.e. the men who have been elected.

113   Restoration of exiles to Mytilene. Mytilene, 332 *or* 324. Two contiguous fragments of a marble stele. Aeolic dialect, Ionic letters, stoichedon (with irregularities).

IG XII (2) 6; Tod 201, pp. 289–94; *Heisserer, *Alexander* 118–31 (with a line drawing and photograph). Cf. Diod. 17.109.1, 18.8.2–7; Curtius 10.2.4–7; Justin, *Epitoma* 13.5.2–5; Arrian, *Anab.* 2.1.4f., 3.2.6.; and cf. no. 122.

E. Badian, *JHS* 81 (1961) 25–31; Hamilton, *Alexander* 136–8; Heisserer, *Alexander* 131–41.

[--] *let* [the] *kings*[1] *vote in favour* [of the restored exil|e, on the grounds that] the one [who was] previously in [the] city *has contrived* [a fraud. But if anyone | of the] *restored exiles* does not abide by these terms of reconciliation, | let him [no longer] *be the recipient* of any property from the city
5   nor [let him en||ter into] any of the (properties) ceded to him by those who [were] previously in the | city, [but] let those enter upon these properties, the ones who cede|d (them) [to him from amongst those] who were previously in the city, and let the generals *once* | *again transfer* the properties *back* to the one who was previously in the city, | [on the grounds that] the restored exile *has* [*not*] *accepted the reconciliation*, and let
10   the kings *vote in* ||*favour* [of the one] who was previously [in] the city, on the grounds that a fraud has been contrived by the *re*|*stored exile*. If

anyone brings a law-suit about these (properties), let (the suit) not be
intro|duced (to the courts) by the peridromoi and the dikaskopoi[2] nor by
any other magistrate at all. | [It shall be the responsibility] of the
generals and the kings and the *pe|ridromoi* [and] the dikaskopoi and the
15   *other* magistrates, if ‖ everything [does not turn out] as *it has been written*
in the *decree*, let them condemn[3] | [the one who disregarded any of the
terms] *written* [in the decree], in order that noth|ing [may be in conten-
tion[4] for the restored exiles] with respect to those who [were] in the
| city [previously, but in concord and] *reconciled* all to *one* | *another* [they
20   may live as citizens] *without intrigue* and may abide by the *i‖nscribed* [edict
and] the reconciliation that in this *de|cree* [has been written. And] *there
shall be chosen* by the People twenty men,[5] ten | [from the restored exiles],
ten from those who were previously in the city. | [Those men] *are to keep
watch* [zealously] and take care that nothing *shall* | *be* [in contention
25   between those] who have returned and those who [were] in the city ‖
previously [for all time],[6] and concerning the disputed properties | (to
take care) [that those who have returned] both with those who were
(previously) in the city and with | [one another] shall [if possible] be
reconciled, but if not, that they shall be (treated) as *just*(ly) | *as possible*,
[and that by] *the* reconciliations that the King adjudged | [in his] *edict*[7]
30   everyone shall abide and shall live in the ci‖ty [and the country] in
concord with one another. And concerning money, | [in order to con-
tribute to the] *establishment* of the reconciliation as much as possible,[8]
and concerning the oath | [that the] citizens [will swear], concerning all
these matters, whatever they[9] *ag|ree* [among] themselves, the elected
men are to bring (this) before *t|he* [People, and when the People] *have
35   heard*, if they consider (it) advantageous, let them take counsel[10] ‖ [con-
cerning the ratification of the] terms that have been agreed (by the
parties) with one another as being *advantag|eous*, [just as similarly for
those] who returned in the presidency of Smithinas | *it was decreed* [pre-
viously by the People]. If there is anything lacking from this decree,
| [let the decision concerning this be] in the hands of the Council.
When ratification has been given to the decr|ee [by the People, the
40   whole] citizen body on the twentieth day of the month ‖ [after the
sacrifice shall pray] to the gods that for the safety and *pros|perity* [of all
the citizens] shall turn out the reconciliation between those who *have
re|turned* [already and those] who were in the city. The priests, *t|hose*
[with public authority, all of them, and][11] the priestesses shall open the
temples and | [the People] *shall gather together* [for prayer]. The sacrifices
45   that the People vowed when it *des‖patched* [the messengers to] the King
shall be paid by the ki|ngs [to the gods][12] *year by year*. And there shall be
present at the sacrifice both | [the whole citizen body and the][13] mess-
engers, the ones who to the King *were* | *despatched*, [the ones from those]

50   who were in the city and the ones from *those who* | [returned]. Once the
treasurers have inscribed this [decree ‖ on a marble stele, they shall set it
up in the temple of Athena].

1   Elected magistrates, perhaps like the tribal-kings (phylobasileis) in Athens.
2   The peridromoi and dikaskopoi are obviously magistrates concerned with the
   legal system.
3   If the restoration at the beginning of line 13 is correct, there is a break
   (anacoluthon) in the grammatical structure of the sentence, for one would expect
   an infinitive at this point.
4   Strictly speaking, Heisserer's text means 'in opposition'. Earlier texts (e.g. Tod's)
   read 'in disagreement'.
5   'Mediators' (Tod and earlier editors).
6   Heisserer. Tod, following earlier editors, punctuates after 'previously', and con-
   tinues '[They shall bring it about] also concerning disputed properties | [that
   those who have returned]'.
7   '[And by the] *agreement*' (Tod and earlier editors).
8   Heisserer, following Klaffenbach. See Heisserer 128. Tod, following Paton, reads
   '[after] the terms of reconciliation [have been accepted] as much as possible'.
9   I.e. the contending parties.
10 'Let the People take counsel in so far as they think it advantageous' (Dittenberger).
11 'The priests, t|he [public ones, all of them, and]' (Tod); 'The priests | [and all the
   magistrates who manage sacrifices and]' (Dittenberger).
12 'At the Ki|ng's [birthday celebrations]' (Tod).
13 '[the twenty men and the]' (Tod.)

**114   Iasos[1] honours Gorgos and Minnion. Iasos (found at Chios,
where it had been taken as ballast; now lost), *c*. 332.** Block of marble,
Ionic letters and dialect, non-stoichedon.

SIG 307; Tod 190, pp. 252–3; *Heisserer, *Alexander* 169–79. Cf. Athenaeus 12.538b; and
no. 127.

Since [Go]rgos and Minnion, Theodot|[os'] sons, have been noble and
good | concerning the public business of the city | and many of the
5   citizens in private have bene‖fited (by them) and (since) concerning the
little | sea,[2] after conversing | with Alexander the king, they recovered
(it) | and gave it back to the People, there shall be given | to them and
10 their descendants exemption from taxation and ‖ the front seat (at
public festivals) for all time. | The decree shall be inscribed on the
| vestibule in front of the record office.

1   On the coast of Asia Minor, south of Miletus. See the map in Heisserer 175.
2   The exact location of the 'Little Sea' is not known, but it was probably an inland lake
   connected with the sea. See the discussion in Heisserer 174–7.

115   Demosthenes' contact with the court of Alexander. 331.[1]

Harpocration, *Lexicon s.v.* Aristion (Diyllus, *FGrHist* 73F2; Marsyas of Pella, *FGrHist* 135F2). Cf. Aeschines 3.162.

E. Badian, *JHS* 81 (1961) 34.

Aristion. Hypereides (in the speech) against Demosthenes.[2] This man is a Samian or a Plataean,[3] as Diyllos says, and (was) a friend of Demosthenes from childhood. He was sent by him to Hephaistion for a reconciliation, as Marsyas says in the fifth (book) of 'Matters related to Alexander'.

1   The date is deduced from Aeschines' reference in 330 (3.162) to the state-galley Paralos and an Athenian embassy to Alexander, from whom he acquired the information about Aristion's activities at Alexander's court. This embassy must be the one that met Alexander at Tyre in 331 (cf. Arrian, *Anab.* 3.6.2).
2   This reference is usually identified with col. 20 lines 10f. of the papyrus fragment of Hypereides' speech against Demosthenes.
3   Aeschines says 'Plataikos', which can either mean 'of Plataea' or 'of Plataean status', in which case it would refer to any foreigner (and sometimes slave) who had been given the same citizen rights as the Plataeans were given in 427.

116   Cyrene supplies grain to Greek states. Cyrene, 331–324.[1]
Marble stele in two pieces, inscribed on the front and both sides (the material translated here is from the right side), Ionic letters, Doric dialect, non-stoichedon.

*Tod 196, pp. 273–6. Cf. Dem. 34.39, 42.20, 42.31; [Dem.] 56, *passim*; [Aristotle,] *Econ.* 2.33e; [Plut.] *Lives of the Ten Orators* (= *Moralia* 845e and 851a).

W.W. Tarn, *CAH* 6.448–9; W.L. Westermann, *AHR* 35 (1929–30) 17–19; M. Rostovtzeff, *The Social and Economic History of the Hellenistic World* (Oxford 1941) 1.90–125; S.I. Oost, *CP* 58 (1963) 11–25.

The priest (was) Sosias, son of Kal[lia]des. | (The following are) all those to whom the city gave grain,[2] | when the grain-shortage took
5   place | in Hellas. || To the Athenians one hundred thousand;[3] | to Olympias[4] sixty thousand; | to the Argives fifty thousand; | to the Larisans
10   fifty thousand; | to the Corinthians fifty thousand; || to Kleopatra[5] fifty thousand; | to the Rhodians thirty thousand; | to the Sicyonians thirty thousand; | to the Meliboeans twenty thousand; | to the [M]egarians[6]
15   twenty thousand; || to the T[enian]s[7] twenty thousand; | to the Les[bian]s fifteen thousand; | to the Therans fifteen thousand; | to the
20   Oeteans fifteen thousand; | to the Ambraciots fifteen thousand; || to the

Leucadians fifteen thousand; | to the Carystians fifteen thousand; | to
Olympias[8] twelve thousand, | six hundred; | to the Atragians of
25   Thessaly ten thousand; ‖ to the Kythnians ten thousand; | to the
Opuntians ten thousand; | to the Cydonians ten thousand; | to the
30   Coans ten thousand; | to the Parians ten thousand; ‖ to the Delphians
ten thousand; | to the Cnosians ten thousand; | to the Boeotians of
Tanagra ten thousand; | to the Gortynians ten thousand; | to the Eleans
35   ten thousand; ‖ to the Palaereans of Acarnania ten thousand; | to the
Megarians ten thousand; | to the Meliboeans eight thousand, | five
40   hundred; | to the Phliasians eight thousand; ‖ to the Hermionians eight
thousand; | to the Oetaeans six thousand, | four hundred; | to the
45   Troezenians six thousand; | to the Plataeans six thousand; ‖ to the
Iulietans on Ceos five thousand; | to the Aeginetans five thousand; | to
the Astypalaeans five thousand; | to the Cytherans five thousand; | to
50   the Hyrtacinians five thousand; ‖ to the Aeginetans five thousand; | to
the Carthaeans on Ceos four thousand; | to the Cytherans three
thousand, one hundred; | to the Ceans[9] three thousand; | to the
55   Ilyrians[10] three thousand; ‖ to the Coresians on Ceos three thousand; |
to the Ambraciots one thousand, | five hundred; | to the Icetyrians[11]
one thousand; | to the [C]nosians nine hundred.[12] |

1   The precise year within this period of these shipments of grain cannot be fixed, but
the famous shortage, referred to especially by Demosthenes, is known to belong to
those years from numerous references in Athenian inscriptions, especially *IG* II[2]
360, in which Athens honours Herakleides of Salamis for his help on several
occasions from the archonship of Aristophon (330/29) to the archonship of
Antikles (325/4). Cf. Rostovtzeff, especially 95.
2   It is not possible that this huge quantity of grain was actually 'given' by Cyrene. It
is probable, however, that the grain was sold at less than the going rate.
3   The shipments are of medimni (somewhat more than the modern bushel) of grain.
4   Mother of Alexander.
5   Sister of Alexander.
6   Oliverio. [Li]paressi or [Eu]pa<li>essi are suggested by Ferri (for these references see the *apparatus* in Tod).
7   The readings 'T[enian]s' and 'Les[bian]s' are quite uncertain.
8   There are eight 'double entries'. They may indicate a second shipment in a subsequent year. For an alphabetical list of the states and persons that received grain
and the total received by each see Tod, p. 274.
9   Of the four cities of Ceos only Poiessa is not specifically named. Perhaps the
Poiessans received grain from this shipment.
10   So Tod, following Wilamowitz. But the spelling is incorrect for 'Illyrians' and they
would, in any case, be unexpected here. Others correct the name to 'Elyrians', the
people of the fairly important city of Elyrus on Crete.
11   The name is otherwise unknown.
12   The total number of medimni despatched by Cyrene was 805,000. For an idea of
the area covered by the shipments see Tod, p. 275.

117   Treaty between Miletus and Sardis. Miletus, *c*. 330 or earlier.[1]
Marble stele, Ionic letters, non-stoichedon.

SIG 273; *SV* 3.407, pp. 17–19.

Resolved by the People. Motion | of the council-members. Botes made
the motion. | The friendship shall be accepted that | is offered by the
5   Sardia‖ns to the Milesians. Let it be voted | by the People that there
shall exist for anyone of the Sardians | who wants (it) the privilege of
entry | into Miletus without violation and without formal trea|ty both
as they sail in and as they sail out, ‖ both for themselves and for any-
10   thing that | they import or expor|t. And there shall also be for anyone
of the Milesians | who wants (it) the privilege of entry into Sar|dis and
15   security according to the sa‖me terms. Care shall be taken of the Sardians
| in Miletus by the preside|nts who on any occasion are in office, (to see)
t|hat the privileges that have been voted for them | turn out well and
20   that they are not wronged, ‖ either when they are staying here or | when
they are going away. At Sardis | care shall be taken of the Milesians by
whom|soever the Sardians appoint from them|selves. There shall be
25   sent by the Sardia‖ns to us a messenger and he shall in|dicate to us (the
men) whom they chose, in order that | we may know (who are) those
who have been appointed. | The decree shall be inscribed on a ste|le of
30   marble and set up in the temple ‖ of Apollo. The magistrates in charge of
wall-build|ing shall hire out the contract. Let the treasurer give | assist-
ance. There shall be inscribed in addition on | the stele the names of the
35   m|en who are appointed by the Sardi‖ans to take care of us. There shall be
sent | also gifts of hospitality to the messenger by the gener|als on
behalf of the city. The following were ch|osen from the Sardians in
accordance with the dec|ree. Potas, son of Papeus; Artimes, son of
40   Pagtyos; ‖ Altis, son of Pagtyos, the priest of Diony|sos. *vacat*

1   This and the other documents mentioned below are usually assigned to the period
after the liberation of Miletus from Persian control by Alexander, but it was not
impossible for Miletus to enter into such relations during the time of the Persians.
Apparently contemporary with this document, to judge from the letter-forms, are
three other Milesian inscriptions: (1) a treaty with its colony, Olbia, confirming the
ancestral relationship of reciprocal rights between the two states; (2) a treaty of
isopolity with Cyzicus; (3) a treaty of isopolity with Phygela. For the text of these
documents see *SV* 3.408, 409, 453.

118   Athens honours Eudemos of Plataea. Athens, 329. Marble
stele, Ionic letters, stoichedon (but syllabic division is carefully
observed).

IG II^2 351+, p. 624; Tod 198, pp. 278–81; *Pouilloux, Choix* 6, pp. 40–2.

A.W. Pickard-Cambridge, *The Theatre of Dionysus in Athens* (Oxford 1946) 137; A. Burford, *Economic History Review* 13 (1960) 1–18; Pečiřka, *Enktesis* 68–70; Mitchel, 'Athens' 34–5; A. Burford, *The Greek Temple Builders at Epidauros* (Liverpool 1969) 184ff.

For [Eudem]os of Platae[a. | In] the archonship of [Arist]ophon (330/ 29), | when Leontis (held) the ninth pry|tany, in which Antidoros, son

5 of Anti[nous], ‖ of Paiania was secretary. On the el|eventh of Thargelion, on the nine|teenth (day) of the prytany. | Of the Proedroi the one who put (the motion) to the vote (was) Ar[isto]|phane[s]^1 of

10 Euonymon. Resolved [by the ‖ People]. Lykourgos, son of Lykophron, | of [Bouta]dai made the motion: Since | [Eudem]os both in the past *promis|ed* to the People that he would contribute for | [the] war,^{2} if there

15 should be any need, *four thousand* ‖ drachmas, and now *has contributed* | for the construction of the stadium | and the theatre of the Panathe[nai]|a^3 one thousand yoke of oxen^4 and these | were all sent by him before the

20 [P]anathe‖naia, just as he had promised, let it be resolved | by the People: Commendation shall be given to [E]udem[os], | son of [Phi]lourgos, of Plata[ea] and he shall be cr|owned with a crown of

25 olive | for his goodwill toward the ‖ People of Athens. And there shall be | for him (a place) among the benefactors of the | People of Athens, for him and | his descendants. And he shall have | the privilege of

30 possession of land and a house and ‖ he shall go out on | campaigns and pay the | capital levies along with Athenians. | Inscription shall be

35 made of this decree | by the secretary of the Boule and ‖ it shall be set up on the Acr[o]polis. For the | inscription of the stele *there shall be given* | by the treasurer of the People [--] | drachmas from the (funds) that on

40 matters related to de|crees are spent [by the] ‖ People.

1 The name of the proedros should be Antiphanes. See Pečiřka 69.
2 The war may either be the war of Agis III (331/30) in which the Athenians in the end took no part or, as Tod believed, the war against Philip of Macedon that ended with the battle of Chaeronea.
3 This is not a reference to the theatre of Dionysos, but rather to the raised seats for the spectators around the stadium. See Pickard-Cambridge.
4 Not 'a thousand carts and pairs of animals' (Tod, p. 279), for it was often necessary to use many pairs of oxen to pull one cart, if it was carrying a heavy object. See Burford.

119   Athens honours Memnon.^{1} **Athens, 327/6.** Marble stele (broken at the bottom), Ionic letters, stoichedon.

IG II^2 356+; *Tod 199, pp. 281–4; B.D. Meritt, *Hesperia* 3 (1934) 4.

E. Badian, *Hermes* 95 (1967) 179ff.; P.A. Brunt, *RFIC* 103 (1975) 22–34 (especially 26–7).

[In] the archonship of [Hegem]on on (327/6), [w|hen Hip]pothon[ti]s (held) [the four|th][2] prytany, [in which Auto|kles], son of [Ph]anias,[3] of
5   [Ach]ar[n]ai was s‖ecretary, on the twenty-n|inth[4] (day of the month), on the six-and-*twent|ieth* (day) of the prytany. (The) *assem|bly* (held) its principal meeting. Of the Proedroi the one who p|ut (the motion) to
10   the vote (was) [-- ‖ --]. Resolved [by the] Peopl|e: *Since* M[e]mnon [-- | (only isolated letters survive of lines 12–22) | --] he chances upon
25   [and] | in the past his ancestors, [Pha‖rn]a[b]azos[5] and Ar[ta]bazo[s],[6] | continually conducted themselves toward the People | of [Ath]ens as
30   benefactor|s and were useful in t|imes of war to the People, [a‖nd] the father of Thymondas,[7] (namely) Me[nt|o]r, brought those in Egypt who were on cam|paign from Greece | to safety, when Egypt was cap-
35   ture|d by the Persians,[8] commendation shall be given to ‖ him and he shall be crowned with a g|olden crown for his excellen|ce [--] |

1   Sometimes identified as Memnon II, son of Memnon the Rhodian who was the most energetic opponent of Alexander in Asia Minor and the Aegean. See the family tree in Tod, p. 282. But Badian and Brunt believe he was the son of Artabazos.
2   Restored to '[eighth]' by W.B. Dinsmoor, *The Archons of Athens in the Hellenistic Age* (Harvard 1931) 371f. and '*seventh*' by Meritt. See *SEG* 21.286.
3   Meritt (*Hesperia* 3) has shown that this name should be [A]utias.
4   29th if the month was 'full'; 28th if it was 'hollow'.
5   The Pharnabazos who campaigned with Konon at Cnidus (394).
6   Son of that Pharnabazos, rebel satrap, who spent some time at the Macedonian court in exile. See Diod. 16.52.3; Curtius 5.9.1, 6.5.2; Tod, p. 283; Hammond-Griffith 484 n. 5 (Griffith).
7   Cf. Arrian, *Anab.* 2.2.1, 2.13.2.
8   Mentor commanded a Greek mercenary army on the Egyptian side. He changed over to the King's side at the siege of Sidon and continued to command his mercenaries in the King's service during the conquest of Egypt. Cf. Diod. 16.42.2, 16.45, 16.47.4, 16.49.7–50.8; Tod, p. 283.

120   Money brought to Athens by Harpalos. 325/4.

[Plut.] *Lives of the Ten Orators* (= *Moralia* 846a–b; Philochorus, *FGrHist* 328F163). Cf. Hyperides 1, *passim*; Dinarchus 1.89; Diod. 17.108.8; Plut. *Dem.* 25.1–26.2; Pausanias 2.33.4–5; Curtius 10.2.2f.; [Plut.] *Lives of the Ten Orators* (= *Moralia* 846a–e).

C. Adams, *TAPA* 32 (1901) 121–53; Jacoby, *FGrHist* 3b.Suppl. 1.539–40, Suppl. 2.434–7; E. Badian, *JHS* 81 (1961) 16–43; J. Goldstein, *The Letters of Demosthenes* (New York and London 1968); Davies, *Families* 3597, pp. 113–39 (especially pp. 133–5); Bury-Meiggs 496–7; MacDowell, *Law* 172–3.

Later when Alexander was on campaign against Asia and Harpalos[1] had fled to Athens with money, at first he (*sc.* Demosthenes) prevented him from being admitted. But when he (Harpalos) sailed in, (Demosthenes,) after accepting one thousand darics, changed his mind. And when the Athenians wanted to surrender him (Harpalos) to Antipatros, (Demosthenes) spoke in opposition, and proposed that (Harpalos) deposit the money on the Acropolis, without telling[2] the People the amount. Although Harpalos said [that he had brought with him] seven hundred [talents, what was taken up onto the Acropolis] was found [to be three hundred][3] and[4] fifty or a little more, as Philochorus says.

1   Alexander's boyhood friend and his treasurer in Babylon, while he was away in the East. As a result of his high living during Alexander's absence, he judged it discreet to flee before Alexander returned. In 324 he took 6000 mercenaries and 5000 talents and sailed for Athens, where he had been made an honorary citizen for his help to Athens during the famine (cf. no. 116). See Badian 22ff., 31ff.
2   This is the reading in most modern texts, but it is an emendation based upon the account of Photius, *Bibliotheca* p. 285. In this reading, Demosthenes is the subject of 'telling'. The manuscripts of [Plut.], however, read 'after he had already told' and the subject is Harpalos.
3   The passages in square brackets are not in our text of [Plut.], but are supplied from Photius. They are confirmed by Hyperides 1.10.
4   Emended by Dübner. The manuscripts read 'or'.

121   Athens sends a colony to the Adriatic. Athens, 325/4. Eleven contiguous fragments of a marble stele, Ionic letters (but o=ou occasionally), non-stoichedon.

IG II[2] 1629 (lines 145–232);[1] *Tod 200, pp. 284–9.

W.W. Tarn, *CAH* 6.449.

A captured *triaconter* (a thirty-oared boat). | [--], the wor(k) of Eudikos. | (The) *trierarch* (was) Demokles | son of [Krates], of Melite | [and his]
150   fellow trierarchs[2] ‖ (were) [Euthykr]ates, son of Charias, | of [Kydath]e(naion): he has equipment | [of wood], a complete set; of *han|ging gear*, girding ropes for a tri|reme in place of those that are unser-
155   vice‖able, they took *two* in accordance with | the decree of the People that was moved | by [Hagno]nides[3] from Pergas(e). | This triacon|ter and
160   the equipment were ta‖ken over by Miltiades[4] | of [Lakia]dai, the founder of the colony | [in accordance with] the decree of the People | [that was
165   moved] by Kephisophon[5] | of [Chola]rgos.[6] ‖ *vacat The decree* in accordance with which there were taken over | by [Milt]iades the tri|remes and the quadriremes | [and] the triaconters | [and] the equipment.
170   ‖ [Kephis]ophon, son of Lysiphon, | of [Chola]rgos made the motion:

with goo|d fortune for the People of | [Athen]s, in order that *as | quickly*
175   *as possible* may be accomplished ‖ the resolution of the People | [concern-
ing] the Adriatic | *colony*, let it be voted by the | People that the
180   sh|ipyard-supervisors shall ha‖nd over to the trierarch|s the ships and
the equipment | [in accordance with] the resolution of the Pe|ople, and
185   the trierarchs, | [those] who have been appointed, shall bring ‖ the ships
alongside the | [jetty] in Mounichion | [month] before the tenth | of the
190   month and have (them) | readied for ‖ [sailing]. The first (trierarch) to
br|ing (his ship) alongside is to be crown|ed by [the] People with a
golden crow|n worth 500 drachmas, | [the] second (with a crown) worth
195   300 ‖ drachmas, and the third (with a crown) w|orth [200]: and procla-
mation is to be ma|de by [the] herald of the Boule at the Thar|[gelia]
200   (about) the cr|owns, and the Apodektai ‖ *shall apportion* the money | [for]
the crowns in order | [that there may be] made manifest the love of
hon|our toward the People (shown) by the | trierarchs. And in order
205   that ‖ [also] the pleas[7] may be introduced (to the law courts), | the
Thesmothetai shall pro|vide (juries) for the law courts, (the number of
jurors) not to exceed | two hundred and one, for the (use of the) | general
210   who has been put in charge of the sym‖mories[8] by election, (and they
shall provide the juries) in the | month of [M]ounichion on the sec|ond
215   and the | fifth days of the month; the | pay shall be given to the ‖ jurors
by the treas|urers of the (funds) of the Goddess in accordance with the
| law. In order that there may exist | for the people for all | time its own
220   commercial outlet and ‖ supply of grain, and, when an anchorage | of its
own has been equipp|ed, there exists[9] a guard against | (the) [Tyr]rhe-
225   nians,[10] and Militia|[des] the founder of the colony and the colon‖ists[11]
may be able to use their ow|n fleet, and those of the Hel|[lenes] and of
230   the barbarians who | *sail* the sea | [they, too,] may sail in ‖ to [the]
anchorage of the Athenians, | *with a view to keeping* [both their vessels] and
their oth|er (possessions) in safety, *knowing* that | (lacuna)[12]

1   Of this document, the continuation of the records of the curators of the dockyards
for the archonship of Antikles (325/4), 1162 lines are extant, inscribed in five
columns, four on the face and the fifth on the right-hand side.
2   The noun is plural, though only Euthykrates is named.
3   For Hagnonides see Tod, p. 289.
4   Miltiades of Lakiadai was a member of the Philaid family. His name recalls the
Miltiades who founded the Athenian settlement on the Thracian Chersonese and
this may explain why he was chosen as founder of the Adriatic colony. See Tod, p.
288, and Davies, *Families* 8429 (XV).
5   For Kephisophon see Tod, p. 289.
6   The first 164 lines of this inscription give the details of nine ships (3 triremes, 2
horse-transports and four triaconters), each of which is recorded as having been
taken over by Miltiades. Only the last is given here as an example. In addition to
these nine Miltiades had some quadriremes (line 167) and possibly other vessels,
though the total is not known.

7   Of those contesting the liturgy.
8   Cf. Aristotle, *Ath. Pol.* 61.1.
9   The mood of the verb here changes to the indicative.
10 Etruscan pirates. See Tod, p. 288.
11 The word 'epoikoi' translated here as 'colonists' often denotes settlers who went
    out to reinforce an earlier colony.
12 At this point there is a break of uncertain length in the text, after which the
    document continues with details of the penalties to be imposed upon any of those
    involved in this enterprise who do not perform their duty. The Athenians obvi-
    ously took this matter seriously and one must presume the colony was actually
    sent out, though there is no literary reference to it nor has its site been identified.

122   Restoration of Tegean exiles. Delphi, 324 *or* 319–317. Stele of
dark limestone, Arcadian dialect (with occasional Koine forms),
stoichedon.

SIG[3] 306; Buck 22, pp. 206–9; Tod 202, pp. 294–301; *Heisserer, *Alexander* 204–19. Cf.
Hyperides 1.18; Dinarchus 1.81f., 103; Diod. 17.109.1, 18.8, 18.56.1–8, 19.35.1;
Curtius 10.2.3f.; Justin 13.5.2ff.

A. Plassart, *BCH* 38 (1914) 101–88; Hamilton, *Alexander* 136–40; Heisserer, *Alexander*
219–29.

[--[1] the K|ing Alex]ander,[2] the edict shall be inscribed in accordance
with the corrections | that were made by the city with regard to the
points in the edict that were ob|jected to. To the exiles that have
5   returned their paternal property ‖ shall be restored, which they
possessed when they went into exile, and (to the women shall be
restored) their maternal property, (that is) to all those who were
u|nmarried and held possession of the property and happened not to |
have brothers. But if for any woman who has been married it turned out
| that her brother, both himself and his offspring, has perish|ed, she too
10   shall have her maternal property, but it shall never go further.[3] A‖s
regards the houses, each man shall have one in accordance with the
e|dict. If a house has a cultivated plot beside it, another (plot) may n|ot
be taken. But if there is not a cultivated plot beside the house but
n|earby there is (one) within (the distance of) a plethron,[4] let him take
15   the plot; | if the plot is more than a plethron, of this ha‖lf is to be taken,
just as concerning the other properties also it has been wr|itten. For the
houses let the price that is to be recovered[5] for each hous|e be two
minas, while the valuation (for tax purposes)[6] of the houses shall be
whateve|r the city decides. For the cultivated plots twice the valu|e[7]
shall be recovered that is stipulated in the law. As for monetary claims,
20   no responsibility shall belon‖g to the city,[8] and it shall not settle[9] them

either for the exiles or | for those who previously stayed at home as
citizens. With regard to the f|estivals, from which the exiles have been
missing, the cit|y shall take counsel, and whatever the city decides is
to be v|alid.[10] The court from outside the state[11] shall pass judge-
25   ments[12] within sixt|y days. All those who within the sixty days do not
| present their claims shall not be permitted to go to law with regard to
t|he properties in the court from outside the state, but (must go to law)
in the | civic (court) for ever (after). If they subsequently discover
anything in addition,[13] (they may present it) within | sixty days from
30   the day on which the cour|t[14] was established. If a person does not
present his claim within this time, let it be no long|er possible for him
to go to court. If later some people | return from exile, when the court
from outside the state is no longer in existen|ce, let them register with
the generals the properties (they claim) within si|xty days, and if they
35   encounter any defenc|e,[15] the court shall be Mantinea. But if a person
does [not] present his cl|aims in these days, no longer shall it be poss-
ible for him to | go to law. With regard to the sacred monies [--] t|he
debts, those that concern the Goddess[16] the city has arrang|ed,[17] the
40   one who has the property is to give back to the returned exile ha|lf (of
the property), just as the others (who possess property are to do). All
those who are personally in debt to the Go|ddess, as guarantors or
otherwise, if on the one hand it is manifest that the possessor of the
| property has settled the debt with the Goddess, let him give back ha|lf
(of the property) to the returning exile, just as the others (are to do),
omitting noth|ing.[18] But if it is manifest that he has not repaid the God-
45   dess, let him give || back to the returning exile half of the property, and
from his ha|lf himself settle the debt. But if he does not wish to s|ettle
(the debt), let him give back to the returning exile the whole property,
and let him (the exile), after he has re|covered (the property), settle the
whole debt with the Goddess. All those | wives or daughters of the
50   exiles who, while remaining at ho||me, married or after being in exile
later married in Tege|a and bought their discharge (from banishment)
while remaining at home,[19] these shall n|ot be disqualified by scrutiny
(from inheriting) their paternal or their maternal property, (neither the
women themselves) n|or their descendants, except that all those who
went into exile later under compulsio|n[20] and in the opportunity that
55   exists at the present are creeping back, either themselves or || their
children, (those) shall be subject to scrutiny, both themselves and
th|eir descendants, regarding their paternal and maternal property in
accordance with the e|dict. I swear by Zeus, by Athena, by Apollo, by
Poseidon that I shall be well | disposed towards the returned exiles
whom the city has decided to receive | back, and I shall not bear a
60   grudge against any of them for whatever he may have pl||otted,[21] from

the day on which I swear the oath, nor shall I ob|struct the safety of those who have returned, either in th|e [--] or in the common council
65   of the city [-- | --] edict [--] toward the return|ed [--] to the city [-- || --] the things that have been written in the edict with respect to | [--] nor shall I plan against anyone. | *vacat*

1   As a restoration of the preceding lines Heisserer suggests: '[with respect to the matters about which the city dispatched the a|mbassadors and the decision that was sent back] *to us* [by the Ki|ng . . . '
2   '[Kass]andros' is also possible here.
3   This is the literal translation. It may mean 'her inheritance shall not go beyond her maternal property' or 'shall not go beyond this (in line of inheritance)'.
4   Following Buck. Heisserer suggests: 'but nearby there is (a field) equal (to the distance) of a plethron'.
5   By whom? For most editors it is 'the exile', but Heisserer argues for 'the one who is giving up the house'.
6   Buck. 'Assessment' (Heisserer).
7   Heisserer. 'Assessment' (Buck); 'tax' (Tod). For the interpretation of this passage see Heisserer 215.
8   Buck. 'The city shall remit the money' (Tod and Heisserer).
9   Buck and Heisserer. 'Without granting a formal receipt' (Tod). See the discussion in Heisserer 215–16.
10 The point at issue was possibly non-performance of liturgies.
11 The word used means 'foreign', but the essential difference between the courts mentioned is that one is manned by citizens from Tegea, the other by citizens of another state, in this case probably Mantinea.
12 On the inevitable disputes over property.
13 Either a new claim or new evidence.
14 Probably the civic court. See Heisserer 216.
15 I.e. 'if they encounter any defence against their claim'.
16 Athena Alea.
17 'Shall settle' (Tod); 'shall make things right' (Heisserer).
18 Heisserer. 'Without retaining anything fraudulently' (Plassart); 'without delay' (Hiller (*SIG*)).
19 'By remaining at home' (Heisserer). I.e. he takes the participle here to express the means by which they secured their discharge.
20 Heisserer (217–18) interprets this difficult passage as follows: 'the contrast is between those women who remained at Tegea or subsequently returned home (and obtained pardon by marrying residents) and those who were later forced into exile'.
21 Buck. 'For any counsel he might give' (Plassart).

123   Alliance of the Greeks against Macedon (Lamian or Hellenic War). 323.

A. *IG* II² 448 (lines 1–31). Athens honours Euphron of Sicyon. Athens, 323/2 and 318/17. Marble stele, Ionic letters, stoichedon. **B.** *IG* II² 467. Athens honours Timosthenes of Carystus. Athens, 306/5. Marble stele, Ionic letters, stoichedon. Cf.

Hyperides, 6.10–13; Diod. 17.111.3, 18.9.5, 18.10.5–11.2; Pausanias 1.1.3, 1.25.3–5, 4.28.3, 5.4.9; Plut. *Demosthenes* 27.1; Justin, *Epitoma* 13.5.1–10.

W.S. Ferguson, *Athens* 11–28; E. Badian, *JHS* 81 (1961) 36–41; F.W. Mitchel, *Phoenix* 18 (1964) 13–17; E. Will, *Histoire* 1.27–30; Mitchel, 'Athens' 49–52; *SV* 3.413, pp. 24–5. Cf. no. 124.

A. *IG* II² 448. Athens honours Euphron of Sicyon

Gods. | In the archonship of Kephisodoros (323/2) when [Pandionis] (held) *the fi|fth* prytany, in which [Ar]chi[as],[1] son of Py[thodoros, from Alopeke] | was secretary. [On the] *sixteenth* of Poseideon, [on the] *tw|o-* and-twentieth (day) of the prytany. [The assembly (held) its principal
5   meeting]. *Of th||e* Proedroi the one who put (the resolution) to the vote. (was) Epame[inon--. Resolved] | by the People, *vv* Euphiletos, son of Euphi[l]e[tos, of Kephisia] *made the motio|n:* Since Euphron, son of Adeas, a man of Sicyon, [continues] to be a *go|od* man toward the People of Athens [and now, having come] *fro|m* the People of Sicyon, *proclaims*
10   [that his city], || being a friend and ally, [will (?) defend against its] *enemi|es* the People of Athens, *first* (to do so) [amongst the Pelo- ponn]|esian cities, *let it be resolved* [by the People: Commendation shall be given to Euph]|ron, son of Adeas, the Sicyonian, for his excellence
15   [and his goodwill] | toward the People of Athens [and the other] *alli||es* and he shall have confirmed the [privileges that were] *previousl|y* granted [to him] by the People of [Athens]. *In ord|er* that all may know that the People [of Athens] *repay|s* to its benefactors gratitude [that befits the] *benefact|ions* that [each man] does [to the People, (Euphron) shall be an
20   Athe]||nian, himself and his descendants, [and it shall be permitted to him] *to enroll him|self* in a tribe and deme and phratry, whichever one [he wants, and] | in the ones that the laws prescribe. [Commendation shall also be given to the People of] | Sicyon [for their excellence and goodwill toward the] P|eople of Athens and they shall be crowned *with a golden*
25   crow||n worth 1000 drachmas and they shall be proclaimed [at] *the gre|at* [Dionysia], at the festival. This decree shall be inscribed [on stelai] of m|arble and set up, one copy near [the (statue of) Zeus,[2] the] | other on the A[cropolis near the temple of (Athena) Polias], and [for] | the inscription [of the stelai there shall be given by the treasurer of the]
30 || People 50 (drachmas) from the funds that are spent (on matters) relating to decrees [by the] P|eople.[3]

B. *IG* II² 467. Athens honours Timosthenes of Carystus

[In] the archonship of Koroibos (306/5) [-- | -] prytany, *vv* | Diotimos, son of Diopeithes, [of Euonymon made the motion: Since Ti]|mos-

5   thenes, who is proxenos [of the People of Athens], co‖ntinues to be
    friendly and *well disposed* [to the People of Athen]‖s and previously, in
    [the war that has been fough|t] by the People of Athens [against
    Antipatros for the] fr|eedom of the [He]lle[nes, when he was sent by his
10 city] as a d|elegate[4] to the *camp* [of the Athenians and their] ‖ allies, he
    strove [for the salvation (of the allies), by saying an|d] doing what was
    advantageous [both to the league of the Hellen]|es and to the
    Car[y]st[i]ans; [and (since) he continued also with regard to the]
    Pe|ople of Ath[en]s *to strive for honour* [and contributed] | also the
15 majority of his property [for their needs], *con‖sidering* that it was the
    common (property) of all [Greeks (for use) against the M]acedonian, and
    (since) [when A]nt[patros -- he did not] | withdraw from *friendship* and
    [he was continually benefitting in public] t|he People of Athens [and
    privately those who] *ca|me* to Carystu[s by providing for their needs and
20 in the] c‖ouncil of the Carystians (he was continually) *saying* [and doing
    what was] *advant|ageous* both to his own *fatherland* [and to the People of
    Ath]|ens; and (since) when [Kassandros] campaigned [against] t|he
    territory of Attica,[5] he gave assistance to the [People --] of his | own
    volition; (for all these reasons) with good fortune let it be resolved [by
25 the People]: *Commendation shall be* ‖ *given* to Timosthenes, son of
    Demopha[nes, for his excellence and] g|oodwill that he continues to
    have *toward* [the People of Athen]|s and [he] shall be crowned [with a
    golden crown worth | 1000] drachmas. [-- | ---]

1   For the name of the secretary for this year see E. Schweigert, *Hesperia* 9 (1940) 338–9.
2   In the agora.
3   This inscription continues for another fifty-seven lines. After a rider to the first
    decree proposed by Pamphilos, son of Euphiletos, to the effect that the matter of
    Euphron's citizenship be brought up at the next assembly, we have a second decree,
    dated to the archonship of Archippos II (318/17). This is necessitated by the fact
    that the oligarchic government at Athens in the period after the Lamian War had
    destroyed the stelai honouring Euphron. The honours of the first decree are con-
    firmed and his actions and death in the war are eulogized in addition. On returning
    from exile he had expelled the garrison from Sicyon, freed the city and made it a
    friend and ally of the Athenians. During the war he had given all possible assistance
    and, when it failed, had chosen to die fighting for democracy against the enemies of
    Greece.
4   As a representative of the Carystians, the only Euboeans to side with the Athenians
    and Aetolians in this war. Cf. Diod. 18.11.2.
5   In 306/5 Kassandros' invasion of Attica was repulsed. See Ferguson, *Athens* 113–14.
    Timosthenes' assistance at this time was the occasion for this decree.

124   The Lamian (or Hellenic) War. 323–322.

A. Suidas, *Lexicon s.v.* Leosthenes. **B.** Justin, *Epitoma* 13.5.12. Cf. Diod. 17.111, 18.8.1–

13.6, 14.4–15.9, 16.3–18.6; Plut. *Dem.* 27–8, *Phokion* 23–6, *Demetrios* 11.4–5; Pausanias 1.25.3– 6; cf. no. 123.

Ferguson, *Athens* 15–20; E. Badian, *JHS* 81 (1961) 36–41; N.G. Ashton, *ABSA* 72 (1977) 1–13.

A. Suidas, *Lexicon s.v.* Leosthenes

An Athenian general. In the war against the Macedonians this man, acting more zealously than was opportune and exploiting the success that had befallen (him), gave no thought for his personal risk in his attacks upon the enemy and in an unguarded moment was struck on the head by a stone and fell in battle.

B. Justin, *Epitoma* 13.5.12

Meanwhile, while besieging Antipatros, Leosthenes, the leader of the Athenians, was killed by a spear that had been thrown at him from the walls as he was passing by.

125   History of the Diadochi. 323/2–322/1.

A. Photius, *Bibliotheca* 82 p. 64a21–b32 (Dexippus of Athens, *FGrHist* 100F8). F. Jacoby, **FGrHist* 2A, pp. 461–2. **B.** Photius, *Bibliotheca* 92 pp. 69a1–71a7 (Arrian, *FGrHist* 156F1 and F9). **Flavii Arriani quae exstant omnia*, Vol. 2 *Scripta minora et fragmenta*, ed. A.G. Roos and G. Wirth (Teubner, Leipzig 1965) 253–69. Cf. Diod. 18.1–19.33.2; Plut. *Eumenes.*

Tarn Griffith 1–11; Cloché, *Dislocation* 10–137; Will, *Histoire* 1.19–47; K. Rosen, *AClass* 10 (1967) 41–94; R.M. Errington, *JHS* 90 (1970) 49–77; G. Cohen, *Historia* 22 (1973) 384–6 and *Athenaeum* 52 (1974) 177–9; R.M. Errington, *Hermes* 105 (1977) 478–504; H. Hauben, *Historia* 26 (1977) 307–39 and *AncSoc* 8 (1977) 85–120; E.M. Anson, *The Ancient World* 3 (1980) 55–9.

A. Photius, *Bibliotheca* 82 p. 64a21–b32

(1) In his History of Affairs after Alexander he (Dexippus) starts from the death of the king itself and describes how the empire of the Macedonians devolved upon both the brother of Alexander, Arrhidaios, who had been born to Philip by the Larisan woman Philine, and upon the son of Alexander who was going to be born from Rhoxane (for she had been left pregnant) and upon Perdikkas and his group, who were made guardians of their rule for them by a decision of the Macedonians. (2) He describes also how the empire of Alexander was divided. The Asian parts were divided as follows: Ptolemy, son of Lagos, was appointed to rule all Egypt and Libya and the territory

beyond, as much as borders on Egypt. Kleomenes, who had been set in charge of the satrapy by King Alexander, was reappointed, (but) as Ptolemy's second-in-command. Laomedon of Mytilene was appointed to be ruler of the Syrians and Philotas of Cilicia, Pithon of Media, Eumenes of Cappadocia and Paphlagonia and of the territories that lie along the shore of the Euxine as far as Trapezous, Antigonos of the Pamphylians and the Cilicians as far as Phrygia, Asandros of the Carians, Menandros of the Lydians and Leonnatos of Hellespontine Phrygia. (3) That was the way in which the Asian parts (of the empire) were divided. Of the European parts, Lysimachos (was appointed to be ruler) of Thrace and the Chersonese, while from the time of Alexander Antipatros had been appointed general with absolute authority over all Macedonians and Greeks and Illyrians and Triballians and Agraeans and all parts of Epirus. (4) Krateros was entrusted with the care, that is the overall protection,[1] of the kingship, which was the highest position of honour among the Macedonians. Perdikkas (was entrusted with) the chiliarchy of Hephaistion. (5) The rulers of all the Indians were Poros and Taxiles. Poros was ruler of all those who live between the river Indus and the Hydaspes, Taxiles of the rest. A man named Pithon was ruler of those who are neighbours of the Indians, with the exception of the Par(op)amisadai. Those who share a border with the Indians and live at the foot of the Caucasus mountains (i.e. the Hindu Kush) were given to Oxyartes the Bactrian to rule, the father of Rhoxane, whose child was born after the death of its father, Alexander, and was called by the Macedonian army Alexander, after its father. (6) Sibyrtios was ruler over the Arachosians and Gedrosians and Stasanor from Soloi was ruler of the Areians and the Drangians. The Sogdians were the domain of Philippos, the Hyrcanians of Rhadaphernes (probably an error for 'Phrat2phernes') and Carmania of Neoptolemos. The Persians were set under Peukestes. Oropius[2] held the kingship of the Sousians, though the domain was not his ancestrally but a gift of Alexander himself. When it happened that he was deprived of his rule, as he was being brought to trial on a charge of rebellion, then Koinos[3] became ruler of these people. Seleukos was ruler of the Babylonians and of the land between the rivers Tigris and Euphrates, Archelaos was ruler of Mesopotamia. (7) Such was the number of the peoples and of the rulers of the peoples, when Perdikkas distributed the commands after the death of Alexander.[4]

B. Photius, *Bibliotheca* 92 pp. 69a1–71a7

He (*sc.* Arrian) is also the author of 'The History of Affairs after Alexander' in ten books, in which he treats the dissent of the army and the public proclamation of Arrhidaios . . . The infantry and the cavalry were at odds with each other. The most powerful of the commanders of the cavalry (were) Perdikkas, son of Orontes, Leonnatos, son of Anthes, and Ptolemy, son of Lagos. Next after them (were) Lysimachos, son of Agathokles, Aristonous, son of Peisaios, Peithon, son of Krateuas, Seleukos, son of Antiochos, and Eumenes, the Cardian. These were the leaders of the cavalry and (the leader) of the infantry was Meleagros. Then, after frequent delegations had passed between them, in the end the infantry, who had proclaimed the King, and the leaders of the cavalry agreed on terms, that Antipatros should be general of the European parts (of the empire), Krateros should be defender of Arrhidaios' kingship, Perdikkas should serve as chiliarch of the chiliarchy that Hephaistion used to administer (and that was the guardianship of the whole kingdom), while Meleagros should be Perdikkas' second-in-command. But Perdikkas, on the pretext of purging the army, arrested the ring-leaders of the dispute and, having arrested (them) as though on the orders of Arrhidaios, put (them) to death in his presence, after instilling fear in the rest. Not much later he got rid of Meleagros also. As a result of these actions Perdikkas was suspect to all and he himself became suspicious . . .[5] And Antipatros went to war with the Athenians and the other Greeks, who were led by the general Leosthenes. At first he was defeated and locked into a desperate situation, but later he was victorious, though Leonnatos, resolving to bring assistance to Antipatros, was killed. And Lysimachos, while fighting desperately for his satrapy against Seuthes the Thracian (for he had few supporters) and distinguishing himself, nevertheless was destroyed.[6] . . . In the sixth (book) he treats the flight from Athens of Demosthenes and Hypereides and their supporters, both Aristonikos of Marathon and Himeraios the brother of Demetrios of Phaleron. At first they went to Aegina. While they were staying there, the Athenian people condemned them to death on the motion of Demades, and Antipatros put the decree into effect . . .[7] And how not much later Demades was taken to Macedonia and killed by Kasandros, after his son had first been slaughtered in his arms. Kasandros brought against him the charge that he (Demades) had insulted his (Kasandros') father in the letter he had written to Perdikkas, (inviting him) to save the Greeks who were hanging from an old and rotten thread and by this phrase ridiculing Antipatros. Deinarchos the Corinthian was the accuser. So Demades, at least, paid a fitting penalty for his corruption and treachery and overall untrustworthiness . . .[8] And Perdikkas, plotting against Antigonos, summoned him to court. But Antigonos, knowing that he was being plotted against, did not obey and they became enemies of one another . . . Antigonos fled to Macedonia to Antipatros and Krateros and divulged

Perdikkas' plot against him and the fact that he was eagerly pursuing the same practice against them all. He described also, with tragic embellishment, the suffering of Kynane.[9] By setting out this information he set them at war with him (Perdikkas) . . . In the meantime also Eumenes brought gifts from Perdikkas to Kleopatra[10] at Sardis and (told her) that it had been resolved by Perdikkas to send Nikaia[11] away and marry her (Kleopatra) in her stead. When this information was made known to Antigonos – the informant was Menandros satrap of Lydia – and made public by him at the court of Antipatros and Krateros, they were all the more provoked to war in their dealings with Perdikkas. Antipatros and Krateros crossed the Hellespont from the Chersonese, bringing those who were guarding the passage under their control by diplomacy. They also sent embassies to Eumenes and Neoptolemos, Perdikkas' generals. Neoptolemos was won over, but Eumenes refused. Neoptolemos was suspicious of Eumenes and they waged war against each other and Eumenes was decisively victorious. Neoptolemos fled to Antipatros and Krateros with a small force and persuaded them into an alliance (on condition that) Krateros should come with him against Eumenes. And they both made war on Eumenes. Eumenes made every effort to achieve the result that the soldiers on his side did not know that it was Krateros who was fighting him in order that they might not be captivated by the reputation that surrounded him and either go over to his side or, if they stayed, be rendered less bold. He was successful in his designs and victorious in the war. Neoptolemos, a soldier's man and one who had gained the highest distinctions in wars, was slain by the hand of the secretary Eumenes himself, and Krateros (was slain) by some Paphlagonians while unsparingly fighting and marching in the forefront so as to be recognized. But he fell without being recognized even though he took the royal cap from his head.

1   The term is ambiguous and could also mean 'supervision'.
2   This name is an emendation and quite uncertain.
3   This name is an emendation.
4   An essentially similar list is given by Arrian (cf. n. 5), though his list does not include the far eastern satrapies and the manuscript of Photius there names the satrap of Caria Kasandros rather than Asandros. There is also a major difference over Krateros in Europe.
5   The narrative continues with the distribution of the satrapies by Perdikkas.
6   Clearly an error.
7   Cf. Plut. *Dem.* 28–30 and [Plut.] *Lives of the Ten Orators* (= *Moralia* 847a).
8   This story is repeated twice by Plutarch in the lives of Demosthenes (31.4.6) and of Phokion (30.9–10), though in the second the letter of Demades was sent to Antigonos. Cf.Diod. 18.48.1–4.
9   Daughter of Philip II and Eurydike. She came to Asia with her daughter Adea

(later Eurydike) to marry her to Philippos (Arrhidaios) and was killed by
Perdikkas. Eurydike later married Arrhidaios. This is described in the section here
omitted.

10   Sister of Alexander and widow of Alexandros of Epiros.
11   Daughter of Antipatros. On this episode cf. Diod. 18.23.1–3 and 25.3–4.

126   Extract from Ptolemy's constitution for Cyrene. Cyrene, 322/1 *or* 313/12 *or* 308/7.

Marble stele, Koine with occasional
Doricisms, non-stoichedon (individual articles of the constitution are
marked off by short lines after lines 15, 29, 35, 31, 33, 43, 56), very
difficult to read in the middle sections.

SEG 9 (1944) 1 (lines 1–46), pp. 1–3, with the corrected readings of P.M. Fraser as
reported in *SEG* 18 (1962) 726, pp. 228–9. Cf. Diod. 18.19–21, Justin, *Epitoma* 13.6.20.

M. Cary, *JHS* 48 (1928) 222–38; J.A.O. Larsen, *CP* 24 (1929) 351–68; Will, *Histoire*
1.32–4; P.M. Fraser, *Ptolemaic Alexandria* (Oxford 1972) 1.48–9, 95, 98–9, 786–8, 2.132;
R. Bagnall, *The Administration of the Ptolemaic Possessions outside Egypt* (London 1976) 28–9.

Good fortune. | Those *men* shall be citizens[1] (who are born) of a
[Cyren]ean [man] and a Cyrenean woman and those who | (are born)
[of] the Libyan women (who live) between the Katabathmos[2] and
Authamalax[3] and those who (are born) of the co|lonists from the cities
(that lie) beyond Thinitis, whom the Cyreneans sent out as colonists, *and*

5 ‖ *anyone* [whom] Ptolemy establishes (as a citizen) and anyone whom
the body politic accepts, in accordance with the following laws. | The
body politic is to be the Ten Thousand.[4] There shall belong to it the
exiles, the ones who have fled to Egypt, | whomever Ptolemy receives
and who have an assessment of possessions (that are) per|manently
secure,[5] together with those of the wife, worth twenty Alexandrian[6]
minas, (an assessment) that the assess|ors rate as unencumbered. And

10 all those[7] who are owed twenty Alexandrian minas, ‖ together with the
(possessions) of the wife that have been assessed as possessions (that
are) permanently secure (at a value) not less than the (capital) of
the de|bt and the interest,[8] and let the debtors on their part swear
solemnly,[9] even if their neighbours[10] do not | hold civic honours,[11]
these also (i.e. the creditors) are to belong to the Ten Thousand, if they
are not younger than thirty years (of age). As ass|essors sixty men are to
be chosen from the Ten Thousand by the members of the Gerousia
(from those) not younger | than thirty years (of age), after they (i.e. the
members of the Gerousia) have sworn the customary oath. Those who

15 have been chosen are to make their assessments, just as ‖ it is written
in the laws. For the first year let political rights be calculated on the
basis of the previous assessments. | Let the Council be five hundred

men, whoever are chosen by the lot, (men who are) not younger | than fifty years (of age). They are to be members of the Council for two years and they are to eliminate by the lot in the | third year half (of the councillors). They are to leave an interval of two years.[12] But if the (required) number is not achieved, | they are to hold an additional lot-
20   tery for the remainder from the forty-year olds. ‖ The members of the Gerousia are to be one hundred and one and (they are to be) those whom Ptolemy appoints. In place of th|e (member) who has died or been removed another shall become a member of the one hundred and one, whom the Ten Thousand are to ch|oose (from those) not younger than fifty years. It shall not be permitted for the members of the Gerousia to be ch|osen for any other magistracy, except as generals in time of war. [And] the | priests of Apollo are to be chosen from the
25   members of the Gerousia from those who have not been ‖ priests (and are) not younger than fifty years (of age). | Ptolemy is to be general in perpetuity. In addition to him there are to be chosen as gener|als five men from those who have not yet been generals (and are) not younger than fifty | years (of age). But if there is a war, (they are to be chosen) from the whole body politic. But if a war | arises in addition, some other one and not a Libyan one,[13] the Ten Thousand are to decide *whether*
30   ‖ [the] same men are to be generals or not. If it is resolved that the same men not (be generals, other generals) are to be chosen from the whole | body politic. |

    There are also to be nine guardians of the laws, (chosen) from those who have not been guardians of the laws, | and five overseers, (chosen) from those who have not been overseers, provided they are not younger than fifty years (of age). |

    The members of the Gerousia are to transact the business that the
35   Gerousia used to transact in time of peace, [and the] ‖ Council (is to transact the business) that the Council (used to transact), and the Ten Thousand (are to transact the business) that the Thousand (used to transact).[14] All lawsuits involving the death penalty are to be judg|ed by the members of the Gerousia and the Council and by one thousand five hundred from the Ten Thousand, who | are chosen by lot. The laws that are to be used are those that were in existence beforehand, all those that are not contrary to th|is edict. The magistrates are to be subject to scrutiny (for their performance in office) in accordance with the laws that are in exist|ence. In the case of any man, upon whom, when he is arrested by the generals, the members of the Gerousia and
40   the Council impose the death penalty in their judge‖ment, it shall be possible for him (to choose) whichever one of two (courses) he wishes, to be tried either under the laws or in (the court of) Ptol[em]|y, for a period of three years. After that he is to be tried under the laws. Against

an exile no | judgement is to be passed without (consulting) the opinion of (the court of) Ptolemy. |

Anyone from the body politic who is employed by the state to be a doctor or a trainer in the gymnasium or a teacher | of archery or of horse-riding or of fighting in heavy armour, or a herald in the Pry-

45   taneion is not elig||ible for the magistracies restricted to the Ten Thousand.[15]

1   I.e. have civic rights, as opposed to the political rights (the vote, eligibility for office) of the body politic.
2   Roman Solum, at the eastern end of the coast of Cyrenaica, east of modern Tobruk.
3   Near the western end of the coast of Cyrenaica, modern Bu Sceifa.
4   The number is reminiscent of the Assembly of the Ten Thousand of the Arcadian League.
5   The word used (athanatos) is an unusual one and has caused much dispute. From its basic meaning 'immortal', it can mean 'held in perpetuity' or 'permanent'. Elsewhere, when used of livestock or slaves it has the sense of something that must be maintained at its original value.
6   This surely means 'minas of the standard current at Alexandria'. See, e.g., Larsen 352–3. The sum of 20 minas (2000 drachmas) is the same as that required for the franchise in the constitution imposed on Athens by Antipatros after the Lamian War (Diod. 18.18.4).
7   The following passage is poorly understood and often left unexplained by the commentators.
8   That is, the wife's possessions are worth at least 20 minas and act as a kind of security for her husband's census.
9   I.e. that they do owe 20 minas.
10   Who, presumably, acted as witnesses to the oath sworn by the debtors.
11   That is, do not have the rights and privileges of citizens. Cf. Aristotle, *Politics* 3.1278a38.
12   I.e. before they can be members of the Council again.
13   I.e. beyond the borders of Cyrenaica; sometimes taken as a reference to the wars of the Successors.
14   The former oligarchic government of Cyrene.
15   The document continues for another forty-five lines. Of these the last 18 are a list of magistrates. Lines 46 to 73 are too mutilated to make a coherent translation possible. For some indication of what they may contain see Cary 235–6.

127   Samians honour Gorgos of Iasos. Samos, *c.* 321.[1] Marble stele, mainly Ionic dialect, non-stoichedon.

SIG 312; *Heisserer, *Alexander* 182–6. Cf. Athenaeus 12.538ab; nos. 114 and 128.

Heisserer, *Alexander* 186–93.

Resolved by the Council and the Pe|ople: Ep[i]kouros, son of Drakon, | made the motion. Since Gorgos and M|inneon,[2] sons of Theodotos,

5   the Iasians, no‖bly and well have behaved | toward the Samians in their
exile; and | (since) by Gorgos, during his residence at the court of
Alexan|der, much goodwill and zea|l was shown regarding the People
10   of Sa‖mos, by working energetically to the end that with all speed | the
Samians might recover their native land; and (since), when it was
a|nnounced by Alexander in his | camp that he would return Samos | to
15   the Samians and on that account the H‖ellenes crowned him, he was
cr|owned also by Gorgos; and (since) a message was sen|t by Gorgos to
Iasos to the magistrate|s to the end that those of the Samians who were
living | in Iasos, at the time when they should return to their native
20   ‖ land, without paying taxes on their possessions should carry (them)
aw|ay and that transport-vessels should be given to them, at the
e|xpense of the city of the Iasians, | and (since) even now a promise is
25   give|n by Gorgos and Minion that they will do what‖ever good they can
to the People | of Samos, let it be resolved by the People that there shall
be g|iven to them citizenship on fair | and equal terms, both to them
and to their descendants, | and they shall be assigned by lot to a tribe
30   a‖nd a thousand and a hundred and a cl|an[3] and (their names) shall be
inscribed into (the register of) whatever clan | they obtain by the lot,
just as also the othe|r Samians (are inscribed), and for that inscription
35   the res|ponsibility shall belong to the five el‖ected men. This decree
shall be in|scribed on a marble stele and set | up in the temple of Hera.
The trea|surer shall do service (as far as the cost is concerned). *vv* |

1   The inscription cannot be dated before the restoration of the Samian exiles to Samos
    in 321. It is, however, normally dated in that year.
2   The spelling of this name is inconsistent in this document. On Iasian documents
    the spelling is Minnion.
3   Presumably subdivisions of the tribe.

128   Samians honour Antileon of Chalcis. Samos, *c.* 321.[1] Three
fragments of a marble stele, mainly Ionic, non-stoichedon.

C. Habicht, *MDAI(A)* 72 (1957) no. 1, pp. 156–64. Cf. no. 127.

C. Habicht, *Chiron* 5 (1975) 45–50; R.M. Errington, *Chiron* 5 (1975) 51–7; E. Badian, *ZPE*
23 (1976) 289–94; H. Hauben, *AncSoc* 8 (1977) 90–1, 119–20.

Fragment A

Resolved by the People: Since, after A[risto]phon had made a mot|ion
and drawn up a bill in Athens | (namely that) the [A]thenian general
who for duty on Samos[2] | had been elected should (in the matter of)

5   those Samians who from Anai‖a³ had returned, both themselves and
their children, | arrest (them) and send them to Athens, | and after the
People of Athens had put this (motion) to the | vote and the Paralos⁴

10   bearing the dec|ree had been sent to Samos, by the gener‖al many noble
and good | citizens were arrested and despatched (to Athens, citizens)
whom the A|thenians confined in prison | and condemned to death;
and (since) when Antileon, son of Leonti|nos, a Chalcidian, one of

15   those from Euripos,⁵ learned ‖ of the dangers that surrounded those of
the Samians | who had been imprisoned in Athens, maintaining the |
friendship that between the Chalcidians and Samians ex|isted and of
the goodwill that he personally had f|or the Samians giving a demon-

20   stration, he sent mon‖ey from his private resources to Athens to the
Boule and the Eleven and saved thes|e men and prevented the
Athenians from p|utting them to death, and, after the men had been
brought safely | to Chalcis [-- | ---]

Fragments B, C

5   [--- | --- | --- | - of the] money [that has been expended ‖ by him] on the
preservation [of the men. In | order that] *we may honour* Antil[e]on [for this
benefa|ction] with *fitting* favours [and ho|nours (?)], let it be resolved by
the People: [There shall be set up] of Antil[eon | a statue] of bronze in

10   the temple [of Hera and he shall be crow‖ned] with a golden crown [on
account of his excell|ence, (a crown) worth -] drachmas, at the time
when [the contest] for the *Kings*⁶ | *is celebrated* by us. [This] decree [shall
be inscrib|ed by the] Auditors on a stele [of marble and | set up] in the

15   temple of Hera, [and the responsibility ‖ for the] inscription of the stele
[shall belong to the Five]⁷ | *vacat*

1   For the date see no. 127 n. 1.
2   Aristotle does not mention a general for Samos, but he does know that the Athenians
     sent out magistrates to Samos (*Ath. Pol.* 62.2).
3   Samian territory on the mainland.
4   One of the best-known state-galleys at Athens. For an account of these ships, their
     primarily religious duties, their origin and the nature of their crews see B. Jordan,
     The Athenian Navy in the Classical Period (Berkeley and Los Angeles 1975) 153–81.
5   Cf. Pausanias 5.23.2.
6   Philippos III (Arrhidaios) and Alexander IV, in whose name, presumably, Perdikkas
     had restored Samos to the Samians (Diod. 18.18.9).
7   Cf. no. 127 lines 33–5.

**129   The deme Aixone honours Demetrios of Phaleron. Athens,
317/16.** Marble stele, Ionic letters, stoichedon (except line 1, which
forms a heading).

IG II² 1201+, p. 672; S. Dow and A. Travis, **Hesperia* 12 (1943) 149. Cf. Diod. 18.74.3.

Ferguson, *Athens* 36–94; Dow and Travis, *Hesperia* 12 (1943) 144–65.

Gods. | [Aristok]rates, son of Aristophanes, made the motion. Sinc|e [Demetr]ios, son of Phanostratos, of Phaleron [is] a man | of excellence
5   toward the People of Athen||[s and the] deme Aixone; and (since,) when war | [arose] in the land and a division existed between [t|he Peiraeus] and the city on account of the [wa|r (?)],[1] [by his negotiations] he reconciled the Athenian[s and once | again] *restored* (them) to unity
10   and *a state of peace* [was p||rocured] (by him) for the [A]thenians and their territory; [and] | (since) when he had been elected [lawgiver][2] by the People [of Ath|ens] he made [laws] (that were) good and [advan-t|ageous for the] *city*; [and] later [--] |

1   The war between Kassandros and Polyperchon in 318/17. Cf. Diod. 18.68.1–3, 74.1–3.
2   In Greek 'nomothetes'. For the various suggestions for restoring the title that Demetrios held and the arguments in favour of this one see Dow and Travis 145–56.

130   Rise of Kassandros to the throne of Macedon. 317/16.

Justin, *Epitoma* 14.5.1–5. Cf. Diod. 19.11.1–9; no. 1 (*MP*) under 319/18 and 316/15.

G.H. Macurdy, *Hellenistic Queens* (Baltimore 1932) 40–2, 48–52; Cloché, *Dislocation* 95–119; Will, *Histoire* 1.43–6; G. Cohen, *Historia* 22 (1973) 384–6.

Meanwhile Eurydike, wife of King Arrhidaios, when she learned that Polyperchon was returning from Greece to Macedon and that Olympias had been summoned by him, struck by feminine jealousy and taking advantage of the ill health of her husband, whose duties she arrogated to herself, wrote to Polyperchon in the name of the king, (telling him) that he was to hand over the army to Kassandros, upon whom the king had transferred the administration of the kingdom. By letter she announced the same information in Asia also to Antigonos. With his hands tied by this benefaction, Kassandros did nothing that did not accord with the judgement of her womanly arrogance. Following this he set out for Greece where he made war on many states.

131   Donations for the rebuilding of Thebes. Thebes, after 316.[1]
Marble stele (inscribed in two columns), Boeotian dialect, non-stoichedon.

IG VII 2419; *SIG* 337; **M. Holleaux, *Études d'épigraphie et d'histoire grecques* 1 (Paris 1938) 40. Cf. Diod. 19.53.2, 54.1, 63.4; Pausanias 9.7.1.

M. Holleaux, *Études d'épigraphie* 1.1–40; I.L. Merker, *Historia* 19 (1970) 143–50; J. Seibert, *Historia* 19 (1970) 337–51.

Col. 2.[2] Philo[kles, --][3] | [-] talents [of silver coin] | of the Alexand[er
20   type].[4] ‖ The Eretrians: | [-- drachmas] | of the Attic standard. | The
25   Coans: four [--]. | The Melians: [--] *talents.* ‖ The Aeginetans: [--] | of the
Aeginetan standard. | Philokles [--][5] | dedicated [--][6] *talen|ts* one
30   hundred. ‖ King [Demetrios[7] | -] drachmas [-][8] | oil-tax [-- | -][9] from
35   the Rhod[ians] | as a tithe [--].[10] ‖ The kings [--][11] | to the city [--].[12] |
King [-- | ---]. King [-- | ---].

1   The donations that were recorded on this stone most likely began at the time of
    the re-founding of Thebes in 316. They were, however, made over a period of
    several years and this stele was not inscribed until the end of the fourth century or
    even possibly the beginning of the third.
2   The remains of col. 1 are too mutilated to make coherent translation possible.
3   Usually restored to read Philokles, son of Apollodoros, later king of Sidon. If the
    same patronymic is given to the Philokles in line 27, the peculiarity is created of
    two donations from the same source. But Seibert (344) correctly points out that
    the name in line 18 could be restored in many different ways and need not be the
    same as in line 27, on whom see n. 5. Since Philokles is the only private individual
    listed as making a donation, Merker (144) wants to restore 'King of the Sidonians'
    here.
4   See Merker 145–6.
5   Against the standard identification of Philokles as the son of Apollodoros, the
    Phoenician general who later became king of Sidon, Seibert proposes the Athenian
    Philokles, son of Phormion, of Eroiadai (*op. cit.* 344), on whom see Davies, *Families*
    14541.
6   Probably 'to the Gods'.
7   I.e. Poliorketes. For this restoration and the explication of the following lines see
    Holleaux 20–4.
8   '[for the]' (Reinach).
9   '[from the | spoils]' (Reinach).
10   '[dedicated to the gods]' (Reinach).
11   '[made the following gifts]' (Reinach).
12   '[for its foundation]' (Reinach).

**132   Letter of Antigonos Monophthalmos to Skepsis,[1] announcing
the peace concluded with Kassandros, Lysimachos and Ptolemy.
Skepsis, 311/10.** Marble stele, Ionic letters, stoichedon (in ruled
squares, except that iota sometimes occupies a square with another
letter and there is occasional crowding at the end of the line), now lost.

RCHP 1, pp. 3–12; **SV* 3.428, pp. 40–4. Cf. Diod. 19.105.1, 20.19.3.

R.H. Simpson, *JHS* 74 (1954) 25–31; P. Cloché, *Dislocation* 170–8; Ryder, *Eirene* 112–14,
163–4; Will, *Histoire* 1.54–7; K. Rosen, *AClass* 10 (1967) 82–4; Wehrli, *Antigone* 52–5.

[--]² we exerted [our efforts for the] | liberty [of the Greeks]; some other
major points [for | this reason] were conceded by us and money [- | -]³
5   *and* for this purpose we sent out ‖ Aischylos [along with Dema]rchos.⁴
As long as there was agree|ment [on] this⁵ the meeting at the
Helle[s|pont]⁶ was participated in by us, and if some trouble-mak|ers
had not got in the way,⁷ this matter would have been settled at that
time. | [And on the present occasion], when negotiations had begun
10   between Kassandros and Pto‖[lemy]⁸ for a cessation of hostilities (and)
to us had | come Prepelaos and Aristodemos⁹ | on this matter, although
we saw that some of the points that were demand|ed by Kassandros
were rather hard to accept, (nevertheless), since the matter | concern-
ing the Greeks was agreed upon, it was nec‖essary to overlook (these
15   points), we thought, in order that the over|all agreement be settled as
quickly as possible. For | we should have considered it a matter of
overriding importance that everything be managed | for the Greeks in
accordance with our preference, but on account of the fact | that this
20   was a rather long-term project, and that in del‖aying sometimes many
unexpected things happ|en, and because we were eager that during our
lifetime¹⁰ affairs concerning the | Greeks be settled, we thought it
necessary not | to risk over small points the conclusion of the overall
settlement. | Of the extent to which we exerted ourselves on these
25   negotiations, clear ‖ proof will, I think, be (given) both to you and to the
others, | all of them, by the terms of the settlement themselves. After
o|ur negotiations with Kassandros and Lysimachos had been con-
|cluded, for the accomplishment [of which]¹¹ Prepelaos had been sent
30   by them with ab|solute authority, Ptolemy despatched to u‖s ambas-
sadors, asking both that the hostilities against him be brought | to an
end and that he be a signatory to the same agreement. | We perceived
that it was no small thing to give up pa|rt of an ambition¹² over which
no little trouble | had been taken and much money had been spent by
35   us; ‖ and at that when affairs with Kas[s]andros and [L]ysi[ma]|chos
had been settled for us and easier (for that reason) | was the rest of our
business; yet in spite of that, | on account of our belief that, when affairs
40   with him | had been settled, affairs with Polyperchon¹³ ‖ might be man-
aged the faster, if there was nobody bound to him | by an oath; and
because of the relationship that ex|isted for us with him;¹⁴ and at the
same time when both you, as we s|aw, and the rest of the allies were
45   being trou|bled by both the campaigns and the expen‖ses, we thought
that it was good to yield and | to conclude the cessation of hostilities
with him also. | For the conclusion of the agreement we sent
Aris|to[de]mos and Aischylos and Hegesias. These men | have returned
50   with the pledges and the men ‖ from Ptolemy, Aristoboulos and his
colleagues, have co|me to take (the pledges) from us. Know therefore

that there has been acc|omplished a cessation of hostilities and peace
has | been concluded. We have written in the agreement | that all the
55 Greeks shall swear to join in protect‖ing for each other their freedom
and auto|nomy, thinking that in our time, so far as (they can be pro-
tected) by h|uman calculation, protection would be given to these
thi|ngs, but for the future, if oaths were b|inding both all the Greeks
60 and those‖ in power, far more secu|re would remain freedom for the
Greeks. | And the act of swearing jointly to join in protecting the
(terms) that w|e have agreed with each other is not disgrace|ful nor
65 disadvantageous to the Greeks in our view. ‖ Indeed it seems to me[15] a
good thing that you should swear | the oath that we have sent. And we
shall attempt | for the future also whatever we can that is of advan|tage
to both you and the other Greeks to pr|ovide. About these matters both
70 to write (to you) was my ‖ resolve and to send Akios to conver|se (with
you). He brings you, both of the agreement that we h|ave made and of
the oath, copies. Farewell.

1 It is hardly likely that the little town of Skepsis was the only recipient of this clearly
propagandistic letter.
2 The upper part of the stele is broken off.
3 Emendations, all of which can be found in the *apparatus criticus* to *SV*, are as follows:
'[for negotiations]' (Dittenberger, Schubart); '[for the cessation of hostilities] or
[on the communications]' (Munro); '[apportioning]' (Köhler); '[distributing in
addition]' (Welles). See also Welles (*RCHP*) 9 *ad loc.*
4 Antigonos' ambasssadors to Kassandros. See Welles 9 *ad loc.*
5 I.e. the liberty of the Greeks. Other emendations (see *SV*, *app. crit.*) are: 'so long as
there was agreement, [in] the meanwhile' (Munro); 'so long as there was [some]
agreement with these men' (Dittenberger). The reading here is that of Schubart,
followed by Welles (*RCHP*) and Schmitt (*SV*).
6 Cf. Diod. 19.75.6.
7 See Welles 9 *ad loc.*
8 The mention of Ptolemy here is rather surprising, since elsewhere Kassandros is
linked with Lysimachos (lines 27 and 35) and Ptolemy is treated as a third party.
See Welles 9 *ad loc.*
9 Ambassadors of Kassandros. See Welles 10 *ad loc.*
10 Antigonos was now 71, if we accept the figure for his age at death given in no. 140.
11 Supplied by Dittenberger (*ap. SV*); 'to [Ptolemy]' (Munro).
12 See Welles 10 *ad loc.*
13 Polyperchon was not at this moment a serious contender, but in 309/8 he managed
to strike a bargain with Kassandros that occasioned no. 133. Cf. Diod. 20.20, 28.
14 Ptolemy and Demetrios, son of Antigonos, had both married daughters of Antipatros.
15 Here and in line 69 Antigonos uses the singular pronoun. See Welles 10 *ad loc.*

133 Alliance of Ptolemy with Antigonos and Demetrios. 309/8.

Suidas, *Lexicon s.v.* Demetrios; *SV 3.433, pp. 49–50.

Cloché, *Dislocation* 184; K. Rosen, *AClass* 10 (1967) 85–6; Will, *Histoire* 1.60–1; Wehrli, *Antigone* 58–9.

Demetrios, son of Antigonos, and Ptolemy agreed that there should be a treaty of friendship between them; the terms were that the whole of Greece should be free and each would defend the other's territory . . . But the agreement between Ptolemy and Demetrios regarding the treaty was not of long duration.

134   Renovating the walls of Athens. Athens, 307/6. Marble stele, Ionic letters, stoichedon.

IG II² 463 (lines 52–74); *Maier, *Mauerbauinschriften* 11, pp. 49–56.[1]

L.D. Caskey, *AJA* 14 (1910) 298ff.; W.S. Ferguson, *Athens* 113; L.B. Holland, *AJA* 54 (1945) 337–56; F. Winter, *Phoenix* 13 (1959) 161–200; A.W. Lawrence, *Greek Aims in Fortification* (Oxford 1979) 368–70.

[--]. And he shall build a roof for the wall-walk | [of the] *wall* around [the city, excluding] the compartment wall[2] and the dipylon above the gates,[3] | [and for the][4] Long Walls, after removing the cornices from the
55   screen-wall. And all the parts of the parapet that h‖ave been *damaged* for more than six fingers he shall build with brick, leaving embrasures two bricks wide, making the height | [of the] parapet three feet, of the embrasure ten courses (of bricks). And he shall set upon (the embrasures) lintels of wo|od the thickness of the wall, one course high, eight feet in length, having fastened (them) with nails. And he shall set blocks of wood beneath the li|ntels and upon (the lintels) he shall lay bricks six courses high. And he shall build off the inward side[5] | piers two bricks wide, where they are not built, spaced seven feet apart, and
60   into (these) he shall b‖uild two cross-beams, spaced three and a half feet apart, making the height of the pier so as to be | level toward the inner side.[6] And he will set beams upon the piers. Where a roof has not been built, he will build a roof with small | beams and planks, laying (them) crosswise, or with cross-beams[7] driven down upon nails, spacing (them) three pal|ms apart, from above.[8] And after closing off (the gaps between the rafters) on the wall with brick, he shall trim the eave strai|ght along the edge, (the eave) that extends not less than a foot and a half. And he shall hammer on a cornice-top, making (it)
65   s‖traight at the top, (its) width (being) seven fingers, thickness one palm, cutting from the inner side the thicknes|s of a plank and making the face (conform) to the slope. And toward the interior he shall hammer on pla|nks, at intervals of three palms, one finger thick, in width

168

five fingers, (using) nails of iro|n. And having cast on (these) rush stripped of its bark under which have been spread beanpod or rush, he shall coat with clay mixed with | chaff, three fingers thick. And he shall tile with Laconian tile the whole extent of the city-wall's wall-
70 w||alk; and wherever the lead-tiles[9] of the Long Walls are not in place, (he shall tile these with Laconian tile) after setting (them) whole in clay upright al|ong the edge; and he shall cover (the joints) in tile, setting the cover tiles whole in clay. And he shall set a cornice [on] | the exterior, of Corinthian cornice-tiles, smoothing off the joints fitting together and setting (them) *straight* [along the] e|dge and at the top. And after making a protective cove[10] he will cover it with clay mixed with chaff, (making) [its width] run | in a straight line, its height four courses of brick.

1   This long inscription is for the most part badly mutilated. The lines translated are amongst the best preserved and contain material of importance to the history of fortification. That is not to say that there is universal agreement about their interpretation, as will be evident from two such different proposals for the roofing-system as those of Winter (p. 182) and Maier (p. 61), who is followed by Lawrence (p. 369); quite apart from the fact that Holland can maintain that we are not concerned with a roofing-system at all, but with the pavement of the wall-walk.
2   See on this wall H.A. Thompson and R.L. Scranton, *Hesperia* 12 (1943) 303–12 and 333–40.
3   See Thompson and Scranton 312–24.
4   '[in the sector facing toward]' (Winter 171).
5   A most troublesome phrase. Cf. Lawrence 369.
6   For different ways of interpreting this phrase see Winter 174–5.
7   'or else with (small beams and) stretcher-poles' (Winter 177).
8   To be taken with 'driven down upon nails'. For the process see Winter 178, following Holland 351–2.
9   'Hegemones'. On these see Winter 180–1.
10 '(For the base of the screen-wall)' (Winter 178).

135   Athenian artillery on the Acropolis.[1] Athens, 307/6.[2]
Fragment of a marble stele, Ionic letters, non-stoichedon.

IG II[2] 1487 fr. A (reverse), lines 84–90. Cf. [Plut.] *Moralia* 851d.

Ferguson, *Athens* 114; E.W. Marsden, *Greek and Roman Artillery: Historical Development* (Oxford 1969) 69–70.

85 [--] a cata||pult that throws stones and *shoots sharp bolts* [-], | four-cubit, complete, [the work] of Bromio[s]. | Another catapult, three-cubit, [--], | complete. Another catapult, three-cubit, *sine*|*w-sprung*, with an aper-

90   ture, complete. Another catapu‖lt, three-span, sinew-sprung, [com-
plete]. |

1   The document is one of the accounts of the treasurers of Athena and the Other Gods
on the Acropolis. There was nothing exceptional about their having artillery in their
charge. They had done so at least since the time of Lykourgos (338–326). The parts
were stored in the Erechtheion or the Chalkotheke. Cf. Marsden 56 and 68.

2   The date is established by line 53: 'In Anaxikr[ates' archonship]' (307/6) and
confirmed by line 91, where a new entry begins under the heading 'In the archonship
of Koroibos' (306/5). At this time Athens was preparing for the Four Years' War,
with help from Demetrios and Antigonos. Evidence for this support is often found
in another treasury-account (*IG* II² 1492 B), where in lines 99–103 there is recorded
a transfer in the archonship of Koroibos of some 140 talents of gold and silver that
were '*from* [Anti]g[onos]'.

136   Establishment of the Demetrieia on Delos by the Island League. Delos, *c.* 306/5. Marble stele, non-stoichedon.

IG XI 4.1036.

Ferguson, *Athens* 190; Tarn, *Antigonos Gonatas* (Oxford 1913) 432–9; Wehrli, *Antigone*
113–18; I.L. Merker, *Historia* 19 (1970) 141–60 (especially 141–2).

[--] the Greeks. [Honours shall be given | by the League of the][1]
Islanders worthily in accordance with its ability | [to Demetrios] with
honours that *befit* him. *There shall be cel|ebrated* [by them on] Delos every
5   second year the *fes‖tival* [of the An]tigone[i]a that they now celebrate,
and in | [every other] (year there shall be celebrated) [a sacrifice] and
games and a convention (to which) *they have given* | *the name*
[Dem]e[tr]ie[i]a, and delegates shall be se|nt [to] *these* just as they are
sent to the | [Antigoneia], *and* [the] preparation of the sacrificial victims
10   and ‖ [--][2] and the hiring of the crafts|men [--][3] of the prizes for the
| [Demetrieia from the] *common* monies in accordance with | [the con-
tribution] that exists at present for the Islanders *for the* | *sake of* [the
15   Antigo]neia; and if any of the Islanders ‖ [do not pay] for these the con-
tribution that *has been imp|osed* [--] | (The inscription here becomes
incomprehensible. Translation resumes in line 35.)
When the citie|s [choose the] *delegates* who during the follow|ing [year]
are to attend the Demetrieia, | [they shall contribute] the amount of
money that for the Antigone[ia] | [was assessed]. *Thought shall be taken*
40   and consideration given whence it shall be possible to *pr‖ovide* [the]
money from which the Demetrieia *shall be cele|brated by them* [for the] time
hereafter. However these matters are manag|ed [by themselves], that
shall be final. As for those who after th|is are sent out as delegates, in

accordance with what was assessed | [originally] they shall make [their]
45   payments. Inscription shall be made by the ‖ [delegates of this] decree
and it shall be set up by the *al*|*tar* [of the] *Kings*.

1   Restorations are by Durrbach, *BCH* 28 (1904) 93 n. 1 and *BCH* 31 (1907) 208f., with
    modifications by P. Roussel, the editor of *IG* XI (4).
2   '[Of the games] *shall be managed*' (?) (Durrbach).
3   The remains are too corrupt to make restoration possible, but most likely contain
    some reference to the cost of the prizes.

137   The tribe Akamantis decrees a sacrifice for the safe return of its soldiers. Athens, 304/3 *or* 303/2. Marble stele, stoichedon.

ISE 1.5, pp. 8–10. Cf. Diod. 20. 102.1–103.7; Plut. *Demetrios* 25.

W.S. Ferguson, *Hesperia* 17 (1948) 112–36; J. and L. Robert, *Bulletin Épigraphique* in *REG*
62 (1949) 109–13; Wehrli, *Antigone* 65.

5   [--- | -] *by sea* [- | ---] | of the People of A[thens -] ‖ *and* of *all* the Greeks [-
    | -] Pleistarchos[1] and [-- | -] Greek cities [-] f|or slavery having cap-
    tured (them), in accordance with [the agreements free][2] *an*|*d* autonom-
10 ous he has made (them). *In order that,* [therefore, all that] *rema*‖*ins* may
    be accomplished *advantageously* [for the whole Peop|le] of Athens and
    for the [other allies,[3] and that the] s|oldiers on campaign safe [from the
    campaign[4] may retur|n] to the city after *defeating* [the enemy, it was
    resolved]: | *oxen*[5] shall be sacrificed by the prytaneis [of the tribe
15 Akamantis] ‖ for the safety of their [fellow-tribesmen], *who are away on
    campaign,* | to Athena Nike and A[thena Polias and] th|e Saviours.[6] The
    treasurer [and the superintendents of the moment] | shall apportion to
    them for [this sacrifice and the] *de*|*dication* to the Eponymous Hero 300
20 [drachmas of silver, and shall giv‖e] to them for the [--][7] | year in [the
    month] of Elaphebo[lion for the] *sacrif*|*ice* to the Saviours and [--][8]
    dr|achmas as a memorial of the [--][9] | during the [prytany] of
    Akamanti[s. Let it be voted by the | tribe] that the *secretaries* [--] | .

1   Brother of Kassandros. His departure from Europe for Asia Minor early in 302/1
    (Plut. *Demetrios* 31) provides the lower terminus for dating the inscription.
2   Restored by Ferguson. The remaining restorations in the text are by J. and L.
    Robert, except where noted.
3   Moretti, *ISE*; '[all the other Greeks]' (Robert).
4   Moretti, *ISE*; '[from the war]' (Ferguson).
5   The restoration of lines 14–19 is by Ferguson, with the exception of the word 'give'
    at the end of line 19 (Robert). Ferguson restored 'apportion'. In line 15 Robert
    restore 'citizens' in place of 'fellow-tribesmen'.

6 Antigonos and Demetrios, whose cult as Soteres was introduced in Athens in 307/6 (Diod. 20.46).
7 'year [following the campaign]' (Moretti); '[time thereafter, year by] year' (Robert); '[for the great festival of the Saviours year by] year' (Ferguson).
8 '[the festival of the Saviours 200]' (Moretti); '[the procession for the Saviours 100]' (Ferguson).
9 '[successes that have been reported]' (Moretti, following Robert); '[concessions that have made by Demetrios]' (Ferguson).

138   Foundation of the Hellenic League under Antigonos and Demetrios. Epidaurus, 303/2.
Twelve fragments of a limestone stele, inscribed both front and back in the upper part,[1] late fourth-century lettering, non-stoichedon.

IG IV² (1) 68; *ISE* 1.14, pp. 105–18; **SV* 3.446, pp. 63–80, 393. W. Peek, *Abh. d. Sächs. Akad. Wiss., Phil.-Hist. Klasse* 60.2 (Leipzig 1969) 19–22 (fragment *m* with discussion of other fragments). Cf. Diod. 20.102.1; Plut. *Demetrios* 25.3; no. 99.

Ferguson, *Athens* 121–2; Ryder, *Eirene* 114; Larsen, *Government* 47–65; Will, *Histoire* 1.66–7; Wehrli, *Antigone* 122–6.

5 [--- | --- | --- | --- ‖ --]. It shall not be p|ermitted *to seize goods in reprisal, neither* [in the case of those] who are on embassy [from the Greeks][2] to the members | of the council [nor] *in the case of those* who are despatched [by the] members of the Council nor in the case of those who on the Lea|gue's *military business*[3] are sent out [nor] (those) *who set out*[4] each on the duties assigned to them | nor (those) *who are returning home* to their [own cities],[5] nor (shall it be permitted) to seize their bodies in reprisal
10 nor to hold them as se‖curity [for] *any* charge *at all*. But if anyone [does these things],[6] *both* [the] magistrates in each of the | cities are to stop (him) and the *members of the council* are to [sit in judgement].[7] There shall be meetings of the members | of the council in peace-time at the [sacred games], but in wartime (there shall be meetings) as often as is thought | beneficial by the members of the council and [by the] *general* who by the kings for the Lea|gue's protection has been left behind. Meetings of
15 the council shall last as many days as the presidents ‖ of the council ordain. Meetings of the council shall take place, un|til the League's war is ended, wherever the presidents and the king or the ki|ngs' appointed general ordain. But when peace is made, | (meetings of the council shall take place) whenever the crowned contests *are held*.[8] To the resolutions of the council [ultimate authority] | shall belong. Business is to be transacted when over half (of the members of the council) are present,
20 but if fewer (than half) convene, ‖ business shall not be transacted. Regarding the resolutions made in the council it is not to be permitted [for the] | cities to hold the delegates they despatch to account. Pres|i-

dents shall be five whoever are chosen by lot, from among the coun-
cillors once the war [is ended].[9] | *More* than one (president) is not to be
chosen[10] by lot from a (particular) tribe or city. [And] these shall
conv|ene the members of the council *and* [the][11] secretaries *at the*
25   *League's expense* [and their][12] ‖ attendants and shall set forth (the
matters) about which [it is necessary] to take counsel *and* [shall --
the][13] resolutions | to the secretaries, keeping also themselves [legible]
copies, and [all] law|suits they shall introduce and they shall supervise
the transaction of business in every way[14] *as necessary,*[15] full authority | belong-
ing to them for punishing the disorderly. [Whoever][16] wishes *to propose*
[anything] that is | advantageous to the kings and [the] *Greeks,*[17] or to
30   impeach certain individuals on the grounds that ‖ they are acting contrary to (the interests of) the allies [or] are not being obedient to the
resolut|ions, or to transact any other business with the *members of the
council,* let him apply in writing to the presidents, | and they are to set
forth (the matter) before the members of the council. Liable to account
shall be those who are chosen by lot (to be) | presidents, for any business
they handle. Let any man bring suit against *them* before | those who
have been chosen as presidents to succeed them. [And they], *taking over*
35   (the indictments) are to introd‖uce (them) before the members of the
council at the first meeting that shall take place *under* [their super-
vision]. Until the League's war is ended, the presidents shall [at all
times][18] be [those] *appointed by* the kings. If | any city does not send in
accordance with the [agreements] delegates to the | meetings, it is to
pay a fine *for each of these* of two [drachmas] for each day, | until the
council is dissolved, except if a *member* swear in excuse that he was ill.
40   ‖ And if a city does not send the *military force* it was assessed in accord-
ance with what is or|dained, it is to pay a fine for each day; [for] a
cavalryman half a mina, fo|r an infantryman twenty drachmas, for [a]
light-armed soldier ten drachmas and fo|r a sailor [ten][19] drachmas, until
[the] duration of the expedition [has expired] *for all* | the other *Greeks.*
[--] *vv* | *vacat*

---

1   Of the twelve fragments (*a–m*), only two (*l* and *h*) are inscribed on both front and
back. It is reasonable to assume they belong to the upper part of the document.
They do not join one another, nor do they join the part formed by the combination
of the other fragments. The text of the inscription as it stands breaks, therefore,
into five parts: (1) *l* (front); (2) *h* (front); (3) *a–g* + *i–k* + *m*; (4) *l* (back); (5) *h*
(back). Of these the only part that lends itself to translation is 3. Since there is no
physical connection between part 3 and those around it, I have numbered the lines
independently, but in a composite text with lines numbered consecutively the
passage here translated would be lines 56–99.
2   For the source of all alternate restorations given in the notes below consult the
apparatus criticus and bibliography in *SV*, p. 64, pp. 70–1. For this line other restorations are: '[to prevent either the members of the council or those] *on embassy*'

(Wilhelm); '[for anyone to detain either the members of the council or those] *on embassy*' (Kougeas). The present restoration is by Hiller and has in its favour the fact that the verb ('to seize goods in reprisal for some act') is precisely balanced by the verb in line 9 ('to seize a person's body in reprisal').

3   Kavvadias; *'security'* (Swoboda).
4   '[nor] (those) *who go out*' (Wilamowitz); '[infantrymen and] *sailors*' (Kougeas).
5   'their [cities]' (Kavvadias); 'their [own hearths]' (Wilhelm); 'their [fatherlands]' (Wilcken).
6   '[he does any] *of these things*' (Wilhelm).
7   *'the allies* are to [stop]' (Kavvadias); *'the members of the council* are to [judge]' (Wilhelm); *'the members of the council* are to [punish]' (Wilcken); *'the members of the council* are to [give assistance]' (Roussel); *'the members of the council* are to [make atonement]' (Peek).
8   'are celebrated' (Kavvadias); 'take place' (Kougeas).
9   '[there is] war [in the] | land' (Kavvadias, Wilhelm, Kougeas).
10   '[Not] more than one (president) is to be chosen' (Wilhelm, Wilcken, Kougeas).
11   '[two]' (Kougeas).
12   'from the *League* [chosen and their]' (Wilhelm); '*at the League's expense* [to hire and their]' (Roussel); '*as a result of the League's* [resolution and their]' (Hiller).
13   '[shall hand over the]' (Wilhelm, Kougeas).
14   'supervise *those wishing* [to speak] or *to transact business*' (Wilhelm).
15   '*in* [an orderly manner]' (Kougeas); '*in a well-ordered manner*' (Roussel).
16   '[and if anyone]' (Wilhelm).
17   '[the] *cities*' (Kougeas, Roussel).
18   'shall be [five] *appointed by*' (Levi, Bengtson).
19   '[five]' (Wilhelm).

139   Athens honours Nikandros of Ilium and Polyzelos of Ephesus. Athens, 301. Two fragments of a marble stele, Ionic letters, stoichedon (except line 1, which forms a heading).

IG II² 505; *Maier, *Mauerbauinschriften* 13, pp. 69–73.

R. Thomsen, *Eisphora* (Copenhagen 1964) 237–42; Pečiřka, *Enktesis* 80–1 and *Eirene* 6 (1967) 23–6.

Gods. | In the archonship of Nikokles (302/1), when Aiantis (held) the twe|lfth prytany, for which Nikon, son of Theodoros, of Plotheia was |
5   secretary, on the twenty-first of Skirophorion, on the t‖wenty-first day of the prytany, a meeting of the assembly (was held); of the P|roedroi the one who put (the motion) to the vote was Epikrates, son of Diokles, of Achar|nai and his fellow-Proedroi. Resolved by the Boule and the | People, Euphiletos, son of Aristeides, of Kephisia[1] made the motion: S|ince Nikandros, son of Antiphanes, of Ilium and
10   Polyz[e‖l]os, son of Apollophanes, of Ephesus have continued on e|very occasion to be well disposed to the People of Athen|s and, whilst resi-

dent at Athens, in many cases of a|dvantage to the People have been
good men, both in the case of | the building of the ship-sheds and the
15 arsen‖al[2] contributing the capital levies year by | year into the Ten
Talent fund[3] nobly and eage|rly from the archonship of Themistokles
(347/6) up to (the archonship) of Kephisod|[or]os (323/2), and during
the Hellenic War[4] in the case of the ships | [that] sailed out with
20 Eue[ti]on[5] for the firs‖t *review* nobly and zealously they helped to see to
| it that they did sail out, and again after the naval bat|tle, when the
25 ships sailed [back -- | --- | --] they cr‖owned along with the *others* [-- | -]
those of Euet[ion --] they cr|owned jointly *along with the* [--] | with a
golden crown worth [300] *drachmas;* [and when the Atheni|ans] paid their
30 contributions[6] towards [the preparation for the] ‖ war and the security of
the *city* [they contributed], b|oth of them, 1000 drachmas; and [in the
archonship of] K[oroibos] (306/5), | when Hege[sias the general][7]
called upon them | and asked them together with the others *to join in
35 facing the dan|ger* and to help in rebuilding the towers [of the] *south‖ern*
wall that were assigned to them, [nobly a|nd] zealously the part (of the
wall) that fell to their share they reb|uilt; and they joined in the cam-
paign|s, all of them both naval and infantry, [in company | with] the
40 People bearing their arms nobly and zealously at t‖heir own expense
and all the duties that at any time to them the People ass|igned, all (these)
nobly and zealously they have perform|ed: in order therefore that it
may be manifest to all that the Boule and the | People of Athens know
how to repay gratitude | of a fitting kind to those who strive earnestly
45 on their behalf, with g‖ood fortune, let it be resolved by the Boule that
the Proedroi | who are chosen by lot to be Proedroi introduce before the
People at the *f*|*irst* assembly the matter concerning them just a|s they
themselves request[8] and communicate the opinion [of the Boul|e] *to* the
People that it is resolved by the Boule that commendation shall be
50 given ‖ to [Nika]ndros, son of Antiphanes, of Ilium and Poly[zel]os, son
of [Apo|lloph]anes, of Ephesus and that they shall be crowned with an
olive cro|wn, each of them. And there shall be granted to them also *the
right of equality of tax|ation* by the People, both to them and to their off-
sprin|g, and the privilege of possession of land and a house and (as for)
55 the capit‖al levies they shall pay these together with the Athenians and
milit|ary campaigns shall be undertaken by them when the Athenians also
go out on | *campaign.* And care shall be taken of them both by [the] Boule
[tha|t] on any occasion is in office and by the generals, in order that
| they may not be wronged by a single man. And they shall have the
60 right of approac‖h to the Boule ₐnd the People whenever they request
it. In|scription of this decree shall be made by the secretary for | the
prytany on a marble stele and it shall be set up on the Acr|[opolis]. For
the inscription of the stele there shall be given | [by the] treasurer of the

65   People[9] [4]0 drachmas from the funds that on matters || [related to] *decrees* are spent by the People. |

1   For his family see Davies, *Families* 6067.
2   The arsenal of Philon in the Peiraeus.
3   Possibly to be identified with the fund mentioned in nos. 35 and 40. See no. 35 n. 14.
4   I.e. the Lamian War.
5   Most likely Euetion, son of Pythangelos, of Kephisia. See Davies, *Families* 5463. He was defeated by Kleitos in the Hellespont (Diod. 18.15.8–9).
6   The technical term is *epidosis*. For the difference between this and the capital levy (*eisphora*) see Thomsen 237f.
7   Hegesias is known from *IG* II[2] 1487, lines 92–3, to have been general in 306/5.
8   This suggests that Nikandros and Polyzelos had requested these honours. Cf. Pečířka 81.
9   The last known instance when this official defrayed the cost of inscribing and erecting a stele.

140   Death of Antigonos Monophthalmos at Ipsus. 301/0.

[Lucian] *Macrob.* 11 (Hieronymus of Cardia, *FGrHist.* 154F8). Cf. Diod. 21.1.4; Plut. *Demetrios* 29.

Cloché, *Dislocation* 210–20; Will, *Histoire* 1.68–70; Wehrli, *Antigone* 68–72; G. Cohen, *Athenaeum* 52 (1974) 177–9.

Antigonos the One-Eyed, son of Philippos, while king of the Macedonians, after encountering many wounds in battle near Phrygia with Seleukos and Lysimachos, died in his eighty-first year, as is recorded by Hieronymus who campaigned with him.

GLOSSARY

Most technical terms and official titles are explained in the notes to the individual documents, where it is hoped they will be most useful. The student should also consult the Index of subjects and terms. Some, however, occur so frequently they are better collected together in the glossary, which is basically an abbreviated and modified version of that in volume 1.

Apodektai ('public receivers'). A board of ten men at Athens, elected by lot, who collected public revenues such as war taxes, tolls, and state debts, and immediately dispensed them to the appropriate authorities. Arist. *Ath. Pol.* 47.5–48.1, 52.3; see Rhodes, *Commentary* 557–8.

Archon (eponymous). Originally the most important of the nine archons at Athens. The powers of the archon waned as the state developed, but the oath he took upon entering office to confirm people in the possession of their property, however superfluous in historical times, gives an indication of his earlier authority. His principal duties were to supervise family affairs – the rights of parents and children, widows and orphans, and the maintenance of family lines. He conducted the major religious festivals and appointed choregoi for the Great Dionysia. He gave his name to the year (hence the title 'Eponymous'), regulated the calendar of the lunar year, and he lived in the Prytaneion, the hearth of the state. Arist. *Ath. Pol.* 3.2–3, 56.2–7; see MacDowell, *Law* 24–6, 93–4, 102–3, 144, 162, 235–7, and Rhodes, *Commentary* 622–36.

Archons (governors). The word *archon* is the term for 'ruler' and so can designate anyone at the head of affairs.

Areopagus ('[the Council of] the hill of Ares'). This Council (Boule), named from the hill on which it sat, was Athens' most ancient. In early Athenian history it exercised the dominant power in the state as overseer of the laws and magistrates. By the fourth century it had become little more than a homicide-court, although in 403/2 Teisamenos proposed to restore its guardianship of the laws (Andocides 1.84) and in the period of the battle of Chaeronea it had the power to investigate treasonable activities (cf. Dem. 18.132f. and the Harpalos affair). Its members were the subject of severe strictures in the law of Eukrates (no. 101). It was composed of ex-archons. Isocrates, *Areopagiticus*, *passim* but esp. 37, 43–6; Arist. *Politics* 1273b–1274a2, *Ath. Pol.* 3.6, 4.4, 8.2, 4, 25.2; see Rhodes, *Boule* 200–7.

Assembly (ekklesia). After Kleisthenes' reforms, the Assembly was open to all Athenian citizens, thetes included, who had completed their eighteenth year. It sat regularly four times in every prytany, one of those meetings (kyria ekklesia = principal assembly) having a fixed agenda; special meetings also could be called. The Assembly was the sovereign body of the state (and thus is sometimes referred to simply as 'the People'): it passed decisions on all major questions, elected major magistrates and could recall them from office; on occasion it tried important political cases. Although no matter won final approval from the Assembly unless it had first been cleared by the Boule, it could modify propositions submitted to it by means of amendments, and it could instruct the Boule

Glossary

to initiate a desired proposal. Any Athenian could participate in debate or offer amendments; voting was by show of hands. Thuc. 4.118.11, 122.6, 7.20.1, 8.9.2; Xen. *Hell.* 1.7.7ff.; Arist. *Ath. Pol.* 42.1, 43.4–6, 54.4; *Politics* 4.14.1298a3ff.; see Rhodes, *Boule* 52–85, and M.H. Hansen, *GRBS* 17 (1976) 115–34.

Ateleia (immunity from public burdens). Freedom from certain public duties and liturgies (such as choregia and trierarchy) involving the expenditure of money. Some such immunities were based on laws of general application to Athenian citizens – e.g. that which freed members of the Boule from the obligation of military service, or the archons from regular liturgies or the trierarchy. But metics and foreigners as well as citizens (in Athens and elsewhere) could specifically be decreed exemptions from regular burdens for services rendered. For metics the dispensation normally would apply to the special burdens imposed on them by the state (see Metics). Dem. 20.18, 107.

Athlothetai (of the Panathenaia). Ten cult officials, picked by lot in the fourth century, who held office for the four-year cycle from Great Panathenaia to Great Panathenaia and had the responsibility of directing the Panathenaic contests and furnishing the prizes for the victors. In the final weeks before the festival was held they dined in the Prytaneion at state expense. Arist. *Ath. Pol.* 60.1, 62.2; Rhodes, *Commentary* 668–76.

Basileus (king archon). Whatever the connection of the basileus (as he was simply called) with the kings of the ancient Athenian state, his duties in the fourth century were to supervise matters of ancestral cult – sacrifices, ceremonies, temple-precincts, the state religion, disputes about the succession of hereditary priesthoods. In his judicial capacity he presided over the homicide-courts. Arist. *Ath. Pol.* 57; see MacDowell, *Law* 24–9, 117–18, and Rhodes, *Commentary* 636–50.

Boule of Five Hundred. Kleisthenes formed the Boule of Five Hundred; it was open to all citizens over thirty years of age, and they were selected by lot from a larger group appointed by lot by the demes, each of the ten tribes being represented by fifty men. It met daily, except for holidays, prepared the Assembly's agenda, fixed the time of the meetings, presided over it, and attended to the execution of its decisions. The Boule supervised the magistrates (e.g. the generals), introduced envoys to the Assembly, and oversaw the financial administration of the state. Arist. *Ath. Pol.* 24.3, 43.2–5, 45–9; see Prytaneis and Rhodes, *Boule, passim.*

Bouleuterion. The primary meeting-place of the Boule. The original building, constructed probably at the end of the sixth century and located on the west side of the Agora, was replaced by the 'New Bouleuterion', a building begun at the end of the fifth century. It contained a raised platform from which men spoke, with special benches for the prytaneis. Aristophanes, *Knights* 625ff.; Antiphon 6.40; Lysias 13.37f.; see Rhodes, *Boule* 30–5.

Cavalry at Athens (hippeis). Though the name hippeis denoted the second of the Solonian census-classes (an annual income of between 500 and 300 medimnoi of wheat or its equivalent), it also refers to an aristocratic body of 1000 cavalry organized about the middle of the fifth century. The 'knights' provided their own mounts and the state provided equipment-money. The cavalry was divided according to tribe, each tribe headed by a phylarch, and the whole corps by two hipparchs (*q.v.*). Thuc. 2.13.8; Aristophanes, *Knights* 225; Andocides 3.5, 7.

Choregoi. The richest citizens were required to undertake certain liturgies or public burdens (cf. trierarchs) of which the choregia was one. Like the others, it was a sort of progressive tax, working as an indirect source of revenue for the state. The

178

choregos assembled a chorus, required at dramatic, comic, and musical competitions held at the festivals; he equipped and paid it, and hired a trainer for it.
Lysias 21.1–4; Dem. 20.130; Arist. *Ath. Pol.* 56.3ff.; see Rhodes, *Commentary* 623.

Cleruchs ('allotment holders'). Athenian settlers of the poorest classes (though the
more affluent may not always have been excluded), who were granted a piece of
land (kleros) in a territory taken by conquest. The cleruchs maintained Athenian
citizenship with all its privileges and responsibilities and, because of their new
status as landholders, could serve as hoplites when needed. Thuc. 3.50.2; Aristophanes, *Clouds* 203; Xen. *Memorabilia* 2.8.1; Isocrates 4.107; Plut. *Pericles* 11.6.

Council of Elders (Gerousia). The establishment of the Spartan Council was ascribed
to Lykourgos' famous rhetra bidding the Spartans 'to tribe the tribes and obe
the obes, (and) establish a thirty-man council of elders including the two kings'.
The twenty-eight men, over sixty years of age, were chosen by the People's
acclamation. Their function was to propose legislation which the People in
assembly would ratify; except in cases where the Council was divided, sub-
mission of a proposal was tantamount to its acceptance. For its use outside
Sparta see no. 126. Hdt. 6.57.5; Plato, *Laws* 3.691; Arist. *Politics* 1270b; Plut.
Lycurgus 6, 26.

Darics. The gold coinage of Persia. Of excellent quality, and bearing the image of
Dareios I armed with bow and spear.

Demes. Local communities that formed the basis for the political organization of the
Athenian state. Some 150 are known from the late fourth century. Membership
in a deme was a requirement of citizenship, and it was inherited regardless of
where one (later) happened to live in Attica. The practice of identifying oneself
by deme-name (demotic), as well as by patronymic, was common in the fourth
century, especially in official documents. Arist. *Ath. Pol.* 42; see J.S. Traill, *The
Political Organization of Attica* (Princeton 1975) *passim*.

Demiourgoi. Magistrates of high rank among the Dorians, chosen from leading
families, with a fixed number and term of office. Virtually no detailed information about them exists.

Dionysia. The City or 'Great' Dionysia was a festival celebrated in honour of Dionysos
Eleuthereus, so named from the town of Eleutherai, from which it was introduced
into Athens, probably by Peisistratos. It was celebrated in March and lasted for
about five days. Foreigners and envoys of Athens' allies attended the celebration,
which consisted of religious ceremonials, tragic, comic, and dithyrambic contests. The eponymous archon, together with other functionaries, supervised the
procession, in which phalli were borne. Isoc. 8.82; Aesch. 3.32ff.; Pausanias
1.29.2, 38.3.

Eisangelia (impeachment). A procedure for dealing with subverters of the constitution, acts of treason, irreligion, and bribery, whether or not specifically prohibited by law. Final decision of guilt or innocence was made by the Assembly or
the law courts. Arist. *Ath. Pol.* 43.4, 59.1; see Rhodes, *Boule* 162–71,
MacDowell, *Law* 58, 64, 238, 251, and M.H. Hansen, *Eisangelia* (Odense 1975)
passim.

Eisphora (property tax). A special tax on capital (not income) that was levied on
Athenian citizens and metics by decree of the Assembly after a vote of 'immunity'
(adeia) was passed. Cf. no. 39 and see R. Thomsen, *Eisphora, passim*.

Eleven (the). This board was selected by lot and charged with the conviction and
punishment of ordinary malefactors (kakourgoi). They were empowered to put

criminals to death when they were caught in the act of committing certain crimes. If a criminal protested his innocence, they presided over his trial by jury. Antiphon 5.17; Arist. *Ath. Pol.* 7.3, 52.1; see MacDowell, *Law* 237–8, and Rhodes, *Commentary* 579–82.

Enktesis. The grant by the state of the privilege of possession of a house in Attica to a foreigner in return for services rendered. See Pečiŕka, *Enktesis, passim.*

Ephors ('overseers'). The ephorate, which consisted of five men elected annually by the People at the beginning of winter, was the 'democratic element' of the Spartan government, and it became the preponderant political body of Sparta by the late sixth century. The college, presided over by the eponymous ephor, and following the principle of majority rule, was the administrative arm of the state. It presided over the Gerousia and Assembly, served as both prosecutors and judges in criminal cases, controlled the education of young Spartans, mobilized the army after a declaration of war, supervised generals on campaign, and accompanied the kings. Hdt. 1.65, 5.39; Thuc. 5.36; Arist. *Politics* 4.9.1294b19ff., 5.11.1313a25ff.; Diogenes Laertius 1.68–73; Plut. *Lycurgus* 7, *Lysander* 30, *Agis* 16, *Cleomenes* 10; see H. Michell, *Sparta* (Cambridge 1952) 118–34.

Generals (strategoi). Of great political as well as military importance, the ten Athenian generals were directly elected by the People, and they could be re-elected continuously. Each general originally represented his own tribe, but already by the middle of the fifth century instances occur of a tribe's double representation. Apart from their command in the field and defence of home territory, the generals enrolled soldiers, appointed trierarchs, made treaties (provisionally) with other states, and helped in general to shape public policy, for they had access to the Boule and could summon special Assemblies. Thuc. 4.118.4, 6.8.2, 62.1; Arist. *Ath. Pol.* 22.2–3, 62.3, 66.1; see C. Fornara, *The Athenian Board of Generals from 501 to 404* (Wiesbaden 1971), *passim*, and Rhodes, *Commentary* 676–84.

Graphe paranomon. A lawsuit that could be brought against any proposed law or decree and its proposer on grounds of unconstitutionality. Implementation of the law or decree was stayed until it had been cleared by the courts. See M.H. Hansen, *The Sovereignty of the People's Court in Athens in the Fourth Century B.C.* (Odense 1974) *passim.*

Heralds (kerykes). Anyone in private life could serve as a herald (e.g. in the market-place), but they were regularly appointed and paid by the state to serve as subordinate officials for magistracies where proclamations were frequent (Boule and Assembly, law courts, the nine archons, poletai). When in foreign parts, they were believed to stand under God's protection and were thus inviolable, even in cases of war (except when the war was 'truceless'). A notable and special group at Athens was that of the Eleusinian heralds, who regularly proclaimed a 'Truce of God' in foreign cities in order to ensure the peaceful participation of all Hellenes in the celebration of the Eleusinian Mysteries. One of the heralds was always a member of the clan of the Kerykes, a long-descended family, heredi-tarily entrusted (together with the Eumolpidai) with the conduct of the Mys-teries. Hdt. 7.133ff., 137; Andoc. 1.36; Aesch. 1.20; Arist. *Politics* 4.15.1299a19, *Ath. Pol.* 62.2.

Hipparchs. Leaders of the Athenian cavalry, normally two in number, the hipparchs were elected to office and served as subordinates to the generals but as superiors to the phylarchs. They maintained the cavalry register and had disciplinary

Glossary

powers over the men. Lysias 15.11, 16.13, 26.20; Xen. *Hipparchicus* 1.7; Arist. *Ath. Pol.* 43.1, 61.4; see Rhodes, *Commentary* 685–6.

Knights. See Cavalry at Athens.

Logistai ('auditors'). Two boards, of which one (ten in number) was chosen by the Boule from its own members, the other (twenty) from the Athenians at large. The first (Arist. *Ath. Pol.* 48.3) checked the accounts of magistrates each prytany, the second (Arist. *Ath. Pol.* 54.2) audited the books of magistrates handling public money when their books were closed or when they underwent their scrutiny for performance in office (euthyna). See Rhodes, *Commentary* 560–1, 597–9.

Metics. Resident aliens in Athens, who numbered 10,000 at one time in the fourth century; their status and obligations were strictly defined in exchange for the privilege of permanent domicile. They paid an annual tax (metoikion) and, it is said, could be enslaved if they failed to pay it. They were prohibited from owning landed property in Attica, though they could be granted enktesis. In most legal disputes they required the sponsorship of a patron (prostates). Like Athenian citizens they were liable to military service and subject to some liturgies. Pseudo-Xen. *Ath. Pol.* 1.12; Lys. 12.4; Xen. *Poroi* 2.6; Dem. 20.18, 20.

Oath-Commissioners (horkotai). Envoys chosen *ad hoc* to administer oaths to a community when a treaty dictated such mutual oath-taking. In the fourth century, at least, it was not necessary for (all of?) them to be magistrates (*IG* II² 16, lines 18–20).

Opisthodomos. This building (probably not a back room of the Parthenon) served at times as the bank of the treasurers of Athena and the Other Gods. It housed coined money, bullion, and dedications. Cf. no. 10.

Panathenaia. An Athenian festival celebrated every year in July/August. Every fourth year the celebration was on a grander scale and so was named the Great Panathenaia. Lasting six to nine days, it consisted of musical and athletic competitions, torch and boat races (the latter held at the Peiraeus), and of a grand procession, pictured on the frieze of the Parthenon, when the robe (peplos) of Athena was brought up to the Parthenon. Plut. *Theseus* 24.3.

Paredroi. Assistants to various magistrates, namely, the three major archons, the scrutineers (euthynoi, who had two each). The archons named their own paredroi, those of the euthynoi were selected by lot. Andoc. 1.78; Arist. *Ath. Pol.* 48.4, 56.1; Rhodes, *Commentary* 561, 621.

Phratry ('brotherhood'). A political subdivision of the pre-Kleisthenic tribe in which membership was limited to citizens, whose names were catalogued on phratry-lists. Each phratry had its leader (phratriarchos), priest, and special place of assembly. The major festival for all phratries was the Apatouria, when votes were taken on the admission of new members. Arist. *Politics* 6.4.1319b19ff., *Ath. Pol.* 21.6; see Rhodes, *Commentary* 68–71.

Phylobasileis ('tribe-kings'). Whatever their earlier role as heads of the four archaic Athenian tribes, in historical times they exercised religious functions and, with the king archon, were in charge of the homicide court at the Prytaneion for cases in which the slayer was unknown or death the (accidental) result of contact with an inanimate object. Arist. *Ath. Pol.* 8.3, 57.4.

Polemarch. This Athenian archon formerly commanded the Athenian military. In the

181

fourth century he retained sacrificial duties and judicial competence over foreigners and resident aliens. Arist. *Ath. Pol.* 3, 58; see Rhodes, *Commentary* 650–7.

Poletai ('sellers'). Ten officials, selected by lot from each tribe, who farmed out state contracts – for tax-collection, mining-rights, rent, etc. – and sold off confiscated property. Arist. *Ath. Pol.* 7.3, 47.2; see Rhodes, *Commentary* 552.

Probouleuma. It was an essential element of the legislative process at Athens that the Boule consider matters of business before including them on the agenda for a meeting of the Assembly and normally prepare the wording of any motion to be voted upon. This was called probouleuma. Arist. *Ath. Pol.* 45.4; see Rhodes, *Boule* 52ff.

Proedroi. Some time between 403/2 and 378/7 the duty of presiding over meetings of the Boule and Assembly at Athens, which had belonged to the prytaneis, was transferred to a new board of Proedroi. This board of nine men was chosen by lot by the chairman (epistates) of the prytaneis, one from each tribe not in prytany. He also selected one of them by lot to be chairman, and this was the man who put motions to the vote. Arist. *Ath. Pol.* 44.2–3; see Rhodes, *Boule* 25–8, and *Commentary* 533–4.

Proxenia, proxenos. A person became a proxenos when he was made a 'public friend' or official 'guest' of a state. As such he would naturally represent the interests of that community in his own. This status was also granted to metics by decrees of the People (Athenian and others) and, in Athens, entitled the recipient to access to the court of the Polemarch without need for the normally obligatory introduction by an Athenian acting as Patron (prostates) of metics. Frequently conferred together with proxenia were other privileges such as freedom from liturgies, the right to possession of a house in Attica (enktesis), and isoteleia (the condition of being subject to no more burdens than were the citizens themselves). Thuc. 2.29.1, 8.5; Dem. 52.5; Aesch. 3.42; Plut. *Alcibiades* 14.1.

Prytaneion. The town hall of a Greek state, originally the meeting-place of the magistrates and the location of the sacred hearth of the polis. In Athens it was used to entertain dignitaries, certain magistrates, and even seers, and it was also the residence of the eponymous archon. A law court at Athens also was known as the 'court at the Prytaneion' (Andoc. 1.78). Hdt. 1.146.2; Thuc. 2.15.2; Pausanias 1.18.3.

Prytaneis ('presidents'). The Conciliar year, or year of the Boule, was divided into ten parts so that the fifty men of each of the ten tribes served collectively as the prytaneis or presiding officers of the Boule for one tenth of the year. The presiding tribe was named 'the tribe in prytany'. During their prytany, the prytaneis lived and dined at state expense in the Tholos, a circular building next to the Bouleuterion. The order of the prytanies followed no set pattern but was determined by lot; nine separate sortitions were held in the course of the year so that the order of the tribes could not be known until the allotment of the ninth. The prytaneis convened the Boule and Assembly, presided over them, fixed the agenda of the Boule, and heard judicial complaints that fell in the Boule's purview. Until some time between 403/2 and 378/7, one member of the tribe in prytany was picked by lot to serve every twenty-four hours as epistates or presiding officer, and he chaired the Boule and Assembly. On duty continuously, he kept in his possession the keys of the state treasuries and the public seal. (See also under Proedroi.) Arist. *Ath. Pol.* 43.2; see Rhodes, *Boule* 16–25.

Satrap. The title of the governors of the Persian satrapies or provinces, who possessed wide authority in their domains, even to the point of acting quasi-independently or rebelliously, though military and civil officials were appointed by the Great King to keep them in check. The subdivision of the empire into satrapies by Dareios the Great remained fundamental in subsequent times and was largely adopted by Alexander the Great.

Secretary of the Boule. The most important of the public secretaries, his name appears on the prescript of Athenian decrees. Until the 360s, when the secretary was elected annually, a new secretary was elected in each prytany and, though he was always a member of the Boule, none was a member of the tribe in prytany. The secretary was responsible for drafting and publishing decrees and maintaining an archive of related records. Arist. *Ath. Pol.* 54.3–5; see Rhodes, *Boule* 134–7.

Thesmothetai. The six junior archons at Athens. Unlike the other archons, they seem to have been concerned solely with the administration of justice. Their major duties were to fix trial dates and assign courts to the appropriate magistrates, preside over law courts in a variety of cases involving wrongdoing against the state (e.g. eisangelia). Arist. *Ath. Pol.* 3.4–5, 59.

Treasurers of Athena. The 'treasurers of the sacred monies of Athena' (though their nomenclature varies) were magistrates/cult officials of great antiquity, ten in number (after Kleisthenes), of the highest census class, and elected by lot according to tribe. They were annual officials, whose tenure of office ran from Panathenaia to Panathenaia, though they rendered accounts to the logistai collectively in four boards at the time of the Great Panathenaia. They superintended the funds of the Goddess, dedicatory offerings (see Opisthodomos) and the great statue of Athena. Arist. *Ath. Pol.* 7.3, 8.1, 47.1; see Ferguson, *Treasurers of Athena* 96ff.

Trierarch, trierarchy. A form of public service involving the maintenance of a warship by the wealthy, who were selected by the generals. (Late in the Peloponnesian War, because of relative impoverishment, two trierarchs were allotted to each vessel and in the fourth century this happened quite frequently, even reaching the point where groups (synteleiai) of as many as sixteen managed one ship.) This duty could be evaded only if the designee had already performed it within the past two years, possessed an exemption, or could demonstrate that someone else was better able to perform it (antidosis). The ship, normally its equipment, and the pay of the crew were provided by the state; the trierarch was required to keep the vessel in good repair during the year of his trierarchy. If he did not (barring unavoidable disasters), legal action was taken against him. The trierarch(s) served as the captain of his ship. Aristophanes, *Knights* 911ff.; Thuc. 6.31; Lysias 21.2, 32.26f.; Arist. *Ath. Pol.* 61.8; cf. no. 47; see Rhodes, *Commentary* 679–82.

APPENDIX I

Athenian archons 403/2–301/0

403/2	Eukleides		360/59	Kallimedes
402/1	Mikon		359/8	Eucharistos
401/0	Xenainetos		358/7	Kephisodotos
400/399	Laches		357/6	Agathokles
399/8	Aristokrates		356/5	Elpines
398/7	Euthykles		355/4	Kallistratos
397/6	Souniades		354/3	Diotimos
396/5	Phormion		353/2	Thoudemos
395/4	Diophantos		352/1	Aristodemos
394/3	Euboulides		351/50	Theellos
393/2	Demostratos		350/49	Apollodoros
392/1	Philokles		349/8	Kallimachos
391/90	Nikoteles		348/7	Theophilos
390/89	Demostratos		347/6	Themistokles
389/8	Antipatros		346/5	Archias
388/7	Pyrgion		345/4	Euboulos
387/6	Theodotos		344/3	Lykiskos
386/5	Mystichides		343/2	Pythodotos
385/4	Dexitheos		342/1	Sosigenes
384/3	Dieitrephes		341/40	Nikomachos
383/2	Phanostratos		340/39	Theophrastos
382/1	Euandros		339/8	Lysimachides
381/80	Demophilos		338/7	Chairondas
380/79	Pytheas		337/6	Phrynichos
379/8	Nikon		336/5	Pythodelos
378/7	Nausinikos		335/4	Euainetos
377/6	Kalleas		334/3	Ktesikles
376/5	Charisandros		333/2	Nikokrates
375/4	Hippodamas		332/1	Niketes
374/3	Sokratides		331/30	Aristophanes
373/2	Asteios		330/29	Aristophon
372/1	Alkisthenes		329/8	Kephisophon
371/70	Phrasikleides		328/7	Euthykritos
370/69	Dysniketos		327/6	Hegemon
369/8	Lysistratos		326/5	Chremes
368/7	Nausigenes		325/4	Antikles
367/6	Polyzelos		324/3	Hegesias
366/5	Kephisodoros		323/2	Kephisodoros
365/4	Chion		322/1	Philokles
364/3	Timokrates		321/20	Archippos
363/2	Charikleides		320/19	Neaichmos
362/1	Molon		319/18	Apollodoros
361/60	Nikophemos		318/17	Archippos

184

317/16	Demogenes	308/7	Kairimos
316/15	Demokleides	307/6	Anaxikrates
315/14	Praxiboulos	306/5	Koroibos
314/13	Nikodoros	305/4	Euxenippos
313/12	Theophrastos	304/3	Pherekles
312/11	Polemon	303/2	Leostratos
311/10	Simonides	302/1	Nikokles
310/9	Hieromnemon	301/0	Klearchos
309/8	Demetrios of Phaleron		

APPENDIX II

Athenian time reckoning

The Athenian year began in midsummer.
The twelve Athenian months are:

Hekatombaion	Gamelion
Metageitnion	Anthesterion
Boedromion	Elaphebolion
Pyanepsion	Mounichion
Maimakterion	Thargelion
Posideon	Skirophorion

The Athenians counted time in two ways. The 'archon' or 'festival' year followed the tale of the months and was the 'official' year for the preponderance of the magistrates, e.g. archons, generals; others, such as the treasurers of Athena, seem to have held their tenure from Panathenaic festival to Panathenaic festival (Hekatombaion 28). Since the 'ordinary' year of twelve lunar months of twenty-nine or thirty days falls short by a little more than eleven days of the solar year, the practice was to intercalate a thirteenth month from time to time. In addition, the eponymous archon was free to intercalate days into the year (in order, for example, to postpone a festival on a day of ill-omen). Time was also reckoned by the Conciliar calendar. Each of the ten Athenian tribes served in the Boule as prytany (see Glossary) for approximately one-tenth of the year. In the fourth century, at least, the first four prytanies served thirty-six days, the last six served thirty-five days each.

APPENDIX III

The ten Athenian tribes in their official order

I Erechtheis	VI Oineis
II Aigeis	VII Kekropis
III Pandionis	VIII Hippothontis
IV Leontis	IX Aiantis
V Akamantis	X Antiochis

APPENDIX IV

Numbers and coinage

The Attic system of numerals worked, like the Roman, by the combination of different

185

units, each a multiple of the next. A different symbol existed for each of the numerals 10,000, 5000, 1000, 500, 100, 50, 10, 5, 1, and in the written form of a sum the largest symbol always appeared first, with the others juxtaposed in descending order. No smaller numeral was repeated when a larger would serve instead (e.g. never two fives instead of a ten).

The Attic system of coinage and weights was based on the drachma.

6 obols (ob.) = 1 drachma (dr.)

100 dr. = 1 mna (mina)

6000 dr. (60 minas) = 1 talent (T.)

The same symbols as for the notation of numerals (with the addition of the drachma sign and of signs for obols and fractions of obols) applied for the notation of sums of money. Consequently, in the restoration of inscriptions involving sums of money, this system of numeration permits assured references as to the maximum and minimum figures allowable when the beginning of a series of numerals is preserved but not its end. For example, if a series started with the symbol for 1000 and six letter-spaces were known to be missing after it, in no case could the sum be less than 1019 or more than 4700. In the first case, the figures would be 10, 5, and 1 (this last repeated four times); in the second, 1000 repeated thrice, 500, and 100 repeated twice. Similarly, one can work backwards when only the last portion of a figure is preserved and calculate at least the minimum possible sum. On this matter of numbers the serious student could profitably consult A.G. Woodhead, *The Study of Greek Inscriptions*[2] (Cambridge 1981) 107–10.

It would be idle to attempt to calculate the value of the drachma in terms of any modern currency. In absolute terms, however, the usual assumption is that in the fourth century average wages fluctuated between a drachma and a drachma and a half a day.

INDEXES

All references are to item numbers.

IB. Index of personal and geographical names

191

Methone, 73A.12, B, and n. 6
Methymna, Methymneans, 35.81, and n. 17; 37 *passim*; 53.28
Miletus, Milesian(s), 24 *passim*; 114 n. 1; 117 *passim*
Milon, harmost of Aegina, 11A
Miltiades, 55.37, 50, 53; 121.166, 223, and nn. 4, 6; of Lakiadai, 121.160, and n. 4
Minion, 127.24
Minnion (Minneon), 114.1; 127.3, and n. 2
Mnasidamos, 88.25
Mnasilaos, 46.3, and n. 3
Mnasimachos, 60 n. 1
Mnesarchos, 70.6
Mnesiergos of Athmonon, 10.7
Mnesikl[--], 19A
Mnesilochos the Athenian, 88.27
Molon, archon 362/1, 56.1; 58.1
Monounios, 70.9, 14, 29
Morychos of Boutadai, 10.12
Moschos of Kydathenaion, 52.2; 53.4; son of Thestios, 53 n. 2
Mounichion, 121.186, 211
Mousike, 47.91
Munychia, 3.7; 108 n. 3
Myesians, 24 *passim*
Mykonians, 35.115
Myrina, 81.2, 7, 12
Myrseloi, 106.9
Mysia, 79 n. 6
Mystichides, archon 386/5, 29.1
Mytilene, Mytilenean(s), 33 *passim*; 35.80, and n. 17; 53 *passim*; 83.7, 11, 14; 90A
Myus, 24 n. 4

Na[-7-], 47.88
Naukratis, 47.99; 60.37
Naulochum, 106.2, and n. 2
Nausigenes, archon 368/7, 1A at 368/7; 52.1, and n. 1
Nausinikos, archon 378/7, 35.1, 35; 38.3; 39C(1)
Naxians, 60.16; 99 n. 16
Neaichmos, archon 320/19, 1 nn. 13, 14
Neaira, 83 n. 3
Neapolitans, 35.130
Nellos, 35.134, and n. 21
Nemea, 14 n. 3; 18 n. 1
Neokleides, 19B
Neon of Halai, 29.4
Neoptolemos, 35.110; 125A, B; king of the Molossians, 62A
Nicaea, 96B
Nikaia, 125B
Nikandros, 139 n. 8; son of Antiphanes, of Ilium, 139.9, 50
Nikanor, 1A at 317/16

Niketes, archon 332/1, 1A at 332/1
Nikokles, archon 302/1, 139.2
Nikokrates, archon 333/2, 111.2, 26
Nikolaos, 74.16
Nikoleos, 55.16
Nikomachos, 9 nn. 1, 4; 19B; archon 341/40, 1B at 341/40; 92; 94.1; 95B, C
Nikon, 88.26; son of Theodoros, of Plotheia, 139.3
Nikophemos, 12C; archon 361/60, 59.2; 77 n. 1
Nikophon, 45.2
Nikostratos of Pallene, 55.2, and n. 1
Nobas, Axioubos' son, the Carthaginian, 48.5
Notians, 5.8
Nymph[--], 24.44

Ochos, king of Persia, 1B at 341/40
Odrysian(s), 29 n. 1; 64 n. 2
Oetaeans, 99A fr. B.9; 116.18, 41
Oineides, 7
Oineis, 19A; 54.4, and n. 2; 55 n. 1; 56.4
Oion Dekeleikon, 31 n. 3
Oion Kerameikon, 31 n. 3
Olbia, 117 n. 1
Olympia, 67 n. 4
Olympias, 1A at 316/15, 1C at 355/4; 62A, and n. 1; 116.6, 22; 130
Olympion, 88.30
Olynthus, Olynthian(s), 61; 67.9; 70 n. 3; 80; 81 n. 1
Ona[-]mes, 3.16
Onesippos of Araphen, 94.5
Onetorides, 19B
Onomarchos, 62E, F; 84.113
Opisthodomos, 10 n. 2
Opuntians, 116.26
Orchomenus, 15; 51 n. 4
Oreus, 91A, B
Oropius, 125A
Oropus, 99 n. 1
Orthoboulos from Kerameis, 34.21
Oxyartes the Bactrian, 125A

Paidikos, 3.12
Pairisades, 82 *passim*
Pagasae, 62D
Pal[-7], 35.85
Palaereans of Acarnania, 116.35
Pamphilos, son of Euphiletos, 123 n. 3
Pamphylians, 125A
Pandionis, 2 fr. A.3, and n. 2; 5.1; 7.7, 77, and nn. 3, 6; 19 n. 2; 20.1; 72A.3; 94.2; 100.1; 111.27; 123A.1
Pandios, 19B; 52.6, and n. 3; son of Sokles, from Oion, 72A.4
Pankon of Thebes, 60.75
Pantaretos, 38.6

Pithon, 125A

Plataea, Plataean(s), 15; 109 n. 2; 115, and n. 3; 116.44

Plataikos, 115 n. 3

Platon of Phlya, son of Nikochares, 2 n. 2; 20.3

Platthis of Aegina, 10.39

Pleistarchos, 137.6

Pleisteas, 88.31

Ploutarchos, 92

Poiessa, Poiessians, 35.82; 55 n. 3; 116 n. 9

Polemon, archon 312/11, 1A at 312/11

Poliagros, 26.3

Pollis, 12C

Polyaratos of Cholargos, 56 n. 3

Polyeuktos, son of Timokrates, of Krioa, 82.65, and n. 8

Polyhippe, daughter of Meleteon, of Acharnai, 10.27

Polykles of Anagyrous, 47.105, and nn. 28, 29

Polyperchon, 1 n. 16; 129 n. 1; 130; 132.39, and n. 13

Polyxenos, 9.68; brother-in-law of Dionysios I of Syracuse, 20.9

Polyzelos, 139 n. 8; son of Apollophanes, of Ephesus, 139.9, 50; archon, 367/6, 54.7

Pontus, 95B

Poros, 1C at 327/6; 125A

Poses, 5 n. 1; 7 n. 6

Potas, son of Papeus, 117.39

Potidaea, Potidaeans, 54 n. 3; 58.5, 9, 10; 61B

Praxagora, 14 n. 2

Prepelaos, 132.11, 28

Priene, Prienians, 24 n. 4; 103.4, 7, 13; 106 *passim*

Pronnoi, 35.108; 41 n. 5

Prophetes, 54.12

Propontis, 95 n. 3

Protias, 108.45

Protokles of Ikaria, 10.4

Prytaneion, 5.11, 15, and n. 3; 8A (front) .12; 25 BC.16; 31.38; 33.3, 9, 12; 34.16; 40.27; 43.16; 53.26, 27, 30, 34; 55.55; 59.38; 65.9, 12; 70.31, 32, 34; 82.52; 93 n. 1; 94.17; 126.44

Psammis, 3.14

Psessoi, 27C.5

Ptolemais, 43.7

Ptolemy, 1A at 319/18 and 312/11, 1C at 308/7, and n. 19; 125A; 126 *passim*; 132 *passim*; 133; son of Lagos, 125A, B

Pydna, Pydneans, 61A, B; 102.13

Pyrrhandros, 38.7; from Anaphlystos, 34.24; 35.76

Pyrrhans, 53.29

Pythagoras, 60.38

Pythian, 104.3 nn. 1, 3

Pythias, 90 n. 1

Pytho, 67.15

Pythodelos, archon 336/5, 1A at 336/5, and n. 10

Pythodoros, 88.32; archon 404/3, 3 n. 2

Pythodotos, archon 343/2, 1B at 343/2; 89A, B.1

Raidios, 73 n. 3

Rhadaphernes, 125A

Rhodes, Rhodians, 12C, and n. 13; 35.82, and n. 17; 71; 116.11; 131.33

Rhodonia, 47.109

Rhoxane, 125A

Rhusiades, 41.27

Rome, Roman, 1 n. 9; 47 n. 1; 126 n. 2

Royal Stoa, 9 n. 1

Sadokos, 29 n. 1

Samos, Samian(s), 4.5; 5 *passim*; 12 n. 23; 24 n. 4; 47 n. 13; 77, and n. 1; 99 n. 1; 115; 127 *passim*; 128 *passim*

Samothracians, 35.104; 99A fr. B.5, and n. 15

Saraukos of Arcadia, 60.42

Sardis, Sardians, 12C; 13 n. 8; 117 *passim*; 125B

Satibarzanes, 12A

Satyrides, 55.36, 49, 53

Satyros, 55.16; 82 *passim*

Scyros, 99 n. 1

Scythia, 96B

Seleucia, 1C at 304/3

Seleukos, 1A at 312/11, 1C at 304/3 and 301/300, and n. 44; 125A; 140; son of Antiochos, 125B

Selymbrians, 35.125

Seuthes, 29 n. 1; the Thracian, 125B

Sibyrtios, 125A

Sicily, 1 n. 27; 52.40

Sicyon, Sicyonians, 116.12; 123A *passim*

Sidon, Sidonians, 40 *passim*; 119 n. 8; 131 nn. 3, 5

Sikinetans, 35.127

Simon, 37.2

Sindoi, 27C.4

Siphnians, 35.126

Sitalkes, 29 n. 1

Skaphai, 15

Skepsis, 132 n. 1

Skolos, 15

Smithinas, 113.36

Smyrna, 26.19

Sochares, son of Chares, 73A.1, 9, 18

Sodamos, 88.20

Sogdians, 125A

Soizousa, 47.83

Sokrates, 1A at 400/399; of Lamptrai, 10.14

Solum, 126 n. 2

Sophocles, 75A

II. Subjects and terms

II. Index of subjects and terms

City of final judgement (ekkletos polis), 55.49, and n. 7
Clan(s), 28B.16; 54 n. 1; 127.30; register of, at Samos, 127.31
Cleruch(s), 54 n. 3; 58.9; 77; 81 n. 2; 94 n. 3. *See also* Glossary
Cleruchy, 47 n. 13; commanders, 47.89
Coins: Attic silver, 45.3; base alloy, 45 n. 10; bronze, 45 n. 10; lead covered with silver, 45 n. 10. *See also* Currency; *under* names of coins; Appendix IV
Colonies and colonists: 117 n. 1; 126.3, 4; Athenian, to Adriatic, 121.161, 176, 224, and nn. 11, 12; founder of, 121.161, 224, and n. 4
Commanders of the cavalry, *see* Hipparchs
Companions (hetairoi), of Hermias, 79.2, 10, 13, 15, 20, 24, and n. 2
Confederacy: Boeotian, archon of, 48.2, and n. 2; Councils, 15, and n. 2; councillors, 15 *passim*; delegates of the Byzantines to (?), 74.11, 24; Federal council, 15 n. 8; Federal Government, 15 n. 9; Federal Treasury, 15
  Second Athenian, 37 n. 1; 56 n. 5; 66.16; 74 n. 2; 'Charter of', 35; 37 n. 1; entry of Corcyra into, 42 n. 1; foundation of, 31 n. 1; growth of, 35 n. 21; number of allies in, 35 n. 17
Contest for the Kings, 128 fr. B, C.11
Coppers (chalkoi), 84.105, and n. 6
Cornice(s), 134.54, 71; -tiles, 134.72; -top, 134.64
Council: of the allies of Athens (synedrion), 35.34; 41.19, 23, and n. 7; 65.9; 97 nn. 6, 8; of the Arcadians, 51.2, and n. 4 (presiding committee of); of the Areopagus, 78A.19; 101 *passim*; *see also* Glossary; of Arkesine, 68.1; of the Carystians, 123B.19; in Chios, swears oaths, 31.32; at Cyrene, 126 *passim*; at Eresus, 112E.31, F.4, and n. 10; Eretrian, swears oaths, 2 fr. B.6; at Erythrae, 28 n. 7; Hellenes', 107.14; 107.13 (resolution of); of the Hellenic League under Antigonos and Demetrios, 138.11, 12, 14, 15, 18 (meetings); 138 *passim* (members); 138 *passim* (presidents); 138.18, 20 (resolutions); 138.24, 26 (secretaries); of the League of Corinth, 99B; at Mytilene, 113.38; at Priene, 103.1; of the Samians, 127.1; of the Syracusans, 52.36; at Tegea, 122.62
Council-members, at Miletus, 117.2
Courier (hemerodromes or hemerodromos), 110.2, and n. 1
Crowns: of gold, 10.29, 31, 33, 34, 36, 37, 40;

68.16; 82.24, 26, 34, 36, 40, 43; 97.36; 100.14; 108.30, 32, 57, 60; 119.35; 121.192, 194, 195, 198, 201; 123A.24, B.27; 128 fr. B, C.10; 139.28; of olive, 97.40; 108.40, 42, 48; 118.23; 139.51; unspecified, 81.8
Cubit, 135 *passim*
Curator, 81.4, 9
Currency: Aeginetan, 60 *passim*; 84 *passim*; 131.26; Alexander type, 131.19; Attic, 60 *passim;* 131.22; Lampsacene, 72.44; non-Attic silver, 45 n. 7. *See also* Coins

Dadouchos, 78A.13, B.54, C.42, and n. 3
Damiorgoi, 51.9, and n. 4. *See also* Glossary 'Demiourgoi'
Darics, 120. *See also* Glossary
Dekadarchia (dekadarchy), 87B
Delegates (synedroi), to the League of Corinth, 99 nn. 1, 9
Demarch(s), 78A.21
Deme(s), 7 nn. 1, 5; 8 n. 5; 19 n. 6; 35 n. 3; 39 n. 2; 85 *passim*; 100.21; 108 n. 1; 123A.21; 129.5; deme-name (demotic), 3.1, 2; 7, and n. 3; 8 n. 5; 47 n. 5; 52 n. 1; 65 n. 4; demesmen, 85 *passim*; 108.45, 52, 61. *See also* Glossary
Demetrieia, 136 *passim*
Demokratia, 8 n. 2
Denunciation (phasis), 45.18, 23, 29, 32, and n. 13
Dialect: Aeolic, 112 (heading); 113 (heading); Arcadian, 122 (heading); Attic, 6 n. 2; 51 (heading); 57 (heading); Boeotian, 48 (heading); 74 (heading); 131 (heading); Doric, 42 n. 3; 57 n. 5; 116 (heading); Ionic, 63 (heading); 114 (heading); 127 (heading); 128 (heading); Koine, 6 n. 2; 106 (heading); 112 (heading); 122 (heading); 126 (heading)
Diapsephisis (Diapsephismos). 85A, and n. 1
Dikaskopoi, 113.12, 14, and n. 2
Dinner (deipnon), at Prytaneion at Athens, 5.11, and n. 3; 33.9, 12, and n. 6; 43.15; 53.25, 33; 70.32; 94.17. *See also* Hospitality
Dionysia, 8B.30; 75A; 81.5; 123A.26. *See also* Glossary
Dipylon, 134.53
Drachma(s), 8 n. 6; 10 *passim*; 35.67; 45.24, 25, 28, 36; 53.24; 55.26, 75; 59.41, 45; 60 *passim*; 65.13, 16, 18; 75A, C; 82.25, 49; 84 *passim*; 97.37; 100.37; 101.28; 102.9; 108.30, 33, 57, 60; 118.15, 38; 121.193, 195; 123A.25, 30, B.28; 126 n. 6; 128 fr. B, C.11; 131.21, 31; 137.19, 22; 138.42, 43; 139.28, 31, 64. *See also* Appendix IV

II. Index of subjects and terms

Edict(s), 113.20; 126.38; of Alexander, 112A.18, C.35, F.10, 13, 23, 25; 113.29; 122 *passim*; of the Kings, 112F.32

Eisangelia, *see* Impeachment

Eisphora, *see* Capital levy

Ekklesia, *see* Assembly

Elaphebolion (month), 82 n. 6; 137.21

Eleusinia, 9 n. 7

Eleven, the (at Athens), 128 fr. A.20. *See also* Glossary

Embassies, 5.9; 11 n. 9; 25A.12, and n. 1; 31.37; 33.5; 37.11; 40 n. 1; 57.4; 70.15; 72C; 86; 89A; 91A; 96B; 115 n. 1; 138.6, and n. 2

Enactment formula, 2 nn. 1, 6

Eparchai, 60.15, and n. 5

Ephebes, Ephebeia, 108 *passim*; 109 *passim*; guard duty of (at Eleusis), 108.46, and n. 3; (at Munychia and Akte), 108 n. 3; 109B; law about, 108 n. 4

Ephebic dedication, 108.43, 49, 62, and n. 4

Epidosis, 139 n. 6

Epimeletai of the market (in Peiraeus), 45.21, 41, and n. 16

Epimenioi, 28B.3, and n. 7

Epoikoi, 121 n. 11 *See also* Colonies

Eponymous Hero, 137.19

Eunuch, 1B at 341/40 and 338/7; 90A

Exile(s), 26.12; 28A.7; 107.3, 6; 112D.23; 113 *passim*; 122 *passim*; 126.6, 41

Exports: from Chalcidice, 21 (reverse).9; dues, 21 (reverse).6; of fir, 21 (reverse).3, 4; from Macedonia, 21 (reverse).9; of other commodities, 21 (reverse).7; of pitch, 21 (reverse).1; of timber, 21 (reverse).1; of wheat, 82.15

Faction, democratic, 28 n. 4

Families, aristocratic, 70 n. 7

Famine, *see* Grain (shortage)

Five, the (elected men): responsible for inscriptions at Samos, 127.33ff.; 128 fr. B, C.14ff.

Freedom (Free), 31.20; 35.10, 20; 38.21; 53.42; 64.16; 106.4; 123B.7; 132.2, 55, 61, and n. 5; 133; 137.8

Freedom from taxation, *see* Tax, exemption from

Freedom to import or export/sail in or sail out etc., 12D.6ff.; 28B.12; 103.11ff.

Friendship, 31.9; 61A; 76A, and n. 1; 80 n. 2; 82.9; 86; 117.3; 123B.17. *See also* Proxenos

Funds: Decree, 55.26, n. 6; 65.4, 13; 82.41; 100.37; 101.28; 118.38; 123A.30; 139.64; Military, *see* Stratiotika; Ten Talent, 35.69, n. 14; 40.18, n. 4; 139.16; Theoric, *see* Theorika

Garrison, 26.14, 24; 35.22; 38.23; 68.9; 69.10; 83 n. 6; 96B; 106.15; 107.17, 19; 123 n. 3

Generals, 12 n. 21; 28A.4, B.2, 3; 97.26; Athenian, 69.13ff. (in charge of Andros); 121.209 (in charge of the symmories); 78A.19, B.50, and n. 5 (for the country); 128 fr. A.3, and n. 2 (for duty on Samos); 26.21 (to negotiate treaty); 37.15 (oaths sworn to); 2 fr. B.4; 31.31; 34.10; 37.18; 41.16; 52.33; 55.57; 56.38; 59.14; 65.6, 19 (swear oaths); 100.30 (take care of Acarnanians); 139.57ff. (take care of honorands); *see also* Glossary; at Cyrene, 126.23, 26, 27, 30, 39; Eretrian, 2 fr. B.6; at Erythrae, 79.19, 21; of the Hellenic League, appointed by the Kings (Antigonos and Demetrios), 138.13, 17; of the Iulietae, 55.15, 19, 42, 47; at Miletus, 117.36; at Mytilene, 113.7, 13; of Philip, 103 n. 1; Royal, 95B; Syracusan, 52.36; at Tegea, 122.33

General with absolute authority (autokrator): Agathokles, 1A at 319/18; Antipatros, 125A; Philip II, 1B at 337/6; 99 n. 12

Gerousia (Cyrene), 126 *passim*

Goddess, the (at Tegea), 122.38, 40, 42, 44, 48

Governor, 26.13, 24; 35.22; 38.25; 68.4, and n. 1; 69.19

Governorship, 68 n. 1

Grain: market, 45.18, 22; shortage, 116.3, and n. 1; 120 n. 1; supply, 121.220

Graphe paranomon, 68 n. 1. *See also* Glossary

Guarantors, 55.46; 122.41

Guardian of Apatouron, 26B.4

Guardians of the laws (Cyrene), 126.32

Hegemon, 99A.21

Hegemones, 134 n. 9

Hekatombaion (month), 9.31

Herald(s), 9.42, 55; 12C; 54 n. 1; 56.6; 58.6; 81.5; 126.44; of the Boule, 121.197. *See also* Glossary

Hieromnemons, 59.19; 88.21; 104 n. 1

Hierophant, 78A.13, B.53, C.41, and n. 3

Hipparchs: Athenian, 34.11; 37.16, 18; 43.17, n. 2; 52.34; 56.39; 59.15; *see also* Glossary; Thessalian, 59.19

Hoplite(s), 13, and n. 2; 15; 22 n. 2; 80; 99B; 125B; 138.42, and n. 4; armour, 109 (heading); census, 15 n. 3

Horse-transports, 80; 121 n. 6

Hospitality (xenia), at Prytaneion at Athens, 5 n. 3; 25B, C.17; 31.38; 33.3, and n. 6; 34.15; 37.25; 40.26; 43.13; 53.27, 29; 59.38; 65.9; 70.30, 33; 82.52. *See also* Dinner

II. Index of subjects and terms

Hostages, 26.9, 10; 76A
Hydria(i), 10 n. 8; 78 n. 6
Hypaspist, 102.9

Immunity from taxation (ateleia), *see* Tax, exemption from
Impeachment (eisangelia), 45 n. 18. *See also* Glossary
Infantry, *see* Hoplites
Inviolability, personal by land and sea, 48.9
Isopolity, 117 n. 1
Isoteleia, *see* Tax, equality of

Juries and jurors, 24 *passim*; 121.207, 210, 215

King, the (Alexander), 105; 106.1; 107.1, 18; 110.1; 112A.18, F.10, 25; 113.28, 45, 47, and n. 12; 114.7; 122, and n. 1; 125A
King, the (Great/Persian), 11A 7.1; 12 *passim*; 23A n. 5; 24.9; 31.11, 15; 35.18, and n. 5; 40.3, and nn. 1, 2; 44.63; 57.8, 11; 72A, C; 86; 90A, B; 119 n. 8
Kingdom: Odrysian, 64 n. 2; of Philip, 99A.11; Western Thracian, 70 n. 1
Kings, the (Antigonos and Demetrios), 138.16, 29, 36
Knights: Athenian, 2 fr. B.5; 41.17; 56.40; 59.15; Eretrian, 2 fr. B.6; Thessalian, 59.19

Law: -code, at Athens, 9; concerning tyrants, at Eresus, 112B.25, F.16, 26, 31; established, 109A, B; -giver (nomothetes) at Athens, 129.11, n. 2; on homicide, 9 n. 1; of Periandros, 39 n. 7; sacred, 9 n. 1; trierarchic, 9 n. 1; of universal peace, 99B; writers (Chios), 107.4. *See also* Nomos
Leagues: Aetolian, 54; of the allies, *see* Confederacy, Second Athenian; Arcadian, 27 n. 2; 51; 56 n. 2; 51 n. 2 (assembly of); Chalcidic, 21 (reverse).4, n. 1; 67.3 (magistrates of); of Corinth, 1B at 337/6; 99; of the Greeks, *see* of Corinth; Greek States, 93; of the Hellenes (against Antipatros), 123B.11; Hellenic (under Antigonos and Demetrios), 138 *passim*; Ionian, 24 nn. 3, 4; Island, 136; Thessalian, 49 n. 1; 59.17, 25, 33, 35, and n. 2; 62D
Lenaea (Lenaean Festival), 20 n. 6
Letters: Attic, 9 n. 1; Ionic, 9 n. 1 and *passim*
Lexiarchic lists, 85C; 109B
Liberty, *see* Freedom
Little Sea, the, 114.5, and n. 2
Liturgies, 39B; 121 n. 7; 122 n. 10; choregic, *see* Choregia; trierarchic, *see* trierarchy

Mercenaries, 22 *passim*; 44.68; 50A; 72A, B; 119 n. 8; 120
Messenger(s), 79.19, 25, and n. 5; 117.25, 36
Metics, 40 n. 8; 85C; -tax (metoikion), *see* Tax. *See also* Glossary
Mina(s) (minai), 68.13; 74.7, 17; 104 n. 1; 122.17; 126.8, 9, and nn. 6, 8, 9; 138.41. *See also* Appendix IV
Mint-workers, 45.54
Money-changers, 45 n. 5; 90A
Money-testers, 45 n. 4. *See also* Certifier
Mortgage, 35.40, 42
Mysteries, 54.9, and n. 1; 78 n. 3; Greater Eleusinian, 54 nn. 1, 5; Lesser, 54 n. 5

Naopoioi, 84.2, 10, 111, and nn. 4, 8
Naukrariai, 39C(2)
Navarch, Navarchy, 11A 7.1; 11C, and nn. 8, 16; 12B, C, and n. 16
Nike/Nikai, 10.16, 41, and nn. 3, 4; 47.93
Nomos (law), 45 n. 23; 101 n. 2. *See also* Law
Nomothetai, 45.1, and n. 1; 101.6

Oaths, 2 fr. B.3f.; 31.10, 18, 30, 35; 34.9; 37.11, 16, 21; 38.13, 18; 41.15, 17, 20, and n. 6; 42.15, 25, 36, and n. 3; 43.2; 52.30ff.; 53.44, 48; 55 *passim*; 56.36, 37; 59.14, 16, 20, 23, 26, 29, 30; 64.17; 65.5, 6, 19, and n. 4; 67.3, 4, 5, 6, and n. 3; 78A.9; 79.12, 13, 19, 29; 99A.2, 8, 14; 109 *passim*; 112A.30, B.16, C.9; 113.31; 122.60; 126.14, and n. 10; 132.41, 59, 66, 72; 79.29 (Gods of)
Oath-takers, 33 n. 1
Obol(s), 8 (front).10, and n. 6; 10 *passim*; 60 *passim*; 84 *passim*
Oligarchy (-ies), 56.26, and n. 8
Oracular responses (oracles), 67.7, 9, 12
Orgas (Sacred), 78 *passim*
Orphans, 8 *passim*
Other allies, *see* Allies (the) of Athens
Overseers (Cyrene), 126.33
Oxen, yoke of, 118.17, and n. 4

Panathenaia, Great, 82.24, 27, and n. 4; 118.17, 19. *See also* Glossary
Panhellenic Festivals, 54 n. 1
Patrol, 78 n. 5; 109B; -commanders of, 78A.20; -men, 109B
Pay: for an architect, 84.124; to a clerk, 84.126; to the cooks for sacrificial victims, 84.108; to a herald, 84.122
Peace: 31.9, 18, 22; 44.63, 65; 102 n. 3; 107.12; 44.70 (altar of); 44 n. 2 (cult statue of); Common, 35 n. 5; 57 *passim*; 99.20; King's, 23 (of 392/1); 16 n. 1, 25 n. 1, 26

204

Shekel(s), 10.43, and n. 7
Ships: quadriremes, 121.167, and n. 6; state-
    galleys, 83 n. 4; 115 n. 1; 128 n. 4;
    triaconters, 121.145, 158, 168, and n. 6;
    triremes, 11A 6.1; 12B–D; 47.88, and n.
    30; 80; 107.8, 9; 121 *passim*
Ship's tackle: hanging equipment for trireme,
    47 *passim*; 121.152; hypoblema, 47.86,
    101, and n. 11; katablema, 47.86, 101,
    and n. 11; oar-timbers, 47 *passim*;
    schoinia (ropes), 47 n. 12; topeia
    (ropes), 47 n. 12; wooden equipment for
    trireme, 47 *passim*; 121.151
Sitophylakes, 45.19, 23, and n. 16
Sixths (Phocaean), 10.42, and n. 6
Skirophorion (month), 17A.2; 55.10; 91A;
    139.4
Slave(s), 45.30, 39, and n. 4; 79 n. 3; 90A;
    public slave-rowers, 82.59, 62
Spondophoroi, 54, and n. 1
Stater(s), 10.42, and n. 6; 74.9, 21; 112A.9, B.3,
    11
Stele of Poseidon, 45.42, 47, and n. 20
Stoas: of Hermes, 45 n. 4; of the King, 35 n. 13
Stratiotika (military money), 75 *passim*; 82.44;
    96A
Successors, the, 103 n. 1
Superintendents (epimeletai) of the shipyards,
    47 nn. 1, 29; 121.178, and n. 1
Superscript (heading), 82 n. 1
Supervisor (tribal), for ephebes (sophronistes),
    108 *passim*
Surveyor (bematistes), 110.3, and n. 2
Syllogeis of the People, 45.15, 20, and n. 12
Syntaxis (-eis) (contribution), 36; 64.16; 69.11;
    83.13, and n. 6; 97.20
Symmory (-ies): for the capital levy, 39C, and
    n. 7; system, 39 n. 7; trierarchic, 39 n. 7
Synoikia (Attica), 9 n. 6

Tagos (magistrate), 59 n. 2
Talents, 12 n. 20; 39A; 55.7; 88.14, and n. 1; 93;
    95B; 108 n. 4; 120, and n. 1; 131.18, 24,
    28; 135 n. 2
Tax: assessment of, at Athens, 39C; equality of
    (isoteleia), 3.6, 9, and n. 10; 139.52;
    exemption from (ateleia), 12D.6; 28B.9;
    48.8; 68.24; 79.2; 82 n. 3; 103.9; 106 n. 3;
    114.9; five per cent, 25 *passim*; 26.8; one
    fiftieth, 79.5; property, *see* Capital levy;
    resident aliens' (metics'), 40.33; 81 n. 1;
    100.26; paying groups, *see* Symmories;
    system, at Athens, 39, and n. 5. *See also*
    Glossary
Taxiarchs, 31.32; 52.34; 56.39
Temples: Aphrodite, foundation or building
    of, at Athens, 111 *passim*; Apollo (the

Pythian) at Delphi, 60; 74.2, 3, 23;
    104.11; Apollo at Miletus, 117.29;
    Athena at Mytilene, 113.50; Hera at
    Samos, 127.37; 128 fr. B, C.9, 14; Isis,
    foundation or building of, 111.44, and
    n. 5; Kekrops, 108.35
Ten Thousand, the (Assembly of the Arcadian
    League), 51.4, and n. 2; 126 n. 4
Tetrarchia (tetrarchy), 87
Thargelia, 121.197
Thargelion (month), 100.3; 118.6
Theatres: of Dionysus, 20 n. 6; 118 n. 3; of the
    Panathenaia, 118.17
Theorika (festival money), 72B; 75 *passim*;
    commissioner for, 72C
Thesmothetai, 45.26; 121.206. *See also* Glossary
Thirty Tyrants, the, 2 n. 6; 3; 8 n. 2; 9 n. 1
Thousand, the, 126.35 (at Cyrene); 127.30 (at
    Samos)
Tithe, 131.34; -collectors, 47.97; to the
    Goddess, 35.56
Treasurer of the People, at Athens: gives
    money for crowns, 82.39ff.; pays for
    inscription of stele, 52.43; 53.23; 55.26;
    59.45; 65.3; 66.19; 82.47ff.; 100.35ff.;
    101.27; 118.37; 123A.29; 139.63; pays
    travelling expenses, 43.12; 59.41; 65.12,
    14, 17
Treasurers
    of Alexander, 120 n. 1
    at Athens, 137.17; of Athena, 10 n. 2; 40.17;
        53 n. 2; 134 n. 1; of the Boule, 25B, C.9;
        of the Goddess, 35.69; 59.40; 121.215;
        of the Other Gods, 10 n. 2; 134 n. 1; of
        the Paralos, 83.7; of the Sacred
        treasures, 10 *passim*; 39 n. 1
    at Miletus, 117.31
    at Mytilene, 113.49
    at Samos, 127.37
    See also Glossary
Tribe(s) and tribesmen, 138.23; at Athens, 3 n.
    7; 7 *passim*; 19; 35 n. 3; 39C(2); 108
    passim; 123A.21; 137.14, 15, 25; Ionian, 9
    n. 5; non-Greek, 106 n. 5; at Samos,
    127.29, and n. 3. *See also* Appendix III
Tribe-kings (Phylobasileis): at Athens, 9.33,
    40, 45, 53; at Mytilene, 113.1, 9, 13, 45,
    and n. 1
Tribute, 35.23; 36; 38.24, and n. 5; 64 *passim*;
    106.13. *See also* Tax
Trierarch(s), Trierarchy: at Athens, 35 n. 1; 39
    nn. 4, 7; 47 *passim*; 121 *passim*; at
    Syracuse, 52.37. *See also* Glossary
Triglyphs, 84.131
Trittys, 9.37
Troops: light-armed, 13; 138.42
Trophy, 46 *passim*; 49.3

III. Translated passages

A. INSCRIPTIONS

III. Index of translated passages

B. LITERARY TEXTS

III. Index of translated passages

Aristophanes
Ecclesiazusae
 193: 14B
Plutus
 173: 22B
Scholion to *Plutus*
 173: 22B
Aristotle
Constitution of Thessaly (fgmt): 87A
Arrian
FGrHist
 156F1: 125B
 156F9: 125B
Callisthenes
FGrHist
 124F2: 90B
Charax of Pergamum
FGrHist
 103F19: 91B
Chronika from Oxyrhynchus
FGrHist
 255F4, 5: 1B, with notes
Cleidemus
FGrHist
 323F8: 39C (2)
Ctesias
FGrHist
 688F30: 12A
Demosthenes, with Scholia
 1.1: 75B
 1.22: 62D
 2.6: 61
 2.17: 50A
 3.28: 71
 3.31: 72B
 4.19: 72A
 10.34: 12B
 11.1: 95B
 11.4: 96B
 11.22: 73B
 18.79: 91A
 20.52: 18
 27.7: 39C (1)
Dexippus of Athens
FGrHist
 100F8: 125A
Didymus
Demosthenes
 col. 1: 91A
 col. 1: 92
 col. 1: 95C (2)
 col. 4–6: 90A–B
 col. 7: 12B
 col. 7: 23A
 col. 7: 44
 col. 8: 86
 col. 10: 95B

 col. 11: 96B
 col. 12: 73B
 col. 13: 78B
 col. 14: 78C
Dionysius of Halicarnassus
To Ammaeus
 1.9.734f.: 80
 1.11.740f.: 95A
 1.11.741f.: 95C (1)
 1.11.761f.: 96A
On Dinarchus
 13:77
Diyllus
FGrHist
 73F2: 115
Duris of Samos
FGrHist
 76F36: 73B
Ephorus
FGrHist
 70F9: 30
 70F209: 18
Eusebius
Chronica (Helm)
 117 23, 119 12, 119 18, 121 12,
 121 26, 124 1, 124 17, 124 19, 124
 21, 124 25, 126 25, 127 3, 127 8,
 127 14: 1C, with notes
Harpocration
Lexicon
 s.v. Amadokos: 76B
 Aristion: 115
 Dekadarchia: 87B
 Diapsephisis: 85A
 Epikrates: 108 n. 4
 Euboulos: 75D
 Hagnias: 11C
 Kineas: 62B
 Mercenary force in Corinth:
  22A
 One thousand two hundred:
  39B
 Pezhetairoi: 51B
 Symmoria: 39C (1)
 Syntaxis: 36
 The dissolution of the
  Mantineans: 30
 Tetrarchia: 87A
 That 6000 talents . . . :
  39A (2)
 Theorika: 75A
 What is the meaning . . . ?
  61A

III. Index of translated passages